# Working Women in
# Renaissance
# Germany

*A Shoemaker's Wife Selling Shoes. Woodcut by J. Ammann from* Beschreibung aller Stände *(Frankfurt, 1568).*

*The Douglass Series On Women's Lives
and the Meaning of Gender*

# Working Women in Renaissance Germany

Merry E. Wiesner

Rutgers University Press
New Brunswick, New Jersey

**Library of Congress Cataloging-in-Publication Data**
Wiesner, Merry, 1952–
   Working women in Renaissance Germany.

   (The Douglass series on women's lives and the meaning of gender)
   Bibliography: p.
   Includes index.
      1. Women—Germany—History—Renaissance, 1450–1600.
   2. Women—Germany—Economic conditions.   3. Women—
   Employment—Germany—History   I. Title.   II. Series.
   HQ1149.G3W54   1986      305.4'3'00943      85–14451
   ISBN 0–8135–1138–0

*For my grandmothers,*
*Belle Nelson and Mabel Bidwell Wiesner,*
*two working women*

# Contents

# Illustrations

# Acknowledgments

I would like to express my thanks to the many individuals and institutions that have helped me over the years in the research, conceptualization, and writing of this book.

The material on Nuremberg was gathered in 1977/1978, and formed the basis of my dissertation at the University of Wisconsin-Madison, "Birth, Death, and the Pleasures of Life: Working Women in Nuremberg, 1480–1620." My research in Nuremberg was supported by a special grant from the University of Wisconsin, which it very generously supplied when another source of funding fell through at the last minute. The helpful staffs of both the Stadtarchiv and the Bayerische Staatsarchiv made my first immersion in German archives much easier. They were surprised to learn that not all Americans studying sixteenth-century Nuremberg came from Ohio State, though I must add that the "family" of Harold Grimm has cheerfully accepted me into the fold. The wonderful people of the Evangelische Freikirchliche Gemeinde in Nuremberg made my year-long stay a pleasant one, for they opened their hearts and homes to me and helped me to love their beautiful city. A special word of thanks to my dissertation advisor, Robert Kingdon, for his light touch in guiding me along and for the chance to focus on women and the Reformation for an entire graduate seminar.

The remainder of the research was carried out in 1981/1982, partly while teaching in Munich and Strasbourg as a faculty member on Augustana College's European quarter and partly while on a leave of absence, which the college was kind enough to grant me. This research was supported by a grant-in-aid from the American Council of Learned Societies and a Kurzstipendium from the Deutsche Akademische Austauschdienst. For this, I used the resources of seven different archives: the Stadtarchive in Munich, Memmingen, Frankfurt, Stuttgart, and Augsburg; the Archives Municipales in Strasbourg; and the Württembergische Hauptstaatsarchiv in Stuttgart. I cannot praise the

# Acknowledgments

staffs of the various archives too highly, for they made my oftentimes short stays and intensive research as easy and fruitful as possible. I will not mention any names for fear of forgetting someone but would like to say a special thank you to the reading-room personnel in each archive, who took an interest in what I was doing and helped me locate and discover obscure sources.

I have talked over many of the issues raised by the book with numerous friends and colleagues and owe a great debt to them for their help and advice: to Jane Schulenburg and Joann McNamara for their expertise on the medieval background; to Philip Kintner for directing me to the rich archives of the small city of Memmingen and for years of wise counsel on a variety of things; to Steve Rowan, for sharing material he discovered in the Freiburg city archives; to Lyndal Roper, Natalie Davis, and Martha Howell for their insights both in theory and in the application of theory to early modern developments; to Sharleen Martenas, Nancy Huse, and Patrice Koelsch for providing links between my work and their respective fields of religion, literature, and philosophy, demonstrating once again that any work on women is by nature interdisciplinary.

Several people read drafts of the entire manuscript before publication and made invaluable suggestions for changes in structure, style, and syntax. Grethe Jacobsen and Heide Wunder read very early drafts, and we have spent many pleasant hours discussing this and many other aspects of early modern women's history. They have made me feel part of an international community of scholars, and my specific debts to them are sprinkled liberally throughout the text. Thomas Brady, Louise Tilly, and Charles Nauert read a much later version and were particularly helpful in strengthening the theoretical framework. Marlie Wasserman from Rutgers University Press read several versions and made suggestions for improving the appeal to nonspecialists. Neil Hanks read every version of every chapter, and his willingness to talk through linguistic nuances, awkward phrasing, and logical jumps gave proof of great patience and care.

I would like to thank the editors of the *Sixteenth Century Journal* for their permission to reprint some material from "Paltry Peddlers or Essential Merchants? Women in the Distributive Trades in Early Modern Nuremberg," vol. 12, no. 2 (1981): 3–13, and the editors of *International Journal of Women's Studies* for permission to reprint some material from "Early Modern Midwifery: A Case Study," vol. 6, no. 2 (1983): 26–43. For their help in preparing the final manuscript, I am grateful to a number of people: to Sue Amacher and Alice Dailing for typing; to my colleagues Bea Jacobsen and Dave Renneke for helping me come to terms with word processors; to Eileen Finan from Rutgers University Press; to my students Roger Miller and Andrea Smith, for their help in preparing the bibliography and index.

If this list of acknowledgments seems unusually long, it is because I have had the privilege of sharing my work with many people, both at home and abroad. The defects which remain in the book are my own, and none of the many people who have shared their knowledge and insights with me are responsible for any of them.

*Mother and Daughter Spinning. Title woodcut from Bartholomaeus Metlinger,*
Regiment der jungen Kinder *(Augsburg: Günther Zainer, 1473).*

# Working Women in
# Renaissance
# Germany

# Introduction

I began this study with the question that must be asked of any historical event or change: What did it mean for women?[1] The sixteenth and seventeenth centuries in Europe saw tremendous economic, social, and ideological changes, changes which greatly affected structures of work and patterns of employment. Most studies of these changes, both rural and urban, have focused on men.[2] Recently a number of scholars have begun to explore how women's lives changed during the period, but their work generally examines women in the context of marriage and the family or popular culture.[3] The central focus of my study is how and why women's work changed during the early modern period.

Alice Clark first addressed this issue in 1919 in her classic study *Working Life of Women in the Seventeenth Century*.[4] Her research was limited to England, but her conclusions have formed the basis of discussion since the book's publication. She found women's participation in the economy steadily decreasing, and she attributed that decrease to the advent of capitalism. As the household workshop was gradually replaced by larger scale production, wages were paid to individuals rather than to families; women were consistently paid less than men, often so little that they retired from paid work altogether if they were married and their husband's wages could support the family. Clark found the range of occupations open to women in the seventeenth century much smaller than it had been during the medieval period, and wages were held down by the large number of women competing for employment in a small number of occupations.

Both older and recent studies have found a similar decline in women's employment in Germany. Karl Bücher, in his exhaustive 1914 study of occupations in Frankfurt, found the range of occupations open to women steadily narrowing from the late Middle Ages on. His only ex-

1

planation was that the proportion of women in German cities must also have declined, for otherwise, he notes, this "narrow-minded exclusion" would certainly have created "strong opposition in society and disturbance of the public order."[5] His own demographic studies, and those of other German historians, reveal that this is not a satisfactory explanation, however, for the proportion of women was not declining.[6]

Helmut Wachendorf, writing five years after Alice Clark, notes that "the beginning of the sixteenth century brought the destruction of economic independence and cultural activity for the majority of women."[7] Rudolph Wissell, in a recent study of guild laws and practices, agrees, though he puts the timing somewhat later: "At the end of the seventeenth century, it was a general principle, except for a few fast-disappearing exceptions, that women were excluded from the crafts."[8] Sibylle Harksen, an East German historian, states this even more emphatically: not only were women excluded from the crafts, but "around 1600, women totally disappeared from the world of work."[9] All of these studies simply trace the decline, however, without offering specific explanations for it.

Unlike Clark's work, most of these German studies are not based on archival materials but rely for their information primarily on printed prescriptive sources. They thus describe not what was happening, but what was supposed to be happening. Despite this weakness, their conclusions about the end of women's economic activities seem to have been accepted. The recent local, intensive studies of women's work in Germany focus on the medieval period, which everyone agrees is the high point of women's employment.[10] If they mention the early modern period at all, it is generally to repeat, without documenting it, the assertion that it was a time of narrowing opportunities.

A closer reading of Clark and more recent studies of women's work in the eighteenth century makes it clear that this lack of interest in the early modern period is ill founded.[11] The exclusion of women was never total and varied significantly both by occupation and in intensity from one part of Europe to another. Moreover, the kinds of work women did were not totally dependent on external forces. Women chose to enter certain occupations in some areas and not in others, and their choices involved status and familial as well as economic concerns.

This study explores the situation in six south German cities—Frankfurt, Strasbourg, Nuremberg, Memmingen, Stuttgart, and Munich—during the period 1500–1700 and in some ways parallels Clark's classic. Like Clark, I have examined occupations which did not change significantly and which continued to offer employment for women along with those which grew increasingly restrictive. I have tested her explanations, but the range of theories in need of examination goes far beyond hers; though there are very few descriptive studies of women's work during this period, theoretical frameworks for explaining changes in women's work have been developed and sharpened since Clark. Some of these theories view changes in women's work as part of more general economic developments; others view them as part of what was happening to women as a social group. Putting it more simply, some studies stress that these were *working* women, others that they were working *women*.

Most explanations for the changes in women's work have been economic. As crafts became guilds during the Middle Ages, they prohibited labor by those who had not been apprenticed. Girls as well as boys were taken on as apprentices in many guilds during the thirteenth and fourteenth centuries, but gradually guild ordinances specifically forbade female apprentices or simply stopped mentioning them. The wife, daughters, and maids of the master continued to work in his shop, and female pieceworkers were hired when needed, but women on their own were no longer part of the guild system. In the sixteenth and seventeenth centuries, enterprising masters and merchant investors began to expand their scale of production and markets, often hiring rural labor for processes previously done by urban workshops. Journeymen and poorer masters felt increasingly threatened by these capitalist industries, and guilds in many cities responded by tightening their regulations. Stringent limitations were placed on the work of maids and female pieceworkers; the rights of widows to continue operating a shop were gradually limited; and even the master's wife and daughters were restricted in what work they could do. Male workers attempted to reduce the number of people competing for jobs, and women were an easy group to single out. Because women were not officially part of the guild structure, they had no way to defend their interests. Women could rarely amass enough capital to invest in large-scale trade or production, nor was it easy for them to travel to oversee business ventures. Thus they could not become merchant capitalists and, like most male workers, became wage laborers if they continued to work at all.[12]

Economic explanations fit women's work into the general economic trends of the period, but they also ignore a number of issues. Why were women singled out as a group to be excluded? Why did journeymen demand restrictions on women's work even when this worked against their own economic interests, as, for example, when their wives were prevented from earning decent wages or their own employment opportunities decreased as widows were forced to close their shops? Why were female workers paid less for the same tasks? Why were women excluded from some occupations in certain cities but allowed to continue in these in others? Answers to these questions cannot be found by looking at economic structures alone.

Recent studies of the impact of industrialization on women's work have suggested another theoretical framework.[13] These studies emphasize that women's work must always be considered in the context of family life. A man's work depended primarily on his social class; level of training; and position in a guild, workshop, or similar institution; a woman's work depended on all these factors and also on her marital status, number and ages of children, husband's occupation, and the availability of child care. For men, the family life cycle and the work life cycle were relatively independent of each other, except in those guilds with marriage requirements for master craftsmen. For women, these two cycles were totally interwoven. Family responsibilities limited most women to work that was close to home and did not require much training or capital nor steady employment throughout a lifetime. Thus, discussions of the impact of economic change on women's employment must be careful to differentiate among single women, married women, and married women with children.

This family framework explains many things about women's work that economic analysis alone cannot, and it also raises other questions. The primary one, why family responsibilities come first for women, is beyond the scope of this study or any study of women's work alone. I can address here some of the narrower questions suggested by this family framework: Why in the sixteenth and seventeenth centuries were women's family responsibilities suddenly incompatible with certain occupations? Which changed, the family responsibilities or the work? Or was there simply a change in perception? Why were single women included in the restrictions? Answers to some of these questions have been suggested both by historical demography and by recent feminist scholarship, which ties changes in women's work to political and intellectual change.

Demographic factors may have played a role in the increasing restrictions on women's work. The surprisingly high percentage of households headed by women in medieval cities has been noted by a number of authors. Bücher finds that independent women were 18–28 percent of the taxpayers in Frankfurt from 1354 to 1495; Annette Winter, that 25 percent of the households in Trier were headed by women; Gerd Wunder, that 22 percent of the households in Schwäbisch-Hall in 1406 were headed by women or children. In Bern the percentage of independent female taxpayers in 1389 was 20.7; in 1429 in Basel it was 25 percent; from 1361 to 1388 in Friedburg in Hesse it was 24 percent.[14] These figures may actually be too low, as they are derived from lists which may include only property holders, not all taxpayers; thus women may often have been left out because they did not own the room or house they lived in. Even standard tax lists may have omitted a number of women because they were too poor to pay any taxes.

This high percentage of independent women is understandable given the highly positive sex ratio found in many medieval cities. Counts of the entire population of Frankfurt in 1385, of Basel in 1454, and of Nuremberg in 1449 show between 110 and 120 women for every 100 men.[15] Of course a number of men chose or were forced to remain unmarried, so the number of women unable to find marriage partners and thus forced to live on their own would easily have been as high as the tax lists indicate.

The sex ratio did not change significantly in the sixteenth century. A 1587 tax list from Frankfurt shows 19 percent of the tax-paying households headed by women, and one from 1607 shows 20 percent. In 1521, 31 percent of all taxpayers in Memmingen were independent women and maids, and one-third of all citizens were widows. A 1545 tax list from Stuttgart shows 24 percent of the tax-paying households headed by women or children, and another from the same year from Schwäbisch-Hall shows 28 percent headed by women or children.[16]

These sixteenth-century tax lists also indicate that households headed by women were often the poorest in the city. Of the 560 households in Frankfurt headed by women in 1587, 266 were valued at less than 50 gulden, the lowest category. Of the 412 headed by women in 1607 in Frankfurt, 177 were valued at less than 100 gulden, again the lowest category. Most of the independent women in Memmingen belonged to the *"Habenichtsen,"* the "have-nothings," who paid only a small head tax. During the fifteenth century female "Habenichtsen" paid a lower head tax than male, but this preferential treatment was ended in the sixteenth century, and both sexes then paid the same small tax. In 1545, 30 percent of Stuttgart's independent women were "Habenichtsen," and the figures were similar for Schwäbisch-Hall. Women not identified as widows were generally worse off than widows, and the widows themselves were poorer than they had been when their husbands were still alive.[17]

During the medieval period, city and religious authorities saw the large number of poor women living independently as an economic problem, if they worried about them at all. They recognized that these women would have to have some way to support themselves or they would require assistance. Authorities thus grudgingly agreed to allow some women to make or sell various simple items and to leave some low-skilled occupations open to them.

In the sixteenth century authorities began to see women living independently as a matter of morality as well as economics. Women who lived alone were "masterless," in other words, they did not live in proper, male-headed households. Laws were passed forbidding unmarried women to move into cities and ordering unmarried female servants who had left one domestic position to leave the city, should they refuse to take another one. Even the daughters of citizens might be forbidden to live alone, to "have their own smoke" ("*ihr eigene Rauch haben*"), or "earn their own bread" ("*ihr eigene Brot verdienen*"), although this was not an easy measure to enforce. In some cases, the city council went even further, requiring grown, unmarried daughters to find service in another household if their widowed mother could not prove need for them at home, or requiring widows to move in with one of their children.[18] Despite all of these measures, the number of female-headed households remained high. Whether there actually were more women living alone in the early modern period, or whether authorities simply thought there were, is difficult to determine given that such women were often too poor to be included on tax lists. What is important, though, is the change in attitude toward and treatment of independent women.

Feminist analysis has placed the roots of this change in attitude in political and intellectual developments, not demographic change. During the early modern period, several political trends negatively affected women's lives. Aristocratic women lost power as the feudal system was replaced by centralized states with professional armies and bureaucracies. Within these states, the line between public and private was drawn more distinctly, and women were relegated to the private realm, except for a few extraordinary queens, such as Mary and Elizabeth Tudor and Mary Stuart.[19] The household in many ways belonged to both the public and private realm, and as women were not to exercise public authority, authorities increasingly felt that the only "proper" households were male headed. Legislation strengthened this patriarchal household as an instrument of social control, and many areas attempted to require all persons to live in male-headed households. The religious and social unrest of the sixteenth century increased the authorities' fear of disorder; thus laws against vagrants, the poor, single women, and other masterless persons grew increasingly harsh.[20]

These political changes were accompanied by intellectual developments detrimental to women. As Joan Kelly has pointed out, women did not share in the educational and cultural advances of the Renaissance.[21] During the medieval period, education had primarily been for religious purposes, and carried out in monasteries, convents, and cathedral schools. Women as well as men could serve God and the church by copying manuscripts, reading the Church Fathers, and writing religious literature, all of which required the knowledge of Latin. With the Renaissance, education increasingly came to serve secular purposes. Humanists saw education as preparation for public service, and as women could not be mayors, officials, or ambassadors, their exclusion from higher education needed no explanation or justification. Though Christian humanists and Protestant reformers decried it, popular ridicule of women increased during the period. The impact of the Protestant Reformation on the status of women has been much disputed, but the Protestant emphasis on marriage as the only proper vocation for women coincided with the political strengthening of the patriarchal household.[22]

This feminist analysis sees restrictions on women's work during the early modern period as part of a more general separation of male and female spheres, accompanied by a devaluation of the female sphere. That devaluation had both an intellectual and an economic basis, the former coming from classical and humanist views of women and the latter from the fact that women's domestic labor was unpaid and therefore had no market value. Marxist feminists stress the latter factor and also point out that men's availability for work outside the home was directly dependent on women being solely responsible for child care and domestic tasks.[23]

What historical demography and feminist analysis have not explained very well is how these restrictions on women's work were carried out locally and how women responded to them. How were theoretical ideas about women transformed into laws restricting their ability to produce or distribute goods? How did authorities justify these restrictions and justify making exceptions? Did women's work vary as the economic structure, political system, religion, and moral climate varied, as one might expect?

The answers to these questions, and a more specific testing of the various theories posited for the restrictions on women's work, can only come from detailed local studies. In selecting the geographic focus of this study, I chose six cities which varied in governmental structure, economic base, population, religion, and level of economic modernization. Each of them had extensive contact with its surrounding rural area, so though the study focuses on cities, it takes into account changes in rural–urban migration and employment opportunities. I chose these particular cities also because they had a wide range of sources from the period, though the extant sources varied somewhat from city to city.

The sources for Nuremberg are found in two different archives, the Bavarian State Archives (Staatsarchiv) and the city archives (Stadtarchiv). Most of the official city documents for the period are actually to be found in the state archives. These include the city council records (Ratsbücher and Verlässe des Inneren Rats), craft ordinances (Handwerkerordnungen and Amts- und Standsbücher), citizen lists (Neubürgerlisten), court records, baptismal records, lists of city officials (Aemterbüchlein), wills, oaths of office (Eidbücher der Nürnberg Aemter), and various other official documents. The city archives contain records of the major city hospitals, collections of inventories taken at deaths or remarriages, municipal law codes, and several collections of craft ordinances and regulations.

The sources in Frankfurt are all contained in the city archives, which were heavily damaged in World War II (as were those of Nuremberg and Stuttgart). They include city council minutes (Bürgermeisterbücher), several volumes of ordinances (Verordnungen), oaths of office, civil court records (Gerichtssachen), midwives' records, and numerous guild records. The latter are divided by occupation and contain not only ordinances and regulations but many supplications by women and men, disputes between various guilds or between a guild and a single individual, and letters concerning guild issues.

In Memmingen the sources are in the city archives and include city council minutes (Ratsprotokollbücher), hospital and midwives' records, citizenship lists (Bürgerbücher), municipal ordinances, wage lists for day laborers (Taglohner Taxe), school ordinances, guild records of all types, and a few isolated tax records. The Munich sources are also in the city archives and include city council records (Ratsitzungsprotokolle), hospital ordinances, wage lists and employee records, municipal mandates, and guild records. Munich has fairly complete tax lists for the period 1410–1640 and excellent court records for cases of slander, debt, market regulation infractions, and disturbance of the peace, though these begin only in the late sixteenth century.

The city archives of Stuttgart were demolished in World War II, though a register volume listing what was there is still extant, to my great frustration, for Stuttgart was one of the few cities which appears to have had a girls' school with female teachers. The city archives do house a variety of records from Cannstadt, a small town near Stuttgart, including isolated tax lists, property records, hospital finances, and court records. The state archives of Württemberg (Württembergisches Hauptstaatsarchiv) contain some pertinent material, particularly criminal ordinances and court records (Malefizakten, Polizeiakten, Strafakten) and regulations pertaining to agriculture and trade. The sources for Strasbourg are in the municipal archives (Archives Municipales) and include city ordinances and statutes, hospital records, and records of the various city councils (Akten der XV, Akten der XXI). I also examined a few of the sources in Augsburg, including city and guild ordinances, municipal decrees, and records from the council of physicians (Collegium Medicum), mostly for comparative purposes.

As this review of the archival sources makes clear, the quality or even existence of any records depends on chance, war, the whim of an archivist or city secretary, and the thoroughness of a city council. At least in these six cities, quantitative analysis of the existing records would be impossible. Even when the records contain large numbers of people and continue unbroken over a long period, changes in the way people were categorized and the total omission of large groups of people make statistical analysis questionable. This is a problem which plagues all social historians, particularly those examining the lives of peasants or lower-class urban groups and even more, those studying women. Records are arranged according to male names and male occupations, and women change names and often occupations when they marry or remarry. It is thus much more difficult to trace the work history of an individual woman than that of most men, whose names appear on apprenticeship contracts, master lists, and property registers. The occupations for which there are the most records are those which developed elaborate ordinances and rigid structures; they are also those which were most likely to exclude women. The majority of women worked at occupations which left no official record.

Because of these problems, I had to extract information on women's work from a variety of different contexts. Rather than focus on one type of document, I looked at everything I could find which might contain some relevant information, both prescriptive and descriptive. The prescriptive sources include the municipal and territorial laws, guild ordinances, hospital regulations, school ordinances, city council decrees, oaths, agricultural ordinances, and wage lists. Often prefaced with a statement as to why this particular law or regulation is necessary, they reflect the values and attitudes of civil and guild authorities toward women working and describe the ideal situation these authorities hoped to create. The descriptive sources include the citizenship lists, city council minutes, municipal tax records, wills, inventories, civil and criminal court cases, supplications and complaints to the city councils, records of municipal expenditures, private household and business records, hospital records, and lists of property owners. These sources provide a more accurate description of the actual, rather than the ideal, situation and include not only the opinions and ideas of the ruling elites but occasionally the ideas, feelings, and actions of illiterate working women and men who left few other traces. Though the records were actually written by city secretaries and private notaries, one can still hear in them the voices of early modern working women. All excerpts from documents are my own translations, as are all translations from other sources.

The study which follows is one about extraordinary women—extraordinary not because they were queens, artists, martyrs, or saints but simply because they made it into the records. Most working women in the sixteenth and seventeenth centuries did not challenge authorities, commit crimes, or ask for special consideration, so they were not mentioned by male records keepers. Thus there may have been many more women doing a wider variety of things than I have discovered; there certainly were no fewer.

This is also a study which views women's work from a variety of perspectives: economic, demographic, familial, political, intellectual. Women's work was affected by changes in all these realms, and no single theoretical framework explains how and why it changed. The men who largely controlled women's work were aware of its political, intellectual, and status implications as well as its economic effects; so were many of the working women themselves. It would be a disservice to their memory to view their work as less complex.

# CHAPTER ONE
# Political, Economic, and Legal Structures

T he work women did in any early modern city was determined to a great degree by the political, economic, and
legal structures of that city. Any understanding of the
changes in women's work requires some idea of those larger
structures. Important, too, are both variations among the
cities and things working women shared in all of them.
Therefore this chapter begins with short sketches of the relevant political, religious, and economic developments in each city and ends
with a more general discussion of citizenship, women's legal person-
ality, and the guilds.

Frankfurt was a free imperial city, ruled by a city council made up
of two-thirds city patriciate and one-third guild masters, which also
had control over the guilds. At the beginning of the sixteenth century,
it had a population of 11,000–12,000 and an economy based on agriculture, crafts, and local trade; only at the time of the fair, twice a year,
was it a major trading center. During the sixteenth century the city
encouraged immigration, especially by Dutch and Walloon (*welschen*)
clothmakers, who brought new methods of cloth production with
them, so that by the end of the century the city's population was about
18,000, one-fifth of whom were not Germans. Empty places in the city
were filled in, and trade blossomed year round. The population declined somewhat as a result of the Thirty Years' War, although the city
fared better in that conflict than most south German cities.

After a revolt in 1525 involving both religious and political demands, and further conflicts between Lutherans and Zwinglians, the
city finally settled for Lutheran Protestantism in 1535. This led, later

*Three Poor Housemaids. Broadside by Anthony, about 1580. Published in Friedrich Zoepfl,* Deutsche Kulturgeschichte, *vol. 2 (Freiburg in Breisgau: Herder, 1930).*

in the century, to conflicts with the Calvinist Welschen and also with Catholics who wanted to remain in the city. The city also had a large (2,000) Jewish population, all of whom lived on one tiny ghetto street. They were often involved in money lending and thus often the target of persecution; in 1612 in the Fettmilch Aufstand, a revolt with a wide range of demands, the Jews were thrown out of the city completely, although they were allowed back in shortly afterward under imperial protection.

Most crafts in the city were carried out by the 130 guilds, but during the course of the sixteenth century, more and more crafts began employing pieceworkers and day laborers in their shops. This was particularly true in the new industries, such as silk production, but occurred in older industries as well. Wages and hours for these workers were extremely low, especially in comparison to food prices, which rose quickly during the sixteenth century despite the city council's attempts to control them. Taxes also rose, especially indirect taxes on basic goods, which hurt the poor most of all, so there were numerous causes for social and economic grievances.

Political power in the city was increasingly concentrated in the hands of the old patriciate, which was really an urban aristocracy, as it lived from rents and had closed its ranks to newcomers. This group set itself off sharply, not only from the guilds, but also from the major merchants and traders, who were often the wealthiest city residents.[1]

Strasbourg was also a free imperial city, ruled by several different city councils, whose members also filled most of the official and supervisory posts in the city. Like many German cities Strasbourg had seen conflicts between the old patriciate—the *Constoffler*—and the guilds during the fourteenth century, and the guilds had gained significant representation on all city governing bodies. By 1482 the city's constitution was set, with political and economic power concentrated in a small group of merchants, guild masters, and professionals.

The guilds were also increasingly rationalized and regulated during the fifteenth century, with power concentrated more and more in the hands of the masters, to the detriment of the journeymen. The number of guilds in the city was set at twenty, with various occupations joined together into one guild. Every citizen had to "serve" (*dienen*) a guild, either actually doing the work of the guild (*leibzünftig*) or simply paying a guild for the privilege of belonging (*geldzünftig*).

The city's economy was broadly based—shipping on the Rhine, grain and wine from Alsace, the manufacture of a wide variety of goods, and especially regional commerce and trade. The level of commerce and manufacturing varied with good and bad harvests, local wars, and competition with other cities. In general the economy was healthy and growing during the early sixteenth century, suffered increasingly from the general inflation during the latter part of that century, and was then disrupted and depressed by the Thirty Years' War, a pattern found in most south German cities. The city's population followed this pattern as well, growing from about 15,000 during the fifteenth century to over 30,000 by 1620 but then shrinking again because of the war and several outbreaks of the plague to about 25,000 by the mid-seventeenth century.

The city accepted a very tolerant Protestantism in the mid-1520s in a movement first supported by intellectuals and the general populace and then gradually co-opted and adapted by the ruling elite. By the end of the sixteenth century, tolerance had been replaced by a stringent Lutheran orthodoxy, with Calvinists as well as Catholics and Jews no longer welcome in the city. During the course of the Reformation, the city councils also took over the administration and oversight of primary and secondary education, reorganized the system of poor relief, and expanded the city hospitals. The ruling patriciate thus assumed control of all the major political, economic, intellectual, and religious institutions in the city, a control which, despite social, economic, and political grievances, was unchallenged to 1789, though the city itself was annexed to France in 1681.[2]

Nuremberg was one of the three largest cities in early modern Germany—along with Cologne and Augsburg—and enjoyed a cultural and artistic importance that was perhaps unsurpassed. Although there is great dispute about the population size, it lay somewhere between 30,000 and 50,000 and seemed to be increasing throughout the period. Its economy was based on an enormous variety of products—leather, cloth, metals, gold, and later, books—and on commerce with all of Europe.

Nuremberg was a free imperial city, governed by a city council made up of twenty-six active members, all of whom were chosen from a very small circle of families. Entrance to this elite group was somewhat open in the fourteenth and fifteenth centuries but was closed tightly in 1521 and limited to forty-three families. The council (*Rat*) made all political, military, economic, and later, religious decisions in Nuremberg, down to the most trivial. Unlike the other cities I studied, Nuremberg had no independent guilds; after an abortive artisans' revolt in 1349, the council never allowed any craft independent powers of supervision or regulation. Anything which hinted at guild-like activities, such as workmen's drinking clubs (*Trinkstuben*), endowments limited to members of one craft, or extraordinary requirements for becoming a master, was quickly suppressed. Many crafts were increasingly regulated, with series of ever-more-explicit ordinances

14

promulgated from the fifteenth century on, but these ordinances were always issued by the council, not by the craft itself.

Despite a lack of political power, artisans and craftspeople in Nuremberg were well off economically until about 1550, as the paternalistic government maintained economic policies which benefited the entire city by promoting local manufacturing, the production of luxury goods, and a steady volume of trade. After the mid-sixteenth century the city began a slow economic decline owing to local wars, shifts in patterns of international trade, and increasing competition.

The council began to take over the administration of public welfare in the city as early as the late fourteenth century, establishing funds for orphans, indigent expectant mothers, lepers, the elderly, and others, and in 1522 it reorganized and rationalized the whole system. In 1525 the city became officially Lutheran, and the council assumed control of church lands and institutions, often using them to expand the municipal welfare system. Of all the cities I studied, Nuremberg was the most conservative and slow to change, for the city council was careful to weigh the effects of any change on the "public good."[3]

Memmingen was a small free imperial city with a population of about 4,100 in 1450. Its economy was originally based on the salt trade, for it stood where the salt road from Switzerland to Bavaria crossed the road from Ulm to Italy. During the fifteenth century it also became a center of fustian (a coarse blend of cotton and linen) weaving, wine production, and regional trade, with a wide variety of crafts.

As the result of an artisans' revolt in 1347, the guilds forced the town patriciate also to form a guild, the *Grosszunft*. The city council was from that year until 1551 about half artisan, half patrician, with the two groups alternating in holding the office of mayor. In 1551 as a result of the city's participation in the Schmalkaldic War, the emperor ended guild hegemony, and the municipal government from then on was purely patrician.

During the Peasants' War, leaders from three large peasant armies gathered in Memmingen, where they adopted the Twelve Articles, the basic list of peasant grievances. Shortly afterward the city threw out the peasants, who were not able to take the city. The Zwinglian Reformation had been introduced early, and in 1530 Memmingen was one of the four cities bringing the Confessio Tetrapolitana to the Diet of Augsburg, a confession which strongly emphasized biblical authority and sharply attacked ceremonies.

The city reached its zenith economically and politically in the mid-fifteenth century and remained relatively strong until the outbreak of the Thirty Years' War; by 1618 the population had grown to about

6,000. During the course of the war, however, the city was first occupied by Wallenstein's army and then besieged and taken alternately
by the Swedes, the imperial forces, the Swedes again, and finally the
Bavarians. By 1648 the city had only 1,500 inhabitants and was never
able to regain its commercial or cultural importance.[4]

Besides these four free imperial cities, I also investigated two ducal
cities. Stuttgart was a typical ducal capital, with few organs of self-
government and many lower level nobility who had land, or even
lived, in the city. Its population had grown from about 4,000 to 7,000
in the fifteenth century and continued to grow to about 10,000 by the
beginning of the seventeenth century. Its economy was based on the
agricultural and natural products of the surrounding Württemberg
countryside—wine, grain, flax, timber, fish—on long-distance trade
in salt, and on a variety of crafts, many of which produced luxury
goods for the ducal court.

During the early sixteenth century Stuttgart was caught in frequent
warfare under the long rule of Duke Ulrich, who also introduced the
Reformation to Württemberg. The duchy became officially Lutheran
in 1534, and the Reformation was further consolidated over the next
several decades under the leadership of Johannes Brenz. The Thirty
Years' War brought disaster to Stuttgart, as the city was occupied by
imperial forces and suffered several outbreaks of the plague, reducing
the population to half its prewar level.[5]

Munich was a very unusual ducal capital, as it had been granted a
city charter and a number of market privileges in the mid-fourteenth
century, during the imperial reign of Louis III (Ludwig der Bayer), a
member of the Wittelsbach family, who was also the duke of Bavaria.
Though these privileges, such as controlling tolls and market regulations and enjoying an independent city council, were usually reserved for free imperial cities, Munich had its charter reconfirmed by
each new emperor until 1641. In governmental structure and political
history Munich in the late Middle Ages was thus more like the free
imperial cities than the pure territorial capitals such as Stuttgart.

Munich saw a long dispute between the artisans and the patrician
city council in the late fourteenth century, which resulted in a short-
lived takeover by the artisans' party and eventually in a compromise
constitution, the Wahlbrief von 1403, which lasted until the eighteenth century. This agreement marked the beginning of a century-
long golden period for Munich. Her patricians grew as wealthy as the
nobility in the surrounding countryside, primarily from regional
trade in salt, grain, wine, cloth, and metals; trade with Venice; and
the east–west trade in building materials. In 1500 the city, with about

13,500 residents, reached a high point of self-rule because the Wittelsbach dukes had very few privileges.

Gradually during the sixteenth century the court began to take over more and more power in the city, assuming control of the salt monopoly and other city privileges. In the 1520s some old Munich families were attracted to Lutheranism, but the dukes remained staunchly Catholic, bringing in the Jesuits in 1559; religious tribunals in 1569 and 1571 broke all Protestant influence in Munich. Economically, the city remained strong in the sixteenth century, not only in regional and long-distance trade but also in the production of Loden, a coarse woolen cloth, and of fine manufactured goods, such as jewelry, clocks, armor, and musical instruments. As the Wittelsbachs increased their power, they began to transform Munich into a cultural and artistic capital, which attracted a variety of artisans to the city. By 1600 the population had grown to over 20,000.

Like every other city in south Germany, Munich suffered during the Thirty Years' War, from the Swedish occupation in 1632, even more from the plague the Spanish army brought into the city in 1634; about one-third of the population died. The city had to provide a number of forced loans to the dukes throughout the war, which ruined it financially. Munich would not reach its prewar heights in trade and manufacturing again until the nineteenth century.[6]

As these short descriptions indicate, the six cities varied in population, political structure, economic development, and religion. I had originally intended this study to be a comparative one, as I expected women's work to be viewed and regulated differently in the different cities. As the research progressed, it became apparent that the similarities were more striking than the differences. Though some types of occupations were found in only some cities, the work that most women did could be found in all communities. Women's work was restricted not only in cities with declining economies and shrinking opportunities but also in those with booming economies and steady immigration from the rural areas. It was restricted in cities occasionally ruled by noblewomen as well as in those whose governing body was elected. City councils with heavy guild membership limited women's work, but so did pure patrician councils, to whom working women represented no status or economic threat. Religious differences also played a lesser role than I expected. Though they disagreed on so many other issues, Protestant and Catholic men united in their growing opposition to women working in certain occupations. It became clear to me that the economic, political, and cultural forces which determined women's work were shared ones.

17

The institutional structures providing the background for women's work were also shared ones. Every city made clear distinctions between citizens and noncitizens, giving citizens great legal and economic advantages. Every city had law codes which enumerated the rights and responsibilities of city residents and controlled their actions. Every city had some form of guild or craft organizations which regulated some occupations and also had certain occupations not controlled by any guild. Within all of these structures distinctions were made between men and women; distinctions were also made among women according to their marital status, which rarely made a difference for men.

Citizenship was the fundamental institution on which all others were based. As cities had grown during the Middle Ages and had won their independence from feudal overlords through negotiation, purchase, or revolution, they had become legal entities, corporate bodies made up of all those living within the city walls. It was therefore extremely important that everyone living within the city, or at least those owning property, renounce all allegiance to other authorities, if the city was to maintain legal and economic independence. Cities therefore required all propertied persons to formally assume citizenship if they moved into the city and to formally renounce it if they left permanently. Cities backed these requirements with taxation demands; noncitizens often paid much higher taxes, and persons renouncing citizenship were often fined heavily as the cities attempted to discourage them from leaving.

Citizenship entailed both obligations and privileges, and cities increasingly denied citizenship to those who could not carry out the obligations or else simply quit requiring everyone living in the city to become citizens. Servants coming in from the countryside to work in the households of citizens were not required to become citizens, nor were wage laborers or pieceworkers who did not maintain their own households. Those seeking citizenship had to prove they were of legitimate birth, free status, and "honorable reputation" (*wohl Verhaltens*) and often had to pay a citizenship fee.[7] By the sixteenth century noncitizens often outnumbered citizens within the city walls, though the privileges accorded to citizens remained. If one wanted a political voice or economic power, one had to become a citizen.

In most cases regarding citizenship, cities treated men and women relatively equally. Unmarried women or widows moving into a city were required to purchase or earn citizenship in ways similar to men and to prove that they were legitimate, free, and had good reputations. They swore an oath on first becoming citizens and were required in most cases to provide soldiers and arms for the city's defense.[8] The number of men and amount of equipment women were required to provide were assessed according to the value of the property they held, exactly as they were for male heads of household.[9] Citizens' wives and daughters often did not swear an oath, as the citizens' oath was only taken by the head of household. After a male citizen died, his widow was often required to take an oath, thus indicating her new status and responsibilities.[10]

Occasionally women were granted citizenship without paying the normal fees, usually if they were maids who had served a long time—ten, fifteen, or twenty years—and "as long as they behaved honorably and without causing any aggravations." Often these women had to swear that they would not ask for public support during their first five years as citizens. This was also true for widows who paid normal citizenship fees; in addition to the fee they had to prove they owned enough property to support themselves without working.[11] Cities also attracted midwives by offering free citizenship to them and their husbands in the same way they offered citizenship to physicians.[12] Women who felt they had performed a special service to city residents occasionally requested a grant of citizenship, as a case in Memmingen in 1571 notes: "She says that she served the people during the Schmalkaldic Wars with her cooking and other services."[13] Such cases were decided individually.

Women also used religion as a means of obtaining citizenship. With the coming of the Reformation, and especially with the Peace of Augsburg, there was an upsurge in those renouncing citizenship and moving elsewhere. In Nuremberg, for example, the decade of the 1510s saw 66 persons giving up their citizenship; the 1520s, 131; and the 1530s, 383.[14] (Nuremberg officially became Protestant in 1525.) Where did these people go? In many cases, to nearby Catholic cities, such as Munich. A woman requested that she and her husband be allowed to become citizens of Munich again, as they could no longer stay in Nuremberg; the Munich city council wanted proof that she "had always held the Catholic religion" even while living in Nuremberg before it would allow them back in. In this case, they only asked about her religious practices, not those of her husband, perhaps because she was making the request. Another refugee from Nuremberg, also Catholic, offered to nurse "sick and infected persons" if Munich would grant her citizenship. Again the city council requested that she bring proof from religious authorities that she had always been a Catholic.[15] Religion was also an acceptable justification for a woman to remain in a city after her husband had left. Even in cases involving the most gruesome wife beating or cruelty, city councils usually ordered women to remain with their husbands; the councils would even try to find men who had deserted their families in order to send the family to them! If the man left for religious reasons, however, the family was often allowed to stay, as long as they agreed to follow the religion of the city.[16]

In some cases involving spouses of differing faiths, a clear double standard emerged in city councils' decisions about whether to allow the couple to remain in the city. In 1631 the Strasbourg council considered whether citizens should lose their citizenship if they married Calvinists. It decided that a man would not "because he can probably draw his spouse away from her false religion and bring her on to the correct path." He would have to pay a fine, though, for "bringing an unacceptable person into the city." A woman who married a Calvinist would lose her citizenship, however, "because she would let herself easily be led into error in religion by her husband and be led astray."[17]

In some cases, cities allowed women to stay without obtaining citizenship at all, usually if they were extremely poor or very old or sick. The city council still wanted to know who and where these charity cases were and sent inspectors out to each quarter of the city. Foreign women who had not received special permission but who were found living in the city were fined, as were the citizens who housed them.[18]

If a woman moved out of the city permanently, she was expected to renounce her citizenship formally and pay the often quite substantial tax (*Nachsteuer*) demanded by the city council. Occasionally she was allowed to retain her citizenship if she married a foreigner and moved away, but only after receiving special permission and under special circumstances, such as the city council's recognition that the new husband was quite elderly and the woman would most likely be moving back into the city after his death. All citizens, male and female, were usually required to live in the city and could lose their citizenship for staying too long outside its walls.[19]

Women, like men, could also lose citizenship for a variety of reasons. One of the most common punishments for a crime was banishment, usually a specific distance away from the city walls. As cities began to enforce stricter moral legislation in the sixteenth and seventeenth centuries, they used the threat of loss of citizenship as a weapon in the battle against adultery and fornication. In Strasbourg in 1620 any citizen-woman, widowed or single, who let herself get pregnant before her wedding was to lose her citizenship once the pregnancy was discovered. This was during the Thirty Years' War, and the city council was especially horrified at the prospect of soldiers impregnating city residents. In 1623 the city council even considered extending this to any male citizen whose wife became pregnant before marriage, although so drastic a step was never taken.[20] Couples who married before they had enough money to set up a household, and thus were likely to become public welfare cases, were also threatened with loss of citizenship.[21]

As cities began to tighten their citizenship requirements, they tried to prevent women from marrying "unacceptable" foreigners. In 1557 the Strasbourg city council forbade citizens' widows or daughters to marry foreigners without its express permission. If they did, they and their husbands would have to leave the city. Memmingen also granted citizenship rights to maids who had served faithfully for many years, but on the condition that if they married, it would be to a citizen "so that two foreign persons do not come into the city in this way." Augsburg, as well, often accepted a woman as a citizen with the note "on the condition that she doesn't marry, unless it is to a citizen." In 1613 Strasbourg sharpened its earlier restrictions and required a male foreigner who wanted to marry a citizen's widow or daughter to obtain citizenship rights on his own before he even became engaged.[22] The situation was the same in Frankfurt. According to a regulation passed in 1614, if a woman married a foreigner who had not received citizenship rights on his own, she would lose her citizenship and be forced to leave the city. In 1623 this was extended to male citizens who married foreign women:

> It has been discovered in the case of citizen's sons and widowers, that many of them marry foreign, propertyless, and even slovenly suspicious female persons and then bring them in [to Frankfurt] and that these persons receive citizenship through this marriage: when the husband dies they then marry someone similar [i.e., a foreigner] and the city and the common good are brought all kinds of problems and difficulties. So we are caused and moved to extend the previous ordinance to include male persons, widowers, and citizen's sons. Therefore they are earnestly admonished that from now on no one is to marry, or even offer to marry or become engaged to, any foreign female person without first bringing us proof of her legitimate birth and her property and means of support. If the marriage is then allowed, these persons are required to purchase citizenship according to the amount of property they own as the law requires.[23]

In regard to the basic rights, obligations, and duties of citizenship, then, cities made little distinction between men and women. Beyond that, however, there were clear legal restrictions on what the female half of the population could do. Some of these restrictions, and the majority of legal cases in which women were involved, concerned private and family matters, so I do not specifically discuss them here. Others concerned legal and economic matters which affected all women, for example, witnessing, inheritance, and guardianship, thus providing the legal setting within which women could operate on public matters; these I mention briefly. Still others primarily concerned working women and are examined in greater depth.

Women could serve as witnesses in civil cases if no male witnesses were available and could appear in criminal cases, though their rights in the latter were somewhat limited.[24] A woman could report stolen goods and could report that she had been raped, although she would usually have to prove that she had tried to resist and that she had a good reputation. Pregnant women were given special rights as witnesses; along with other "dangerously ill" people, they were allowed to give their testimony before a case had been officially opened, in case they were no longer available once it had.[25]

If a woman was ordered to appear before a court as a defendant or witness and refused, she was to be banished. In the case of a married woman, if the refusal was with her husband's knowledge, he was to take the punishment; if he did not know or approve, she was to take it. A married woman was also required to accept a court order that her husband appear; if she refused to take it or took it and then did not tell her husband, she was to be arrested herself.[26]

If there was any suspicion about a woman's character or motivation, however, her testimony in any case was to be discounted: "If a woman is of a timid disposition and fears her husband, then she is to be disdained. If she is a brave woman, who only wants to hide her feelings from her husband out of consideration, then she should be accepted, as long as she is found to have a good reputation [*guten Leumundts*]. Also, if the opposition party will allow her to speak, then she is not to be ignored."[27]

Women could freely make their own wills, although they generally could not serve as witnesses for anyone else's will. In Nuremberg girls could make a binding will at the age of twelve, while boys had to wait until they were fourteen. In the Duchy of Württemberg the legal age for both boys and girls was sixteen. In general, no special requirements were placed on women making wills; the procedure varied from town to town as to the number of witnesses required and the way in which a will had to be registered but was the same for both men and women. This was also the case with inheritance laws. These were often extremely complicated, as they sought to cover every possibility—multiple marriages, stepchildren from a previous marriage, grounds for disinheritance, adoption, and so on—but were roughly the same for men and women. The only interesting difference is that in some cities a son could be disinherited at any time for entering into a marriage against his parents' will, but a daughter could not if it was shown that the parents had not found her a husband before she was twenty-two or twenty-four.[28]

A clear difference between the legal status of men and women emerges in the issue of guardianship. When a man died, his children, even if their mother was living, were usually given a male guardian responsible for their welfare until they came of age. Usually, although not always, the widow was given a guardian (*Vogt*) as well. He was to represent her in court cases and act as her agent if a male voice was needed. Here again, though, there was a difference between legal theory and practical reality. Widows were frequently represented by their guardians but also appeared in court to present their own cases.

For a variety of reasons cities began to tighten up their systems of guardianship beginning in the late fifteenth century. I found it possible to trace this process in Strasbourg and see some of the motivation behind it. In 1465 four members of the city council recommended that a guardian be appointed for every widow within one month of her husband's death:

> Who is to give her useful and well thought out advice: also every widow responsible to provide a horse for the city [i.e., whose property was above a certain value] should not have the right to give away or sell more than 20 gulden worth of her property or goods without the knowledge and approval of her guardian. Every widow should also make a yearly report concerning her property to her guardian. If the widow marries again the guardianship is to be ended.[29]

But the system was not to be limited solely to widows:

> All unmarried women who have come of age but who no longer have a father and mother are to be given a guardian as well. Also if a man or boy who owns property comes of age and handles this property in such a way that he is bringing himself to ruin, which the council can clearly see, then the council will appoint him a guardian from among his own relatives or in some other manner help him to take care of his own interests.[30]

Thus, with the patriarchal attitudes so common among city councils, these four members recommended that those judged to be incapable of handling their own affairs be given guardians "for their own good." Men who were unable to deal with their own inheritance were to be treated exactly like women.

Although at first glance the city council appeared to be protecting gullible widows and spendthrift young men, their real motivation emerged in a discussion six years later. Again the council recommended that all widows and unmarried women be given guardians, but this time expressly to prevent their going into convents and deeding all their property to the convent, "by which their relatives are disinherited and the city loses people who provide it with horses [i.e., taxpayers]." The guardian was to approve any agreements the woman made regarding her property, although she could complain to the council if she felt he was treating her unfairly. If she wanted to go into a convent, she was free to go but could only take in enough property to support her during her lifetime; at her death no more than fifty pounds was to be given to the convent, with the rest to go to her heirs. Covering all angles, the council also noted that women who gave up their citizenship but then came into one of the city's convents were also to follow these rules, "for giving up their citizenship shall not allow them to escape them."[31]

The council adopted these regulations shortly afterward, but not without opposition. One of the most vocal opponents was the preacher and moralist Geiler of Kaisersberg, who saw the regulations as an infringement on individual women's opportunity to do works of charity. In a sermon from 1501 he commented:

> Arranging a guardian for widows who are responsible and sensible persons is a novelty that has arisen in this city supposedly for the common good. In truth, as I will report, it was a self-seeking move by those who were in power. Strasbourg has long stood and been governed without such an inappropriate law. The decline of the city cannot be attributed to it, but to many other things as I have often said before. Everyone who is bothered by something always says it harms the common good, but it really involves his own affairs.
> The opposite is shown to us in the advice of God and the practice of the holy saints, like Saint Elizabeth, who gave two thousand marks at one time to the poor for the building of a hospital, or Saint Paula, who lost everything that she had, and many others too numerous to tell. The Gospel tells us directly: if you want to be saved, go out and sell everything you have and give it to the poor. It does not say to give it to your heirs and relatives. This law is totally against the word of Christ. It is a mockery of God, a haughty service of the devil to forbid a pious person to give everything that she owns for the will of God.[32]

In this and other sermons Geiler constantly stressed the freedom and right of both men and women to do what they wanted with their own money. It is clear, of course, that the underlying dispute is an economic one. The city felt it was losing too much money to the convents; the convents, that they had a right to the property of the women who entered them. What happened as a result of this dispute, however, was that the power of guardians over widows and unmarried women in all economic matters, not simply their going into convents, was increased.[33] As is so often the case throughout this study, restrictions on women came about as a by-product of a dispute between two groups over political and economic power.

The power of guardians was similarly increased in other cities throughout the sixteenth century. In 1578 Augsburg ordered that all widows report to the official in charge (*Oberpfleger*) within one month of the death of their husband, make an appraisal of all goods and property, and choose two men who were not heirs to act as guardians. If the widow did not, the city council would choose these for her "because so often out of stupidity and inexperience, especially in these difficult times, widows have diminished the estate of their children and even sunk into total poverty." The women of Augsburg were apparently not ready to admit to their stupidity or inexperience, however, as this ordinance was reissued in 1615, with the added threat that if any woman out of "disobedience or mischief" did not follow it, she was to be clapped in irons.[34] In 1668 it was reissued again, as a new problem had emerged. Widows had claimed that since their guardians, and not they themselves, swore an oath that the appraisal was complete, they could not be held liable if it were not. After all, they were only inexperienced women who might easily forget to include something. The city council responded by adding the clause that the widows, as well as their guardians, had to swear all oaths, whether they appeared in court or not.[35]

Throughout the entire period, widows frequently took their guardians to court when they felt their rights had somehow been violated. All the city codes allowed them to do so, and city councils were quite willing to order a guardian to take better care of a widow and her children or to appoint a new guardian if the first one was creating problems.[36] In these cases, the widow herself, not some male relative, appeared before the city council to argue her case. Thus, though the power of guardians steadily increased during the period, women were never totally at their mercy.

Along with a strengthening of the role of guardians over widows, the sixteenth and seventeenth centuries saw increasing restrictions on widows' rights to their own children. In a number of cities it was up to the guardians whether a woman should retain control of her children if she remarried. Even with very young children, the deceased husband's father often had more to say about their future than their mother did. Only women whose children were illegitimate had full fatherly force and could appear in court on behalf of their children in all cases.[37]

In addition to these limitations on their ability to be witnesses, make wills, serve as guardians, and handle inheritance, women were often specifically forbidden to make contracts or own, buy, and sell property. The guiding force behind many of the restrictions was the concept of *weibliche Freiheit*, "female freedom" in exact translation. Basically this meant that women had the "freedom" to declare their signature invalid on contracts and agreements in cases where they were acting for any third party, including their husbands. They could simply say that they had been misled or pressured or had not understood what they were doing and thus should not be held liable.[38]

In some cases, weiblich Freiheit acted as protection for a woman. She could even claim it on loans from her own husband and say that he had pressured her into making an agreement. Only if two of her male relatives were present could she legally give up this right, "because wives are so easily persuaded into making such dangerous promises through the duplicity of their husbands."[39] In some cities two impartial judges could be substituted for the relatives.[40]

Generally, though, weibliche Freiheit acted as a protection for the husband, for it meant his wife could not legally pledge his goods or property to pay back any debts.[41] The husband's knowledge and agreement was needed on any major financial decision which involved property held jointly: "Whoever loans a woman money without the knowledge of her husband, be it man or woman, Christian or Jew, shall not have the right to demand it, and her husband will be able to retrieve the letter or pawn for five pounds. Before this, he must prove the debt was made without his knowledge."[42]

There were, however, a number of ways a woman could get around this weibliche Freiheit and make legally binding contracts. First, if she was acting in her own interests, handling her own property, the principle did not apply at all. Even a married woman who owned property in her own name—and this was very common in the sixteenth century—was free to do with it as she wished, to buy, sell, loan, or pawn without the knowledge or approval of her husband.[43] Widows and unmarried women could also handle their property without a co-signer.

Second, if a woman had acted deceitfully (*"gefährlich und betrüglich"*) or had made money off the contract, she could not later plead weibliche Freiheit. This was a protection for those who lent a woman money under the understanding that she would not later claim weibliche Freiheit, only to have her attempt to do so anyway. Cities added this limitation, despite the fact that weibliche Freiheit was a right protected by the emperor, because they found that "good and honorable people, in all good faith" were loaning money and then losing it when a woman refused to pay them back.[44]

Third, a woman could also willingly and specifically give up this right in the presence of two witnesses who were her relatives. In Frankfurt this agreement was to be made in the presence of a Bürgermeister, and the clause noting her renunciation was written into the contract. In Nuremberg she could also do this in the presence of two of her husband's friends and a notary.[45]

Fourth, and most important for this story, exceptions were made for women whose occupations required that they buy and sell goods or loan and borrow money. The earliest city law codes (e.g., Lübeck 1220–1226) made no mention of such occupations, but usually by the late fourteenth century, exceptions were being made for all sorts of women. In Lübeck these women were described as "those who have market rights [*kopschat*], and who loan and sell independently." The Munich city law code from 1340 states simply: "A woman who stands at the public market and who buys and sells has all the rights that her husband does." An Augsburg ordinance from 1432 notes that all female marketwomen (*Krämerin*) lost their weibliche Freiheit.[46]

In the late fifteenth century many cities began to define more precisely who was and who was not a market woman, making exceptions for them in suing and inheritance cases as well. A Nuremberg city ordinance notes: "Also no bailiff may summon a married woman. And no judge or summoner can issue a suit against any married woman. If a suit is written against a married woman, her husband shall be without penalty and can free his wife from any suit with a payment of thirteen pfennige, except for female tailors, shopkeepers, money changers, innkeepers, and market women."[47] Frankfurt and Stuttgart used similar language, and as a case in 1505 in Frankfurt indicates, married market women, not their husbands, were imprisoned for their own debts.[48]

The special status of market women is evident in inheritance laws. On the death of a spouse, most cities allowed the survivor to separate all his or her goods from those of the deceased and pay off the heirs and creditors only from the goods of the deceased. By doing this, the surviving spouse also gave up any claim to a share of the estate of the deceased but was assured of retaining something if the debts were larger than the estate. This was intended primarily as a protection for women, who could thus at least take back and live off their dowry and any other goods they owned separately, rather than see them go to pay off their husband's creditors. This "renunciation and separation" had to be done within a month of the death, and the surviving spouse had to swear that he or she had not taken anything from the estate of the deceased.

Market women were not allowed to do this renunciation and separation. The Nuremberg Reformation from 1564 spells this out: "If a couple practices a craft or business together, with buying and selling, like cloth cutting, money changing, running a stand at the market and the like, or are public innkeepers or wine handlers, then both spouses are obliged to pay all debts in the same manner. Because the wife in such occupations is in the same danger of loss, an equal share of the profits shall also belong to her."[49]

The Frankfurt Reformation from 1578 gives a more elaborate justification for excluding market women:

> Because in selling and at the market stands, the two spouses carry out a common business—the wife as well as the husband goes through the streets or sits at the market stall, sells and buys, takes in and gives out money, keeps the books, and other such things. Also, with people who keep a public inn or hostelry, or a common wine stand, it is difficult to divide or separate the goods. So that the people who do business with them will not be deceived or injured, we have decided that in such cases both spouses will be responsible to pay back all debts in full.[50]

In Frankfurt and Lübeck the common business even included the woman's dowry; if she was a market woman and carried out a common business with her husband, she could make no marriage contract which excluded her dowry from the final reckoning of debts. The reasoning of the Lübeck authorities is illustrative on this point:

> Because this city of Lübeck is a merchants' city and dedicated to trade and commerce [*Handel und Wandel*], honor and trust must always be present, which the oldest and first laws clearly recognized. Thus it is better that private persons, especially women, are somewhat harmed in their inheritance and goods than that the trust needed in trade is weakened or even destroyed in this city, which would bring decline and disaster.[51]

The Frankfurt Reformation, like that of Nuremberg, gave her the slight solace that "because the woman in this sort of common business must stand in the same danger and chance of loss, it is also just [*billich*] that all profits from such business belong equally to her.[52]

Frankfurt later extended this restriction to include wives of "craftsmen, vineyard workers, day laborers, and the like." Why? "Because what they produce and purchase for their craft (with which both spouses support themselves) is common property and is often even acquired without purchase (i.e., by barter with the neighbors, or made by one spouse), and one as well as the other is responsible to pay all debts."[53] With this, the city council recognized that neither spouse would have brought much, if anything, into the marriage and that both worked to produce or purchase any goods, so that dividing things between the husband and wife would have made little sense. Though this is a compliment to the wife of a laborer, as it recognizes her vital contribution to the family income, it actually worked to her detriment, for she was often left with nothing on her husband's death because their debts were so often greater than all the property held.

Strasbourg had passed a similar ordinance in the early sixteenth century, but one vague enough to cause constant problems. In 1552 the city council decided to spell things out more clearly:

> Because a large number of tiresome legal cases have come up frequently between creditors and widows, as to whether these women are market women or not, and on both sides there have been appreciable expenses, we have decided that from now on, all women are to be recognized and seen as market women if they are in business by themselves or alongside and with their husbands (either in salted or other wares, in grain or other things, with nothing excluded). Whether they sell inside or outside the city of Strasbourg, on market or fair days, whether they buy or sell wholesale or retail, or exchange goods for other goods and thus carry out public business (*öffentliche Gewerbehandel*). Those who sell wine, fruit, grain, or other things from their own fields at harvesttime are not to be considered [as market women], but only those who handle these goods as their primary business and derive most of their support from this.[54]

Strasbourg was somewhat more narrow in its consideration of the wives of craftsmen than Frankfurt was: "And as to whether the craftspeople who buy wares and then later distribute, sell, or trade these goods are to be considered market people: so in the same manner if a craftsman or his wife buys other wares and sells them along with the things they have made themselves, she is to be considered a market woman."[55] The council also reserved the right to decide in those cases in which the woman's status might still be in dispute.

Just such a case was brought to the Strasbourg XV, the body which handled all internal affairs, in 1584. This case points up several aspects of the whole issue of weibliche Freiheit and the status of market women. A butcher's widow wanted to separate her goods from those of her husband, a proposal opposed by his creditors, who argued "that the widow, while her husband was alive, stood at the butcher's counter herself, weighed out the meat, took in money, melted tallow, made candles, sold the candles, and other things. After his death she also slaughtered four head of cattle and received the money for them;

therefore she is to be considered a market woman." The widow answered them that she had not stood at the counter or sold at the market. The council asked its lawyers about what to do in the matter, questioned the other butchers, and finally decided that she had not been active enough to be considered a market woman. What is striking about this case is that the woman was playing down her own role, arguing that she had less of a part in the family business than she probably had. It was to her financial advantage to assert, or to pretend, that she knew nothing about butchering.[56]

Thus the whole question of weibliche Freiheit and its limitations takes a very ironic twist. Originally, it appears that any woman could claim weibliche Freiheit, no matter what her occupation. Gradually city councils realized (or claimed) that women were using the privilege to their own advantage in order to make contracts and then break them. The women most likely to have done this, the market women, were gradually excluded from weibliche Freiheit and forced to take full responsibility for all their economic activities. Because in many cases, like that of the butcher's widow, it was detrimental to the woman involved to be considered a market woman, she was forced into the position of denying her own competence and knowledge about the family business.[57] A Munich case from 1595 is a good example. A man demanded payment for a horse from the widow of a butcher, who answered him that she "knew nothing about her husband's business or what he had contracted for." She knew very well, however, that this man had not been there when all her husband's creditors had been ordered to appear shortly after his death to make their claims against his estate.[58] In most such cases, the city councils recognized that such women were economically active and relatively independent; the women themselves tried to deny it in order to claim weibliche Freiheit. What few women's statements there are about their own activities are therefore not always creditable; the creditors may actually be more accurate when they report that certain women did everything their husbands did in running a business.

Though law codes mention only the four exceptions to weibliche Freiheit already noted (women acting in their own interests, women specifically giving this right up, women deceiving their creditors, and market women), actual court proceedings involve many more women. Women were making contracts, buying, selling, and trading land and goods all the time without specific male approval or the co-signature of their husbands. Perhaps some implied renunciation of weibliche Freiheit was understood in each case, or else the whole principle was frequently ignored.[59]

This distinction between theory and practice appears in many types of legal cases involving women. Despite theoretical restrictions on their ability to appear in court, women appeared as plaintiffs and defendants fairly frequently. Many of these cases involved marriage and family issues, but others were strictly economic. Women brought suits to demand repayments for debts owed them, usually quite small but occasionally as high as one thousand florins; to ask for extensions on loans they owed to others; to demand that pawnbrokers return goods they had paid off; or to demand that former or present employers pay them the salary owed them.[60] Though the law distinguished between single, married, and widowed women, women of all marital statuses brought cases to court, evoking no comment that this was somehow unusual.

The difference between theory and practice points out the ambiguity of women's legal position. Women were simultaneously independent legal persons (they owned property, inherited wealth, received wages, paid taxes) and dependent parts of a legal entity, the family, whose financial decisions they did not officially control. On marriage, a woman gave up some of her legal rights in return for greater security and an established status, but not all of them. At no point in the sixteenth and seventeenth centuries did a woman completely lose her legal identity when she married. She could also use the institution of the family to defend her status and rights against other male-controlled institutions, or even against her own husband. On widowhood, a woman's legal status changed again, and not simply back to what it had been before marriage, for the widow's status brought additional responsibilities and opportunities.

This ambiguity stems from the aims and motivations of the men making the laws and also from their views of women. They viewed women as less competent and weaker than men, needing both guardians to protect them and protection from those guardians, should the guardians turn out to be unscrupulous and crafty. City councils also realized that women could be just as unscrupulous and crafty as men, so laws were needed to protect society from women as well as to protect women themselves. The family was seen as the foundation of society, with the husband as its proper head; when strengthening the power of the husband was perceived to strengthen the family, lawmakers built up his power. If his personal interests worked to the detriment of the family, however, the wife's interests might be strengthened. City councils aimed at both social control and full city treasuries, aims which came into conflict when they had to decide whether to allow widows and single women to work independently.

If there were ambiguities in women's general legal status during the early modern period, there were even more surrounding their rights and responsibilities in the workplace. Most production in 1500 was organized by craft guilds, which had grown up in most German cities during the twelfth and thirteenth centuries. During the fourteenth century these guilds began to demand that they be allowed to participate in city government, which was generally controlled by a small number of merchant families. These merchant families, often termed "patricians," dominated the economy of the city and were the only ones allowed on the city council.

The guild demands varied from city to city but generally included seats on the city council, an end to the patricians' special privileges, some control over defense of the city, rights to determine taxation levels and the tax structure, control of the gates into the city, and other economic and political rights. The guilds were often joined in their opposition to the patriciate by day laborers and the poor, and the conflicts were often violent. In some cities, such as Strasbourg and Memmingen, the conflict resulted in the guilds' winning some participation in the city government. In other cities, such as Nuremberg, the guilds were totally defeated, and the city council forbade any independent guilds from that point on; production in Nuremberg was organized by the "sworn crafts," which were completely controlled by the council.[61]

Conflicts between the guilds and the city councils continued throughout the early modern period and frequently involved women's work or, more specifically, whether the guilds or the city council would control what work women would do and when exceptions would be made. Women were rarely actors in these conflicts, for with the exception of a few female guilds in Cologne and Basel, the guilds in Germany were male organizations.[62] They were structured according to the male life cycle. One studied for a set number of years as an apprentice, then became a journeyman and theoretically worked under a number of different masters to perfect one's skills, then finally made a masterpiece. If it was judged acceptable by the current masters (and they felt there was business enough to support another shop), one could settle down and open a shop.

The guilds recognized, however, that a master could not run a shop on his own, and in many cities they required that the master be married. The master's wife and daughters thus often learned some of the skills required for that particular craft, though they were not officially part of the apprenticeship structure. In addition, a master craftsman might hire maids or female pieceworkers during busy seasons, so there were often women working in the shops alongside the journeymen and apprentices. Most workshops were small and attached to the master craftsman's house; thus women could easily divide their time between domestic duties and work in the shop. Women could spend a great deal of their time in production-related tasks, for there was relatively little housework in early modern homes. Clothing and furnishings were few, simple, and rarely cleaned, and a maid or maids assisted in the cooking and washing.[63]

Because women were not officially part of the guild structure, however, their work in guild shops was not dependent on their own level of training but on their relation to past, present, and future guild masters. The work changed when the woman's status changed from daughter to wife to mother to widow, and thus it followed the female life cycle. Because these status changes were personal ones and might occur at any time, it was difficult for working women to perceive themselves as a group with common interests. Unlike apprentices and journeymen, they did not have a clear peer group. Because of the informal nature of women's participation in the guild system, there were no formal institutions which protected their rights in the workshop. Individual women might be granted the right to work at a particular occupation, but there were no blanket statements allowing women per se to work.

Masters' widows were a particular problem for guilds. On the one hand these women were generally skilled at running a shop, and the tools, raw materials, and workers were already in place. In addition, the guilds wanted to make sure that masters' widows and orphans were supported, for they were fraternal welfare organizations as well as economic institutions. On the other hand the widow had not received official training, and by operating a shop she often prevented another master from being allowed to join the guild and open a shop. The fact that she was now giving orders to apprentices and journeymen also contradicted commonly held notions of the proper place of men and women. Guilds thus had to resolve a variety of conflicting aims in their treatment of masters' widows.

The guilds themselves were also in the process of change during the period. Particularly in cloth production, but also in other industries, the independent household-workshop was being replaced by the household whose labor was hired by a merchant investor who owned the raw materials. The investor might hire many households, both in the city and in the surrounding countryside, and his trading network was often international in scope. Guilds often felt threatened because they could not produce products as cheaply, and so they sharply limited the number of workshops by restricting widows or by allowing a journeyman to become a master only if he could inherit an existing shop.[64]

As the opportunities for journeymen to become masters decreased, they became permanent wage workers rather than masters-in-training (*Gesellen* rather than *Knechte*) and formed separate journeymen's guilds. These guilds demanded the right to determine who would work in a shop by refusing to work alongside those who did not have their approval. At first this meant those who were of illegitimate birth, but gradually it came to include women. Journeymen first demanded that masters' maids be excluded from all production-related tasks, then that wives and daughters be excluded as well.[65] Guild shops became increasingly male, as even the master's wife retreated more and more from actual production.

The new capitalist industries offered employment for women, but this was also problematic in the eyes of local authorities. When women—and young male workers as well—worked in guild shops, they generally lived in the master's household and were under his control. When workers were simply hired by the day or by the piece, they might live independently, not under anyone's control. Local and state authorities considered such "masterless" persons a threat to public order and passed laws restricting their movement from town to town or even prohibiting them from living on their own.

Concentrating on guilds and capitalist industries, on economic structures, can, however, be somewhat misleading. Most women worked in occupations which were not highly regulated or in sales and service occupations not directly affected by the rise of capitalism. Even for someone involved in an industry which did change, such as cloth production, the transition may have meant little. The working conditions of a spinner in the home of a master weaver, or in a small workshop organized by a major cloth merchant, were no different. She may have been called a "maid" in the former situation and a "piecework spinner" in the latter, but a close look at her daily tasks shows the two to be identical. An overemphasis on changing economic structures may lead away from the realities of most women's work lives.

This qualification must be kept in mind when analyzing any of the legal and economic restrictions on women during this period. Law codes and guild regulations are only a framework, only a theoretical description of the way one group of men would have liked things to operate. They are not a picture of reality—in fact, they are often the opposite. Any move by a city council or a guild usually came in response to something people were already doing. These bodies were inherently conservative and made changes only after extended grumbling and long considerations. This is certainly the case with women's economic activities; if something was forbidden, it is certain a number of people were doing it. The more frequently a prohibition was repeated, the more often the law was being broken. One must examine, then, not only changes in laws and ordinances, but if and when and why these changes were enforced.

Throughout the next four chapters I examine the work that women were doing and how economic, political, and intellectual changes affected that work. As this chapter has pointed out, generalizations which lump all women together are very dangerous. Women's experience varied according to social class, economic status, and citizenship status—factors traditionally taken into account in social and economic history—but also according to age, marital status, family size, and life span—factors rarely considered. In some cases, the sex of a working person is not an important factor in analyzing the impact of change. More often, however, no matter how much variation there was among women, the fact that they were women was the most important determinant of what work they would do.

*Birthroom Scene with Midwife and Other Women Assisting. Woodcut from Jakob Rueff's* Hebammenbuch *(Frankfurt, 1563).*

# CHAPTER TWO
# Hospitals, Healing, and Health Care

**M**any women worked in health care and healing during the early modern period, for this was considered natural and proper, part of women's sphere. These occupations were viewed as outgrowths or extensions of a woman's function in the home—cooking, cleaning, child care, nursing the sick, care for the elderly. They often required little or no specialized training, so women could stop and start frequently, working only when financially pressed, or work part-time if they had a family to care for. Because of this flexibility and fluidity, the women were often underpaid and rarely organized or protested to get higher wages or salaries.

For a variety of reasons, women working in health care or hospitals were rarely viewed as threatening. They were not an economic threat, as they rarely received more than subsistence wages and sometimes not even that; they were not a moral or status threat, as their occupations were regarded by society as naturally female; they were not a political threat, as they rarely had power over male employees or assistants and so caused little resentment. It is difficult to find precise figures, but the early modern period may have seen a growth in the relative numbers of women employed in these occupations, particularly as other fields were closed to them.

Though health care occupations were generally low status and poorly paid, city governments did not regard them as trivial and unimportant. They were increasingly regulated by ordinances about training, duties, conduct, pay, and responsibilities. Many of the women made reports or brought complaints to the councils, and their suggestions for improvements in their particular occupation or institution were taken seriously and often acted upon. In a few occupations, such as midwifery, the women involved did develop a strong sense of work identity and a clear sense of their own importance to the life and health of the city.

I begin with a look at the women working in medical institutions such as hospitals, infirmaries, pesthouses, and orphanages, then turn to independent practitioners: the healers, midwives, and wet nurses.

## HOSPITALS

During the fifteenth and sixteenth centuries, most cities, both Protestant and Catholic, began either to take over the operation of hospitals, infirmaries, and orphanges from the church or to establish new medical institutions. As they secularized these institutions, they often centralized them, setting up one major hospital to replace a number of smaller care centers. This main hospital, located within the city itself, was not for those with contagious diseases, who were sent to small pesthouses or infirmaries outside the city walls, but for the injured, chronically ill, infirm elderly, and poor expectant mothers. In both the main hospital and the smaller infirmaries, the city councils, or officials appointed by them, hired the staff and set forth the responsibilities and duties of each person.

All of these institutions employed women in a variety of capacities, from administrative and medical to cooking and janitorial. Most of the women, no matter what their position, had to swear an oath of loyalty and agree to follow all directives laid out for the day-to-day operation of the institution. These ordinances and sets of instructions provide a glimpse of the daily life in a hospital and the actual work the women were doing.

In Nuremberg the largest hospital was the Heilig Geist Spital, founded in 1339 by Konrad Gross, a wealthy merchant.[1] It was controlled by the city council and under the direct supervision of a hospital master. Along with this master, there were a number of other male officials and three women, the *Custorin*, *Meisterin*, and *Schauerin*, who actually took care of most of the day-to-day operations of the hospital.

The Custorin was responsible for the physical needs of the hospital and the patients. She was to purchase equipment for the kitchen and bedding for the sleeping chambers, as well as food and other provisions. When patients were admitted, she was to make a list of all they brought in to the hospital and, when patients died, to take an inventory of what they left behind, as all their possessions were to be left with the hospital. She was also to keep careful records of all that she purchased and turn them over to the hospital master each week. She was also in charge of the maids and the cooks, making sure they all did their jobs and helping out wherever she was needed. Throughout the ordinance, she was always admonished to treat the patients "patiently and in a friendly manner." Each week she and the Meisterin were to examine all patients to make sure they were still ill or weak enough to stay in the hospital; the healthy were to be released.[2]

The Meisterin assisted the Custorin in most of her duties, although she was primarily responsible for the operation of the kitchen. She determined how much and what kinds of food were to be cooked, and "at the proper times she should test the food to see whether it is correctly salted and has the right amount of fat." She and the Custorin dished out the portions and ordered preparation of special foods for patients who were too ill to eat regular food. She was to make sure all food coming in to the hospital was "good and suitable, without blemishes and correctly weighed" and also to present the hospital master with "an itemized accounting of her income and expenditures each week." She and the Custorin were both specifically forbidden to give any leftover food from the hospital to their relatives or anyone else or to invite their relatives or other guests to join them for a meal at the hospital.[3]

The Schauerin handled admissions: "If someone asks to be let in, she should examine this person carefully and admit no one to the hospital who has a dangerous, contagious disease, but only those who are suffering from moderate bodily weakness. All of these people should be citizens, children of citizens, or servants of the same, or journeymen who have worked a long time with a master here." She also handed out beer and bread, making sure those who had to pay for their food did not receive any which had been donated to the poor, and was specifically admonished "to take no bread that has been given to the sick and resell it to the pensioners nor to anyone else."[4]

Thus these three women had complete charge of the kitchen, laundry, servants, and most of the maintenance of the hospital. They also had the right to determine who was ill enough to remain in the hospital or, in the case of the Schauerin, who was not too contagious to get in in the first place. This medical function is certainly remarkable given the fact that these women were not required to have any medical training.

Munich had a similar institution, again called the Heilig Geist Spital. The most important female official was also called the Meisterin and had even more wide-ranging duties than her Nuremberg counterpart. Along with overseeing all the maids and the kitchen, she was to be sure any patient who was dying had someone nearby all the time and that all patients received a bath regularly, including those who were too weak to walk. She was responsible for a special children's room and for keeping the mentally ill away from the children. The woman in charge of the hospital kitchen was called a *Kellerin*. She was to sleep in the general sleeping quarters so that if anyone needed help during the night she would be readily available. She and all other officials were ordered to speak "modestly and pleasantly" with the patients and not to insult or make fun of them ("*kein smahe noch scheltwort geben*").[5]

Throughout the sixteenth century the number of women who worked in the hospital increased. Besides the Meisterin and the Kellerin, there were also two cooks, a "vegetable girl," a shepherdess, and at least eight other maids and assistants. One man and one woman were put in charge of the fifteen–twenty mentally ill patients, and another man and woman, usually a married couple, of the children's quarter.[6]

A 1628 Munich ordinance gives some idea of the wages these women earned. The Meisterin was paid 12 gulden annually, one-third of what the hospital master was paid. The two female cooks also received a similar salary, 12 gulden, which was one-fourth of what the male cook was paid. The Kellerin, shepherdess, and "vegetable girl" were all paid 8 gulden, about half of what men in similar positions received. Only at the very bottom of the scale were female and male salaries roughly equal—both male and female servants received between 2 and 4 gulden annually. These salaries seem extremely low, but all these people received their room and board at the hospital as well. They do indicate, however, that hospital workers were viewed very much like domestic servants, whose salaries are comparable.[7] Similar salaries for hospital workers may also be found in Memmingen and in Cannstadt near Stuttgart, and in the latter case, the amount of food female workers received was also specified as about half that given to male workers.[8]

In Memmingen the city hospital had a Meisterin to oversee not only the personnel and the food but also the lands the hospital owned. Her assistant was called the "mother of the needy" (*dürfftig Mutter*) and was to wait on the sick herself, as well as cooking for them and feeding them. In later ordinances this woman was given a religious function as well, as she was required to lead the patients in prayer before and after each meal.[9]

The motherly role of female hospital personnel was also emphasized in Strasbourg. Here the Meisterin in the Grossen Spital (large hospital) was specifically told to treat the patients "as a mother would her children," to do everything "that is appropriate for women to do, with nothing excepted." She and her assistant, again called a Custorin, were to prevent jealousy and bickering among patients by making sure all food and wine was divided equally. The Custorin oversaw the kitchen and sat with those who were dying, praying with them and comforting them. In addition to these two women, the doctor's maid and the "bread mother" also had their duties laid out, the former to administer medicines and salves which a doctor had ordered, especially to female patients "who for reasons of modesty" might object to being touched by a doctor, the latter to distribute bread twice a day to the patients. She was to pick up any "hard little pieces which were left over and give them to the poor three times a week." All of these women were to "act like an honest woman would in her own house in all things, and like a mother would to her children."[10]

The Strasbourg city council was very specific in its demands on hospital maids. Most ordinances simply note that they are to do anything they are asked to "willingly and cheerfully," but in 1547 Strasbourg decided to spell out what this meant in a fourteen-page ordinance. Not only are their duties at each hour of the day described in nit-picking detail, but also the proper attitude and conduct. They were to say their prayers regularly, attend church services daily, and not stand in dark corners talking to young men or sing shameful songs. They were to be friendly and polite to the patients but not to take any presents from them or show any favorites. Decorum, piety, and obedience were stressed, and the maids were warned that they could be punished as the Meisterin saw fit if they disobeyed. The city council clearly envisioned the hospital staff as one big, happy family, with the Meisterin as mother and the maids as "true and loving sisters."[11] In many cases, the city councils got what they wanted, for women were frequently rewarded with cash or goods or even made citizens because of their long service to the hospital.[12]

Unfortunately, this was not always the case. Hospital work was long, physically taxing, and unpleasant; the women who were drawn to it not always motivated by the desire to serve, as the city councils would have wished. Relatively often in city council and court records, the various Meisterinnen and other employees appear accused of neglect, drunkenness, disobedience, or occasionally even worse.[13] In 1557 Katherina Zell, the wife of Matthias Zell, one of Strasbourg's leading reformers, made an inspection of the hospital and was horrified at what she found there. The food was "only salted fish and tough, fatty meat that the healthy as well as the ill wouldn't want to eat," the house "so Godless that when an 'Our Father' is said at the table, it is done so quietly and secretly that no one knows if it's a prayer or a fart. . . . No one knows who Christ is, and no one is taught anything about him . . . they sleep in horrible beds, like a sow in her own manure." She recommended that the entire staff be dismissed and new people appointed, "God-fearing women who will oversee things properly." Sadly for the hospital patients, Zell's suggestions were not followed.[14]

Two of the most dramatic stories about hospital workers come from Nuremburg. In 1469 the Custorin hanged herself in the hospital, supposedly because she had loaned Nikolaus Muffel, a council member and former chief mayor executed that year for embezzlement of public funds, two hundred florins out of the hospital treasury.[15] In 1620 in a story much embellished by frequent retelling, the Meisterin was charged with exchanging her normal serving ladle for a smaller one so that she could feed the patients less. She denied it, but the ladle was thrown into the Pegnitz River nearby with the words "This belongs to the devil!" She cried out, "I do, too!" threw herself in, and drowned. From then on, her ghost was supposed to have haunted the hospital, screaming and breaking bowls and spoons.[16] The supernatural element aside, the story is quite believable, for the women were frequently admonished to keep costs down and were probably easily tempted to shortchange the patients, whether to stay within a budget or to make a profit on the side.

Because these hospitals did not accept those with contagious diseases, they often had some spare beds, and one of the ways they solved financial problems was to take in pensioners (*Pfründnern*) who paid slightly more than their own keep. These pensioners were usually elderly women without an immediate family to take care of them. They paid an initial sum and agreed to turn over their estates to the hospital when they died. Occasionally the city also provided a pension in the hospital for an indigent or handicapped old woman who could prove that she had taken care of the sick herself or performed another similar service. Thus the hospital also served as an old-age home.[17]

The pensioners were a frequent source of discussion and irritation. Though cities tried to limit their number, there were often so many that there were not enough beds for the truly sick. Though they were supposed to pay for their own food, they often coaxed the Custorin or the maids to provide them with food meant for the poor. They occasionally bribed servants to bring them food or wine they were not supposed to have. Finally, most cities wrote special ordinances for the pensioners, requiring them to swear to abide by them and stipulating the same sort of modesty, decorum, and pious behavior expected of female hospital workers.[18] In Strasbourg the pensioners were to elect two of their members to be responsible for the collection of payments and the distribution of food. One of these was to keep records and take an annual inventory of everything the pensioners owned. She was to be paid for this task, although the city council did note, "If neither one of these women can write or read, then someone else must do this and she is to receive nothing." [19]

The pensioners were not the only group that proved difficult for city hospitals to handle. The hospitals also served as housing for indigent mothers during their delivery, and very often the number was greater than the hospital could handle. City councils attempted to find the alleged father, if the mother was unmarried, to make him pay the hospital costs for the woman and his child, and they debated ways to alleviate the crowding, including buying new buildings. [20]

By the end of the sixteenth century, few but prostitutes and unmarried mothers came into the city hospital for delivery, and these often went directly from the hospital to prison for a prostitution or fornication sentence after their children were born. They either took the children into prison with them or sent them out to wet nurses. After release from the hospital and prison, these women were usually banished and had to take their newborn children with them. Even women who were judged deranged or mentally deficient were given their children back again and sent out of town. The care of these women while they were in the hospital was nonetheless considered important, however, as indicated by the order of the Nuremberg city council in 1561 forbidding removal of women from hospital beds to accommodate victims of the plague or other diseases unless "an especially healthful, airy place could be found for them." [21]

The women running the hospital thus dealt with a wide variety of patients—chronically ill, elderly, expectant mothers, handicapped, foundling children, and mentally retarded or psychologically disturbed children and adults—and had more than two hundred patients at a time under their care. [22] They oversaw a staff of servants and were responsible not only for the physical needs of the patients but often for their medical treatment, emotional state, and religious instruction as well—a considerable charge for twelve gulden a year.

### PESTHOUSES

The city hospitals were uniform in their refusal to accept people with contagious diseases, so that some provision had to be made for them elsewhere, especially during epidemics. Cities often set up somewhere outside the city walls temporary plague hospitals or pesthouses, open only when needed, for those with infectious diseases. Many were begun as leprosariums, with such euphemistic names as Guten Lute ("house of the good people"), the name given them in

Strasbourg and Frankfurt. These plague hospitals also provided employment for women, again ranging from administrative to simple maintenance. They were usually presided over by a hospital master and his wife, who both swore an oath to do whatever was necessary to aid the sick. The woman was to buy all food and other supplies needed and to oversee the preparation of meals. A Custorin aided her and handed out sheets and bedding to patients as they were admitted. After patients had been let out or, more likely, after they had died, the sheets and clothing they had used were to be washed out and then used as bandages(!) for patients coming in. In some cases, patients were admitted only if they promised to nurse those who were more sick than they.[23]

During times of an epidemic the number of people employed by such plague hospitals increased dramatically. The report of the director of the Augsburg plague hospital (*Brechhaus*) on measures taken during the course of the plague there in 1563/1564 gives an idea of what cities tried to do. He first took on eight women to care for the sick, "for lifting, turning, and whatever they were needed for, including sewing the dead into their burial cloths. We also used them if the parents of children had died—one was either sent to the children, or the children were sent into their homes until they each had three children." If people needed someone to care for them in their own home, "we knew if one of them was free, or where they were; if one of them did not have a place to serve, she told me, and then I sent her to a house where she was needed. I also used other women when these eight weren't enough—and let these go when they weren't needed more after using them for a long or short time. A midwife was also sent into the Brechhaus and was paid fifteen kreuzer whenever she helped a woman deliver."[24]

Ten months after the plague began, he felt he could finally let the women go, "but with the condition that if they are needed again we will pay them one-half gulden each per week." A month later he let the female cook go, and a month after that he and the four gravediggers and two maids who were left behind burned everything in the building. At the end, the two maids were left to clean up what was left, and the house was locked.[25] (In this particular outbreak of the plague, which lasted eleven months, 954 people died in Augsburg, 446 of them in the Brechhaus.)

In most cities, as in Augsburg, the pesthouses were simply closed when not needed, and people were hired for short periods of time when the need was great enough.[26] Although the work was unpleasant and possibly dangerous, it did provide employment for women as cooks, maids, and serving girls. Women were also hired to take care of the orphaned children of plague victims, both in the pesthouses and in their own homes. In all of these places, actual medical treatment was minimal; the best they could offer was probably a more pleasant place to die.

## ORPHANAGES AND CHILD CARE

Besides caring for the sick in city hospitals and infirmaries, women had various responsibilities in caring for children both in orphanages and in special areas of the city hospital. They also cared for them in their own homes as wet nurses or foster-mothers.

A number of cities in Germany had public orphanages—Freiburg in Breisgau, Augsburg, Ulm, and Nuremberg as early as the fourteenth century. They were usually overseen by a married couple, the *Findelvater* and *Findelmutter*, aided by a variety of cooks, servants, and teachers, many of whom were women. The number of children in these varied according to the space available, from 12–25 in the children's room of the Munich hospital during the sixteenth century, to 25 in the Strasbourg orphanage in 1482, to 90 in the Nuremberg orphanage in 1560. During times of plague or war, the number grew tremendously; for example, in 1563 the same orphanage in Nuremberg had 212 children, and in Strasbourg during the Thirty Years' War, the orphanage had five times as many requests for places as it had space available.[27]

All of the permanent staff of the orphanages swore an oath and functioned under a set of ordinances drawn up during the sixteenth century explaining their duties and responsibilities.[28] The Findelvater and Findelmutter were to keep the children neat and tidy, guard the stock, and maintain the buildings. They were to instruct the children at least three times a day "to praise God and say their prayers." Bad behavior was not to be tolerated but punished "with a sturdy stick."[29]

The Findelmutter was basically responsible for the same things a mother was in a family. She was to teach the little girls to spin and the older ones to cook and care for clothing and laundry. She and the older girls were to bathe the children twice a week and see to their clothing and shoes. She made most food purchases and was to keep a record of her purchases for the city council. All of the servants, from cowherd to cook, were under her direction. The Findelmutter also took care of most illnesses among the children, and her right to do so was defended by the city council against the objections of barbersurgeons and other groups who claimed their territory was being infringed upon. In special cases, people were called in to treat scrofula, eye diseases, or other ailments common among orphanage children, although those called in were often skilled women rather than university-trained physicians.[30]

When the children reached the age of ten or twelve, the girls were to be sent out as domestic servants, the boys as apprentices. Employers often had to be induced to take in children from the orphanage, so they were usually given permission to have one extra apprentice if they took on an orphan. The city councils sought to aid orphanage girls by providing them with a dowry or offering free citizenship rights to any man who married one of them.[31]

The orphanages were supported both by private endowments and public funds, although the funds provided were often not sufficient to cover all expenses. Living relatives or godparents of the children were requested to give some financial support or else take the children into their own homes, for which they would be paid by the orphanage. In the case of illegitimate children, especially if the mother had died, the father was to be sought and made to support the children; in a case in Strasbourg the city council even ordered a man to sell his inheritance and make payments to the orphanage, though he denied being the father of any children there. The Findelvater and Findelmutter were encouraged to find any additional support they could and thus were occasionally involved in land speculation or making products like brooms or brushes to sell. They received only a modest salary themselves but had their room and board provided and often received gifts of food or household goods, so their financial situation was relatively good.[32]

The couple who served as orphanage directors were generally former artisans. Occasionally a widow or married woman was appointed independently as Findelmutter in a girls' orphanage and was thus responsible for the entire operation. The skills and abilities many of these women undoubtedly possessed can be seen in the example of Elisabeth Kraus in Nuremberg. She was herself an orphan, the daughter of simple peasants, and came to Nuremberg alone at the age of ten in 1569. There she worked as a maid until she married Konrad Kraus, a small merchant. They were both industrious, and his business thrived despite the general economic difficulties of this period. During the early seventeenth century she was appointed Findelmutter of the girls' orphanage, and she and her husband purchased land and houses in the city, although they lived in the orphanage. At her death in 1639 (her husband had died several years earlier), she left six houses and monetary capital of 79,000 florins, with the whole estate estimated at over 127,000 florins. Her will set this up as an endowment for the children of the orphanage, to provide them with a yearly feast and day-to-day necessities. This fund was the largest private Protestant endowment in all of Germany.[33]

The other employees of the orphanage were also responsible for the children's spiritual as well as material well-being. The maids were to keep linens and clothing in good repair and serve meals punctually and peacefully and to instruct the younger children in prayer, making sure prayers were said regularly and respectfully. The cook and the seamstress were to be examples of cleanliness, thrift, "obedience, propriety, industriousness, order, and fear of God."[34] Although these high standards were not always met, there were few major complaints about orphanage employees.

Like the hospitals, the orphanages provided public employment for women—married, widowed, and single—who had simple household skills and perhaps a concern for and interest in children. Although life in them would not have been especially pleasant, at least the children were assured of food and clothing, the right to citizenship without payment when they reached maturity, and often the right to work, as city councils declared that all children in orphanages were legitimate and thus could be accepted in any occupation, whether the actual family history was known or not.[35] These were municipal and secular institutions from the start, and their regulations and ordinances were not directly affected by the Reformation. Throughout the period, they remained an important part of most cities' welfare systems.

Besides those children who actually lived in orphanages, there were a great many given to wet nurses, either in the city or in the surrounding villages.[36] If they were hired by the orphanage, these women were paid a salary of five to seven gulden a year and were provided with diapers, clothing, and blankets for the children from the orphanage funds as well.[37] Occasionally there were nearly as many children with wet nurses as in the orphanages: in Nuremberg 43 in 1550 and 114 in 1600; in Strasbourg 31 in 1482 and 121 in 1531.[38] Along with caring for infants who were still nursing, these women took care of children up to age four or five, as very young children were not wanted in the orphanage.

Often these arrangements had begun privately, with a relative or friend asked to care for a child whose parents had died or with a woman taking in a foundling "out of pity with the hope it would be claimed again," but then the financial burden became such that the woman asked the orphanage or city council for assistance. Sometimes these women were simply given gifts of wood or food in recognition for their services without having to ask for assistance.[39]

Occasionally the need for wet nurses was so great that women were given special dispensations if they would agree to serve. They were forgiven of minor crimes, allowed to stay in the city though they had had illegitimate children, or allowed to maintain their own households as long as they would take in some children.[40]

## CARE OF ADULTS

Informal arrangements for care were not limited to children. Women often took care of incapacitated adults or the elderly, either in the home of the patient or their own homes. Occasionally this could lead to disputes between the parties involved. In 1621 a woman came to the court in Cannstadt, a small town near Stuttgart, demanding another woman pay her forty gulden for caring for her and her infant during delivery and a long convalescence afterward. The other woman answered that "such demands were totally unreasonable, as I had to work like a maid as soon as I could walk and had certainly earned my keep." The court agreed, and the case was dismissed.[41] For providing this care women normally were either paid by the city for their services or given special favors, often being allowed to stay in the city without becoming a citizen and without paying the special tax normally required of noncitizens, with the single limitation that they behave "honorably and decently." If a care provider became ill herself, she could be taken into the city hospital, though admission was usually limited to citizens.[42]

Such care of adults could even involve care of the contagiously ill; in 1497 in Nuremberg a woman was given permission to care for syphilitics in her home: "The woman who has asked the council to allow her to take people ill with the French disease [syphilis] into her home is to be allowed to take in citizens and permanent residents but forbidden to take in strangers."[43] These informal arrangements were very common during plagues. Not only were women hired to work in the special plague hospitals but also to nurse people in their own homes; for this they were either paid or rewarded in some other way. Cities were not at all reluctant to take away special privileges once a plague had passed, however, and ask these women to leave the city or find employment as domestic servants somewhere.[44]

War offered special opportunities as well. In 1614 six poor women in Nuremberg were given permission to feed, nurse, and care for soldiers and other people who had fled into the city.[45] Owing to a shortage of meat and medicines in the city, they were allowed to give the refugees only porridge, lungs, and liver, which was all the patients at the hospital were getting at the time, and to treat them only with herb tea and similar things.

The mentally ill and deranged were handled whenever possible in the homes of relatives, with the city council in Nuremberg actually loaning out chains so they could be controlled.[46] If there were no relatives who could take them or if relatives felt they were uncontrollable, they were locked up in a tower, with a woman paid to look after their basic needs. Funds for their support were provided by relatives or by the city. In one instance this woman was praised and rewarded for her work, given six gulden "for the extraordinary trouble and effort she has taken with some lunatic patients, but she [was] also told to use more care when keeping the people clean."[47]

In 1532 the Strasbourg city council decided to organize care for the sick outside the hospital as well, rather than leave it to chance. It named a dozen people in each quarter of the city, mainly poor old widows, as *Berufskrankenwarterinnen* (professional attendants for the sick) whom anyone could call if they needed care. The wealthy were to pay these women a fee, six pfennige a day, and the poor to have their services for free; the city also paid the glorious salary of two pounds per year. The council wanted to find "elderly married men with good reputations and childless widows" for the positions, and it did succeed in appointing six women and two men. Besides the small salary, they were also given places to live in the former Beguinages, which had been dissolved by the city during the Reformation. In many ways these women and men performed some of the functions the Beguines had before the Reformation, caring for the sick and comforting the dying. The council gave the dissolution of the Beguinages as one of the reasons for the need for such people.[48]

## MEDICAL PRACTITIONERS

Thus opportunities for women to be involved in a variety of medical and nursing functions were many. There was no opposition to their serving in hospitals or similar institutions and no tracts declaring them unfit or too delicate to care for even the most horribly afflicted patients. Opposition to women in medicine in the early modern period centered not around their work in hospitals but around their treatment of people for external and internal ailments. Barber-surgeons, physicians, and apothecaries made numerous and frequent complaints about women who were using drugs or methods of treatment they considered to be their province alone.

Most of these treatments grew out of the practical knowledge of herbs, salves, and ointments that was expected of any housewife. Even noble women traded recipes for powders and creams they believed effective against everything from pimples to the plague. In the mid-sixteenth century, Anna, the wife of the elector of Saxony and the daughter of Christian III of Denmark, wrote a "medicine-book" (*Ertzneibüchlein*) with hundreds of recipes for drugs which she had got from many sources; Paul Luther, the physician son of Martin, used it in his work. In 1600 Duchess Eleonore Marie Rosalie of Jagersdorf and Troppau compiled "Six Books of Medicines and Artifices, Chosen for All Human Bodily Weaknesses and Illnesses," which was reprinted under various titles for many years.[49]

Until about 1500 there seems to have been little opposition to women practicing any type of medicine. Women are listed as doctors (*Artztin*) in the lists of citizens from Schwäbisch-Hall in 1433 and 1438–1446 and in Hildesheim in 1425. The ordinance from the Strasbourg plague hospital from 1461 mentions both male and female doctors, and one-sixth of the entries under "doctor" in the Frankfurt tax lists from 1320 to 1500 were women, although the last female doctor appears in 1479.[50] In Frankfurt many of these women were Jewish and specifically described as "eye doctors." Often these women were rewarded for their services by having their taxes reduced; although they were not permitted to live outside the Jewish ghetto, they were allowed to treat both Jewish and gentile patients.[51] A significant share of the apothecaries in Frankfurt during this period were also women. Female apothecaries were also numerous in Schwäbisch-Hall and Mainz, although they were prohibited in Cologne, Schlettstadt, and Überlingen on the belief that they would be inattentive to the proper preparation and mixing of drugs.[52]

Gradually all references to female doctors disappear, and during the course of the sixteenth century, many cities passed regulations expressly forbidding "women and other untrained people" to practice medicine in any way. A decretal from the Nuremberg city council in 1529 reads:

> The *Zuckermacherinnen* and other old women, or whoever they are, make elixers, tonics, and juices and give each one of them a special name, though they don't know what belongs in each of them, or how they are to be prepared; if they simply taste right to them, then they give it that name, sell the stuff, and deceive people with it. So from now on, no one is to sell these juices or elixers unless they have let a doctor see the ingredients and recipe beforehand.[53]

An ordinance in the duchy of Würtemburg in 1552 forbade people to sell medicines or act as doctors unless they had studied at the university or unless they got special permission beforehand, and a similar ordinance was issued in Augsburg before 1581.[54]

Ordinances such as these did not keep women from practicing medicine, however, nor prevent people from going to them if they felt they were skillful and effective. In 1528 the Munich city council forbade a woman to sell medicines or drinks or it would punish her severely; three men immediately came to the council, saying that her medicines had helped them and they wanted to be able to continue buying them. The council compromised and allowed her to sell a specific medicine to these people but no other kind and to no one else.[55] A female eye doctor in Nuremberg was ordered to leave town because she was not a citizen, but some people she had treated came before the council, and she was again allowed to stay and work despite complaints by the city's barber-surgeons.[56]

In 1535 the same barber-surgeons complained of another *Winckel-artztin* (literally, "female doctor who works in dark corners"), and she was limited in what she was allowed to do: "Catherine Koler, the Winckelartztin, is to be told that she is to keep using her medicines and treatments only as she has been allowed to before. Namely, she is only to heal external wounds on the body and not treat anything internal or examine any urine [*prinnen schauen*]." Eight years later her case came up again, and the council ordered her to stop administering medicines, inspecting urine, and giving advice; it did allow her to treat "secret wounds and sores, as those on women's breasts and others on the external body."[57]

The small city of Memmingen offers a number of cases beginning in the last half of the sixteenth century. In 1554 the woman in charge of children in the city hospital was ordered to limit her "healing of heads" (probably for lice or scrofula) to children and occasionally adult citizens. Under no circumstances was she to practice on foreigners. Later that same year another woman was ordered to leave the city for treating people with eye diseases, and a third was forbidden to give anyone a "little drink," unless it was prescribed for them by a doctor.[58]

In 1560, a certain Grethelin Schererlin asked the city council for a reward for healing a woman "in a secret place." The council gave her a small reward but warned her not to ask for any more money or treat people with the hope of being rewarded again. Four years later, she was forbidden to treat any men, even if they asked her to. She apparently paid no attention to the order, for several months later she was ordered to stop all "curing" (*curieren*), whether of men or women.[59]

Toward the end of the century, another woman, Elizabeth Heyssin, became involved with the barber-surgeons in Memmingen in a long dispute from which a number of interesting things emerge. The first complaint was brought against her in 1596 and then repeated in 1598. She answered that she didn't help people with the hope of any reward but only "out of charity for the poor and needy"; most of the people she had treated were in the city's hospital anyway.[60] The council agreed, allowing her to continue "because she does this at the special request of these people and more out of love of God and for free (*vergebenlich*) than for money."[61]

In 1602 the barber-surgeons complained again that she was not only doing this to help people but also receiving the salary of a university-trained physician: "One of us could not even ask for half of what she is now demanding." They gave several examples. She was also giving her patients many drugs (which the barber-surgeons had learned from the apothecaries) and was now going into people's houses offering her services. She denigrated the abilities and services of the barber-surgeons and had even gone so far as to criticize one of the town's university-trained physicians! All of this had created hard times for the barber-surgeons and their families; she was, they complained, "taking the bread out of the mouths of our wives and children."[62]

A month later Heyssin answered them point for point. She had not taken that much money from people, and what she had taken had been used for wood, candles, bedding, and the like. She did not leave patients if they didn't pay quickly nor set broken bones or handle fresh wounds except those of her own children, and she did call a physician if she felt a case warranted it. Witnesses were offered to testify in her behalf on all these points. As to where she had learned her skill, she had gotten the basics from a man who had cured her infant daughter, and the rest came from "God in Heaven, who gave me soul and body, reason and understanding, for which I have to thank him daily." She asked to be allowed to continue, making the comment that such activities "were done by honorable women not only here but also in other cities just as large and important as Memmingen. Such are fine things for women to do." The barber-surgeons countered with the comment that her skills must come from the Devil, not God, a charge she answered with the citation of several Bible verses. She said she would abide by the council's decision but that the barbers were acting "enviously, jealously, and maliciously"; it would be "contrary to Christian and brotherly love not to allow the poor and needy to be helped with help which came from God."[63]

Four months later the council finally made its decision:

> Elizabeth Heyssin is to be allowed to treat external wounds and sores in the same manner that she has been doing up till now, but only on women and children when they request it of her. She should absolutely not handle new wounds, bloodletting, or setting bones and should behave and handle herself with all possible modesty. Her daughter, though, is to be totally forbidden from practicing any kind of medicine.[64]

Both parties were told to quit calling each other names and make peace with each other. The barbers objected to the council's decision but were told it was final. They never complained about her again, although seven years later she was again treating men and the council warned her to abide by the limitations it had set or she would be kept from practicing completely.[65]

The Heyssin case is instructive, as it contains a number of elements which also occurred in similar cases in other cities. Though the barber-surgeons opposed her activities on principle, they objected most strenuously when she appeared to be making a profit from them. One of the first defenses by any woman accused of practicing medicine was that she did it for free or for only a small recompense and only when people asked her. To point out how far Heyssin had gone, the barbers stressed that she was not only insulting and criticizing them but also the university-trained physicians. Women were always specifically and forcefully forbidden to do anything physicians normally did, especially examining urine for diagnostic purposes. The question as to where a woman had learned her medicine was raised in all cases, often with the hint of diabolic inspiration. Usually the woman answered that she had learned it from her brother or father or mother and that she used no incantations, amulets, or any other magical means to bring about a cure. She also promised, or was ordered, to stop teaching medicine to her own children, even if she were allowed to practice within certain limits herself.[66]

In most cases, city councils were willing to let individual women practice, despite objections by other groups, as long as they were effective and successful and as long as people felt better after their treatments. They placated the doctors, barber-surgeons, and apothecaries by forbidding the women to do some things—like examining urine or bloodletting or mixing drugs—which these groups considered their own most important tasks. Even these tasks were allowed if the council had a grievance against one of these groups. For example, during the Thirty Years' War a woman who had taken refuge in Strasbourg because of her religious beliefs asked to be allowed to make medicines and *Zuckerwerck*, or medicinal syrups and cakes. She got a recommendation from the city's pastor "that she is a pious and godly woman who left everything to follow the true word of God," and the city council allowed her to work because it thought the current apothecaries were charging too much for their work anyway.[67]

Councils were also willing to let a woman do things they looked upon as an extension of her job as a midwife. In 1614 the Memmingen barbers brought a complaint against a midwife for practicing medicine. The council allowed her to handle outward illnesses of women and children that were brought to her but not to treat any men, do any cutting, or use any purgative drinks. When she was treating pregnant women and infants, however, there were no restrictions on what she could do. Occasionally city councils actually paid women for their skills; in 1597 the Nuremberg city council paid a woman thirty-two gulden a year for her and her children's support because she was treating the children in the orphanage and the people in the hospital for eye diseases at no cost. The Munich city council made similar payments to a woman over the ten years 1552–1562.[68]

The women practicing medicine defended their right to do so skillfully and ably, and it is best to let one of the women involved have the last word on the subject:

> *Modest answer and obedient report from Katherina Plumanerin Carberinerin*
>
> Honorable, just, careful, highly educated, and wise mayors and council of this electoral capital city of Munich, gracious and serving sirs:
> Because of my humble modesty, I cannot let your honorable and gracious sirs go without an answer: A few days ago your city secretary (with somewhat harsh words) brought me an extract from a council meeting held on December 17 of last year, which included the following: that Plumanerin Carberinerin is to be earnestly forbidden to treat or look at patients. This decision, arrived at because of malice and not through any fault of my own, appears to me not only strange, but also totally deplorable. On one hand I use my feminine skills, given by the grace of God, only when someone entreats me earnestly and never advertise myself, but only when someone has been left for lost, and they ask me many times. I do whatever I can possibly do out of Christian love and charity, using only simple and allowable means that should not be forbidden or proscribed in the least. Not one person who has come under my care has a complaint or grievance against me. If the doctors, apothecaries, or barber-surgeons have claimed this, it is solely out of spite and jealousy.
> At all times, as is natural, women have more trust in other women to discover their secrets, problems, and illnesses than they have in men (as long as no un-Christian means are used)—but perhaps this jealousy came from that. Undoubtedly as well, honorable husbands who love and cherish their wives will seek any help and assistance they can, even that from women, if the wives have been given up (by the doctors) or otherwise come into great danger.
> Because I know that I can help in my own small way, I will do all I can, just as, according to the Gospel, we should help pull an ox out of a well it has fallen into on Sunday.
> So that your honorable and gracious sirs can see that I am trying to follow your directives, from now on—as I have generally done in the

past—I will not promote or advertise my healing. But if someone comes to me in an emergency and pleads with me, I cannot deny them my time or my troubles or the skill which God has given me out of friendship or out of Christian sympathy. Thus I humbly hope that you will not listen to any spite and envy any further but will allow me this out of your grace and wisdom. This is my answer given to you out of my duty of obedience.[69]

## MIDWIFERY

Undeniably the most vital occupation in which women were involved was midwifery. Until the late seventeenth century there were very few male doctors or accoucheurs doing any work in the fields of obstetrics and gynecology; all births, from those of the very poor to those of the nobility, were attended to and helped or hindered by a midwife. City councils recognized very early the importance to a city of having a well-organized system of midwives and devised various means of establishing one.[70] In most cases, women who wanted to become midwives had to apply directly to the city council, which set standards and passed regulations about their training, numbers, and conduct.

The first mention of a midwife anywhere in Germany was in 1302 in Frankfurt, and records from other cities also make note of them during the fourteenth century (Nuremberg in 1380, Stuttgart in 1350). These were private midwives, paid by their clients. Midwives first appeared as sworn city officials in Constance in 1379, Nuremberg in 1417, Frankfurt in 1456, Munich in 1480, Heilbronn in 1486, and Stuttgart in 1489, receiving either an annual salary or else a payment for each woman they handled who was not able to pay herself. Usually one woman was appointed first, and then the number increased as the city felt the need, growing as high as twenty-two for a large city like Nuremberg.[71]

The annual salaries which the cities paid these women were usually very low—2–8 gulden—and the midwives constantly asked that they be raised. They compared rather badly with the salaries city barbersurgeons were paid—10–25 gulden—and are roughly comparable to the salaries of some employees in the city hospital. Rather than increase salaries, however, the city council often gave the midwives grain or wood on a regular basis or allowed them to pay less taxes than normally required. Midwives also received special payments and gifts for services the councils considered above and beyond those normally required, such as caring for pregnant women during times of the plague or caring for women in the city hospital. The city council occasionally even offered to help midwives collect debts owed them for deliveries.[72]

The midwife was also paid for her services by individuals who could afford it. Her fees varied with the social class of the mother involved and were often set specifically according to social class in city regulations. Women from the city's wealthiest families might often pay ten or twenty times what the city paid for indigent mothers. As regulations became more and more specific, fees were also set according to how difficult the birth was. For twins, a breech birth, or any birth which took longer than twenty-four hours, a midwife was to be paid twice as much as for an "easy and natural" birth. The cost of a simple birth was roughly that of a circumcision; the cost of a more difficult birth, roughly that of setting a bone or removing tonsils.[73]

In addition to the midwives themselves, many cities also began to appoint other women, often from upper-class families, to oversee the midwives. These overseers assigned midwives to indigent mothers, helped in the distribution of food and clothing, and could be called on to give advice in difficult cases. They were also to discipline midwives they believed were not living up to their oath and could revoke a license—literally "take down the sign"—if they thought the infraction serious enough. In some cities these women also held the examination for those who wanted to become midwives. This they did either on their own, as in Nuremberg, or with the assistance of several of the city's doctors, as in Frankfurt, Strasbourg, Freiburg in Breisgau, Zurich, Memmingen, and Ulm. They were usually paid for their services, in Augsburg, Munich, and Memmingen roughly the same as the midwives, in Frankfurt significantly more, but in Nuremberg only if they made a special request.[74]

These supervising women were called various things—"honorable women" (*Ehrbare Frauen*), "sworn women" (*geschworene Frauen*), "women assigned to the midwives" (*zugeordnete* or *verordnete Frauen*), "wise women" (*Weise Frauen*)—but their function was the same. Nuremberg began appointing them in 1463, Munich in 1555, Frankfurt and Memmingen some time in the mid-sixteenth century, Strasbourg by 1500.[75] In 1466 the Augsburg city council ordered the guilds to take care of this; each guild master was to appoint "two honorable women who will stand by pregnant women from the same guild whenever they are called upon, giving them help, advice, and assistance."[76] In every city these women made an annual report to the city council, indicating any problems, such as a shortage of midwives in one area of the city.

Midwives themselves also brought problems to the council's attention, problems which occasionally involved the "honorable women," for their relations with the midwives were not always friendly. In 1549 Nuremberg midwives requested that the council appoint yet another group of women to oversee them, to be chosen from the wives and widows of craftsmen, not patricians. Apparently the Ehrbare Frauen would no longer assist at births among the city's poor and were unresponsive to the midwives' requests. This third group was to be paid a slightly larger salary than the midwives and were to be specifically ordered not to neglect poorer women or request too high a payment from mothers or midwives.[77] In Frankfurt in 1696 midwives complained that some of these "sworn women" were acting as midwives themselves without being licensed to do so and thus were depriving some midwife of a fee. The women who were doing so were required to take the normal midwives' exam and then wait until a position opened, exactly like any other woman.[78]

Along with appointing women to oversee the midwives, cities also encouraged midwives to take on apprentices so as to make sure there would always be an adequate supply. They did this by pleading and threatening and also, more effectively no doubt, by offering financial rewards to midwives whose former apprentices were accepted into the office themselves. These rewards could often be as high as the normal annual salary paid to a midwife. Midwives were also offered a delay or reduction in their punishment for various crimes if they would take on an apprentice.[79] Women often responded by taking on their own daughters as apprentices; there were no objections as long as a woman did not send her daughter out alone before her training was over. Cities did pay experienced midwives the normal reward if their daughters were accepted.[80] This is but one example of a mother handing down an occupation to her daughter in the same way a father would to his son.

In some cases, when city councils felt the need for midwives was unusually large, women were taken on before the end of their training period, the length of which varied between one and five years. In these circumstances the woman was accepted with the limitation that "though she has the desire and love [*Lust und Liebe*] for this office, she is in some points rather weak; because she is a beginner and experience comes only through daily practice, especially in this occupation, she must learn a number of things by daily application, and in difficult or precarious situations that she is not ready for, she is to call in another older and more experienced midwife."[81]

To make sure the women trained in the city remained there, city councils rarely allowed midwives to leave, whether permanently or simply to aid in a delivery outside the city walls.[82] Only if someone in a very high position, such as one of the counts Palatinate in 1496 or the duke of Saxony in 1541, made a personal request would the Nuremberg city council send out one of its midwives.[83] A local noblewoman who requested a midwife of the Memmingen city council was forced to use not-so-veiled threats that her husband's "friendship and good feelings" toward the city would certainly end if one were not sent. A midwife was finally sent, and the noblewoman was pleased with her services, commenting that "my husband will now be unsparing in his willingness to serve your city."[84] In 1571 it took five personal requests by the imperial marshall before Memmingen would allow a midwife out to assist a local noblewoman, even though the marshall offered to send a wagon and escort for her. As soon as she left, the city council began asking that she come back, despite the fact that the birth had not occurred.[85] Similar requests were usually met with a similar lack of cooperation, and midwives who went out of the city to serve noblewomen were threatened with a loss of salary or even a loss of position.[86]

Even requests by other city councils who wanted to improve their own systems were turned down, such as those made of Nuremberg by Ulm in 1506 and by Heilbronn in 1606.[87] In 1549 the duke of Württemburg ordered that in all the "leading cities" of his realm, "pious, honorable, God-fearing, and experienced women" be taken on as midwives, with "experienced and capable" women to help them.[88] Getting these women from cities with already developed systems was a problem the solution to which he left, however, to the leaders in each city.

Cities did feel a responsibility to the areas right outside the city walls (*Vorstadt*) and to villages nearby and under the city's jurisdiction. Besides naming women to serve in Frankfurt, the city council there also appointed them for Sachsenhausen, the area across the river. The Nuremberg council sent them to Gostenhof, Wöhrd, and Lichtenau and provided these women with housing, wood, and a salary of eight gulden a year, with an additional bonus of one gulden each for each farmer's wife to whom they taught midwifery. Midwives were allowed to come in and go out of the city gate at night if they were called to serve someone in the Vorstadt, a freedom allowed very few other people.[89] Midwives in Frankfurt were the only gentiles allowed in the Jewish ghetto at night at the few times the Jews did not have a midwife of their own.[90]

How effective was all this in providing trained midwives for a city's residents? A closer look at Nuremberg, which was regarded as having one of the best systems in Germany, gives some idea. The population of the city was somewhere between 30,000 and 50,000; using a rough birth rate figure of between 40 and 50 births per 1,000, one would expect somewhere between 1,200 and 2,500 births per year in the city.[91] With the number of midwives varying between 8 and 22, the number of births per midwife would have varied between 55 and 300 a year. The latter pace, nearly one birth per day, would have been very difficult to maintain and would not have allowed for any postnatal care, which midwives were also often paid to do. Thus one can understand the constant concern of the council that more women be trained, particularly whenever the total number of midwives in the city dropped below 10.

These figures may be somewhat high, as there were undoubtedly many women who gave birth without the aid of a trained midwife. If a woman had already had several children without complications, was generally healthy, and had friends and relatives who could attend to her, she may not have summoned a midwife. If a child was born prematurely, there may not have been enough time for a midwife to reach the mother. Certainly women in the rural areas during this period did not expect the services of a midwife for each delivery. Given that city councils did, however, attempt to provide the services of a midwife for every indigent mother and carefully spelled out the proper charges for women of all social classes, one may assume that most births in these cities were handled by a midwife. The best ratio noted above— about 1 birth a week—could have been easily handled by any midwife, 3–5 a week by the most experienced. Given the number of official midwives in Strasbourg (6), Munich (6–10), Augsburg (19), Memmingen (2–5), and Frankfurt (6–12) and the population of these cities, this pace could usually have been maintained, except during times of war and famine, when the city population swelled.

The one comment by an actual midwife corroborates this assumption. In 1629 a woman applied to the Memmingen city council to be made a midwife, though she had studied only three months in Augsburg. The Memmingen midwives objected, but she answered that she had learned in three months what would have taken a year in Memmingen, as she went with her teacher to all her cases and accompanied other midwives occasionally as well. She had seen 70 different deliveries during this three-month period, a rate of nearly 6 a week. Granted she was probably exaggerating somewhat to argue her case, but the Memmingen physicians and "sworn women" tested her, found her very competent, and accepted her.[92]

Not only were city councils convinced it was important to have a sufficient number of midwives and a structure to control them, but they also expected these midwives to live up to certain standards, which were set out in greater and greater detail throughout the period in the various ordinances for midwives each city promulgated. These ordinances were designed to combine in one comprehensive unit all previous midwife legislation and decisions, so they usually contained little that was new. They were reissued and amended quite frequently, however, as new problems arose or new things came to be thought important.

These ordinances, though many are quite long, were read to each new midwife as she was taken into office, and she then had to swear to abide by all the points in the ordinance. The first was promulgated in Regensburg in 1452; Munich followed in 1488; Freiburg in Breisgau in 1494; Strasbourg in 1500; Frankfurt in 1509; Nuremberg in 1522; the Duchy of Württemburg in 1549; Memmingen in 1578. Many of these are essentially copies of earlier ordinances from other towns, so they all contain a number of nearly identical phrases and requirements. They do give a very clear idea of what was expected of a midwife and how those demands changed during the period, so it is useful to examine them rather closely, always keeping in mind that they are describing an ideal situation yet responding to real problems and difficulties.

The 1488 Munich ordinance is short and simple. The midwife was to swear to come to anyone who asked her, whether rich or poor, day or night, and handle all to the best of her abilities. As long as she was with a woman, she was not to drink anything "so that you keep your senses" and not to attempt to hurry the birth in any way or leave the woman at any time during her labor. If two midwives were called to the same woman, they were to consult with each other in a peaceful and friendly manner and not accuse the other if something went wrong or argue, as this would disturb the pregnant woman. If something went wrong, the midwife was to call one of the "honorable women." She was not to leave the city without the permission of the council, so that she could always be found at home when needed, and was to leave a message as to where she could be found if she was out attending to a woman. "She should also encourage and comfort the pregnant woman and not be sharp or coarse with her, not even with a poor woman from whom she could expect no special reward." If a woman were dying, on no account was she to leave her side but was to encourage her to confess her sins and believe in God and the Savior. If the child was born alive and healthy, she was to care for it and the mother; if it was born dead or nearly dead, she was to perform an emergency baptism or she "would have to answer to God for her laziness and irresponsibility."[93] Thus she had not only medical but also counseling and religious functions.

The first ordinances from Augsburg, Stuttgart, and Strasbourg are very similar, and the Frankfurt oath from 1509 adds that midwives should not demand more than a woman could afford, "and for the very poor the midwife should work for free and wait for her payment from Almighty God, who does not let works of mercy go unrewarded."[94] The first Freiburg in Breisgau ordinance, from 1494, contains most of the same regulations but adds several which discuss intentional and unintentional abortion:

They shall also swear not to destroy any child, whether by doing too little or doing too much, and at all times during the birth try to keep the child alive . . . if one aids in the death of a child, the council will punish her, as this is such a terrible and awful thing out of which much harm and damage comes, some of which cannot even be reported because it is so awful. They are also not to use any gruesome or clumsy tools to damage or pull out the child, like long iron hooks and similar things.[95]

Nuremberg could not let things remain so simple, however, and attempted to cover every conceivable possibility. Its 1522 ordinance began by duplicating the Munich ordinance and then added clauses dealing with what to do if a midwife had to sleep or if she was disobedient. A more significant addition was that which accused midwives of deceiving the city's welfare system, either asking for public support for those who did not need it and then getting a kickback or else demanding payment for handling poor women both from the city and from the women themselves. This ordinance is also quite specific in its description of the apprenticeship system: apprentices were to learn from only one midwife, not switch from one to the other; to be older, experienced women rather than "flighty young girls"; and not to be sent to any woman until they had completed their instruction and had carried out a birth in the presence of their instructor. Most important, midwives were required to report all illegitimate children—whether they were alive or dead; who and where the mother was; who the father was, if possible—and bury no children without telling the city council. "Three or four unsuspected female persons" had to accompany the midwife to the grave when she buried any dead child.[96] Similar clauses were also added to the Freiburg in Breisgau ordinance in 1510.[97] Here emerges a new concern of the city council: illegitimate births. Midwives were to report all they knew about them, not only to keep the children and mothers from needing public support but also to prevent infanticide. The city council included this clause because "recently evil cases have taken place, that those women who live in sin and adultery have illegitimate children and, during birth or before, purposefully attempt to kill them by taking harmful, abortion-causing drugs or through other notorious means."[98]

The Reformation itself brought few immediate changes to midwives' ordinances, and those for Protestant and Catholic cities remained very similar. Beginning in the 1570s, however, there are a number of revisions with quite a different tone from earlier ordinances. The 1578 Memmingen ordinance was issued specifically because "not only the mother but also the child could be injured by the lack of skill or neglect of the midwife, which touches and affects every housefather in his own house." The emphasis on the father and on the fact that he would be more affected by harm to his child than to his wife comes through very clearly. The ordinance is also much more religious than earlier ones, complete with numerous Bible quotations and demands that the midwife be, above all, God-fearing and aware that "her office is a godly, Christian calling."[99] This new emphasis is also seen in the 1585 Württemburg ordinance, which stressed that midwives were to stick to the word of God (*christlicher Trost*) when they advised and comforted mothers and not repeat any superstitions or old wives' tales about births or female diseases. They were to have been instructed in this and in the proper method for emergency baptisms by the pastor of their village, and fidelity to this religious teaching was to be made part of their oath.[100]

The 1578 Memmingen ordinance goes beyond the 1522 Nuremberg ordinance in its discussion of midwives' responsibilities toward illegitimate children. Not only are midwives to report them, but also "when they come upon a young girl or maid or someone else who is pregnant outside of marriage, they should speak to them of their own accord and warn them with threats of punishment not to harm the fetus in any way or take any bad advice, as such foolish people are very likely to do."[101]

In this ordinance the oath the midwives swore was very similar to earlier ones, but the questions they were to be asked in their examinations were spelled out in detail. The questions reveal the level of knowledge the city council hoped every new midwife would have. First came questions about her training and experience: With whom had she studied and for how long? Had she had children herself? How many births had she seen or taken part in? Then came questions about the content of her training: What food, drink, and baths will help a woman have an easy birth? How does she know if a woman is pregnant and does not simply have some other kind of swelling? How does she tell if pains are really labor pains, if the time for delivery has come? How does she know whether the fetus is healthy or sick, dead or alive? What is the normal position for birth, and how is this to be brought about in the case of abnormal presentation? What should be done with the umbilical cord and afterbirth, especially to make sure all of the latter has emerged? How are the new mother and infant to be best taken care of, and what advice should she give the new mother? These questions clearly show that the midwife was responsible for pre- and postnatal care and also for handling somewhat difficult births, such as breech or foot presentation. If a birth proved too difficult and a caesarean section was the only possible means of extracting the child, the city's doctors, the "honorable women," and even the council itself were to be consulted.[102]

The new clauses in the Nuremberg ordinance from 1579 are mainly concerned with the relations between the midwives and their apprentices. Midwives were apparently turning over many of their responsibilities, such as holding children they had delivered at their baptisms, to their apprentices and then taking most of the tips people gave the apprentices. They were also not taking on a new apprentice once one had completed her training. The council intended all of these problems to be corrected, although as later city council records indicate, they were not solved simply by publishing the ordinance.[103]

Thus throughout the sixteenth century midwives' ordinances gradually became more specific and far-reaching in the knowledge and skills they demanded of the midwives and broadened both their legal and religious functions. These same trends continue throughout the seventeenth century, a process that can best be traced in Strasbourg. In the 1605 ordinance midwives were again responsible for reporting all illegitimate children "and also the name of the one that is exclaimed during the pains of birth [i.e., the father]."[104] They were not to use any tools to speed the birth along and were to visit the mother and child in the first weeks after birth. Not only the midwives but also their maids were to swear to abide by the oath.

In the 1635 expansion of the 1605 ordinance, the council reasserted its direct control over the system by requiring that one of its members be present when any midwife was being examined. Midwives' use of medicines was to be sharply limited if it could have dangerous applications: "No midwife or apprentice is to give advice as to how to abort a child through bloodletting, purgatives, or other means . . . children who have died in the womb or the afterbirth are not to be forced out of the mother by medicine or any other means, but a responsible doctor is to be called in." On the other hand, the midwives were to learn to apply "poultices and enemas which pregnant women often need but are embarrassed to ask the apothecary to apply." This is the first mention of female modesty in any of these ordinances, but it may also be the first time such poultices were used at all. Midwives were also to learn the correct way to perform emergency baptisms by "diligently studying and learning" about it in church ordinances.[105]

The 1688 ordinance adds little that is new but further restricts the handling of illegitimate children: "When she [a midwife or an apprentice] is called to an unknown person or a person pregnant out of wedlock who has been overcome by the pains of childbirth, she must then ask her before she gives her a helping hand who the father of the child is so that justice is not neglected and children come in to the orphanage who should be taken care of elsewhere."[106] A baptism ordinance from the same year also requires the midwives to ask permission of one of the city's mayors before performing an emergency baptism, as the council thought too many were being performed. A new Munich ordinance from 1688 also stresses the midwife's responsibility to report any illegitimate children, any they suspected of being illegitimate, or any cases of suspected infanticide or abortion.[107]

During the seventeenth century, then, city councils took over tighter control of the whole midwifery system, expected the midwives to depend more on physicians in difficult cases, and used them increasingly to control morals in appropriate situations. These trends are predictably consistent with trends in city life in general: trends toward more control by the city council of all aspects of life, more respect for university-trained physicians, and attempts to control morals in both Protestant and Catholic cities.

What is surprising is that none of the city ordinances mention any specific superstitious or magical beliefs or practices, such as requiring the midwife to dispose of the afterbirth in a certain way to prevent its being used for magical purposes. This contrasts with contemporary English ordinances, like one from 1559 requiring midwives to be asked "whether you knowe anye that doe use charms, sorcery, enchantments, invocations, circles, witchcrafts, southsayings, or any like crafts or imaginations invented by the Devyl, and specially in the tyme of women's travyl."[108] The only reference to any superstitions at all in the German ordinances is in the ducal ordinance for Württemburg, and that is simply a warning not to scare women with old wives' tales about the dangers of birth.[109] The city councils are much more concerned with the honesty, industriousness, and competence of the cities' midwives than with their possible diabolic connections. This is very different from contemporary discussions of witchcraft, such as the *Malleus Maleficarum*, which often accuse midwives of witchcraft or using their power over life in the service of the devil.[110]

It is interesting to compare these ordinances with those of later periods, for one sees how little the occupation of midwifery changed over centuries. Medical historians often view the mid-eighteenth century as a time of great progress in obstetrics in Germany, as male accoucheurs (physicians specializing in delivery) began to practice in many cities. These accoucheurs often took over the direction of the midwifery system from the "honorable women," and this office then disappeared or dropped to only one or two women.[111]

These changes made little significant impact, however, on the role of the midwife. She still handled most births in any city, and ordinances from the mid-eighteenth century often simply repeat those from the sixteenth century with very few changes. The midwives were still to be of good moral and physical character, married or widowed and preferably somewhat older, and to have had children themselves. They were not to drink too much or to leave town without notifying the council and were to advise new mothers both before and after the birth. They were not to hurry along any birth or use any tools or strong medicines. They were still to perform emergency baptisms when necessary and report all illegitimate births. As Audrey Eccles notes in reference to England, the practice of midwifery was probably slower to change than most other branches of medicine because the patients often had very set ideas about what they expected the midwife or accoucheur to do and would not recommend or go back to one who did not do what was expected.[112]

What did change was the way a midwife was to be educated. Besides her apprenticeship with an experienced midwife, she was to receive some theoretical training from city physicians. This may even have involved watching an autopsy on a female cadaver, a practice first reported in Nuremberg in 1688.[113] Frankfurt and Memmingen specifically requested a city doctor to perform an autopsy if a pregnant woman died in the city hospital and the child was illegitimate, so that the midwives would have a better understanding of female anatomy.[114] All of these eighteenth-century ordinances required that the midwives be literate: "The midwife is not to neglect during boring hours the reading of good books that concern themselves with the art of midwifery. Anything in these that she does not understand, she should have explained by a doctor or capable surgeon."[115]

In many ways, however, even the emphasis on education was not new. During the early seventeenth century several midwives became famous throughout Germany for their high level of education. Maria Colinetia (1560–1634), the wife of the surgeon Fabricius von Hilden, traveled all over Germany performing minor surgery as well as midwifery; she is said to have first advised getting an iron splinter out of the eye with a magnet. Margaretha Fuss (1555–1625), called "Mutter Grethe," had learned midwifery in Strasbourg "with numerous learned doctors" and became the midwife of Duchess Sibylla of Leignitz and Brieg, the daughter of Elector John George of Brandenburg. She was called to many German courts and also to the Netherlands and Denmark.[116] The first midwives' book in Germany by a woman, *Berliner-Hilff-Wehe-Mutter*, was written in 1700 by Justine Siegemundin, who had taken some medical training at Frankfurt on the Oder.[117] On a somewhat less spectacular level, most of the applications to become a midwife or responses by midwives to charges against them, while written in a scribal hand, were clearly signed by the women themselves.[118]

Even earlier than this, a few sixteenth-century ordinances required that midwives read or have read to them one of the midwives' manuals currently being published.[119] The two most popular were Albertus Magnus's *De Secretu Mulierum*, a general discussion of female anatomy and physiology, and Eucharius Roesslin's *Den swangeren frawen und hebammen Roszgarten* [The Rosegarden for Midwives and Pregnant Women]. The latter was first published in Strasbourg in 1513, with later editions in all the western European languages.[120] Much of the information contained in the *Roszgarten* came from classical authors, and much of it was wrong or useless, but it was accepted by university physicians and midwives alike. It sold widely throughout Europe, which indicates that at least some midwives were probably reading it on their own, and a number of items in late-sixteenth- and seventeenth-century ordinances, such as the discussion of unnatural birth positions in the 1668 Memmingen ordinance, are taken directly from Roesslin.[121] As J. H. Aveling, a historian of English midwifery, notes, "During the century following its publication, it was almost the sole book from which midwives gained any knowledge of their art."[122]

Although Roesslin had little regard for the general level of skill among contemporary midwives and accused them of neglect or worse, most of the information in his manual was not new, and much of it, he admits, came from talking with experienced midwives. He gives a wide variety of herbal and other natural remedies for all kinds of problems associated with giving birth, along with some more bizarre treatments like having the mother sit over a smoldering fire of donkey's dung to force a spontaneous abortion of a dead fetus. Most of it is simple common sense: keep the mother warm and away from cold drafts; avoid scaring or shocking her; handle the mother and child carefully and gently; make sure the entire afterbirth emerges; keep up the mother's strength with simple, nourishing foods; avoid using tools or medicines unless it is absolutely necessary. Only his discussions of what to do if problems arose—if the water broke too early, if a mother had been torn greatly during the birth, if a child had died in the uterus—offer what might be new information to sixteenth-century midwives, but his solutions make one doubt if any mother could have survived them. Roesslin himself admits this, and he includes a section instructing midwives how to tell if a mother is dead.

Roesslin's text is useful precisely because it contained little that was new, and so it provides an idea of the normal birth procedure that cannot be obtained from reading ordinances. The mother was seated on a birthing stool, which tipped her back slightly, was padded so that she would be comfortable, and had handles or leather thongs for her to grasp. The midwife was seated directly in front of her to assist in bringing about a normal presentation if the child was turned in the uterus. Often a number of other women—the midwife's apprentice, female relatives, and friends—bustled about preparing broth, wine, and other drinks for the mother and a meal for the midwife. Normally a warm herb bath was prepared for the infant, and care was taken to have clean swaddling clothes.

Dr. Christoph Scheurl, a Nuremberg lawyer, describes just such a scene at the birth of his son, George: "The birth occurred at the back of the house, in our normal eating room along Rosenpadt street. I was banished before the bed was prepared. Frau Margaretha Endres Tucherin, Ursula Fritz Tetzlin, the widow Magdalena Mugenhoferin, and Anna the midwife assisted her." [123] The social position of the midwife is clear from Scheurl's reference to her by first name only whereas to the other women of his own social class he gives complete names.

All of these ordinances together with the midwives' manual form a picture of what city councils hoped the typical, or at least the ideal, midwife would be: a widow or older married woman who had had children, was not wealthy enough to have her own household, but was not absolutely penniless either. In fact, a woman's request to be made a midwife was denied in at least one case expressly because "such poor people as her should not be midwives"; instead she was given support from the municipal welfare fund. [124] The ideal midwife was to be devoted to helping others, godly, modest, and obedient to her superiors. The clauses dealing with the consumption of wine and attempts to defraud the public welfare system do indicate that not all women lived up to these standards, however.

Midwives were occasionally accused of leaving women before the delivery was completed or of refusing to treat poor women or of hurrying along the deliveries of their poorer patients in order to have more time for wealthier ones. The "honorable women" sometimes claimed they were not being obeyed and asked the city councils to increase their power to punish disobedient midwives. Councils themselves were not afraid to follow through on their threats of punishment, scolding, fining, and removing midwives from office. [125]

In several cases, midwives were even banished: one from Nuremberg for three years for not reporting that an unmarried maid had killed her own child; a second from Munich for general disobedience and being so inattentive as to carry a child she had delivered to its baptism and allow it to be baptized "George" although it was later discovered to be a girl; a third from Memmingen for arranging to give an illegitimate child to a woman whose own child had died at birth without the knowledge or permission of the city council. [126] Midwives who were removed from office for negligence often protested, bringing women they had served to plead for them, and occasionally succeeded in being reinstated. Midwives arrested for other crimes also brought testimonials from women they had served when asking for reductions in their sentences.[127]

The number of serious cases against midwives is surprisingly small, however, given the number of women involved and their opportunities to injure either mother or child. In Nuremberg, in one tragic case, a woman killed herself because of the pain after being mishandled by a midwife; there were other reports of this midwife's ineptitude, and she was removed from office and another set in her place.[128] This is the single such case, however, among the more than two hundred midwives working in Nuremberg in the early modern period, and I can be relatively sure that the sources are complete on this account.

The only malpractice case in Frankfurt for which the sources are still extant is one from 1656. A shoemaker brought a complaint against "Mutter Mackell" after his wife had died in childbirth, charging her with "irresponsible negligence and ineptness" and asking that she be removed from office. He called for an autopsy, hoping to get a report from the doctors that the midwife had indeed caused the death, but then found that she had talked to the doctors first and convinced them to decide in her favor. He then asked other women who were present at the birth, and they said they had heard the wife cry out, "Oh, Mother Mackell, you have never hurt me so much before! Oh, my stomach! Oh, my stomach!" The women also admitted that Mother Mackell had not called on God for help and had used "illegal means to draw out the afterbirth." The child had lived, and the shoemaker pled in the name of this one and his other children. He maintained the midwife had killed his wife intentionally and had then lied about it; if the council did not punish her for it, it would have "agreed to a murder, and to further murders without fear of punishment."[129]

The doctors did finally perform an autopsy and found that the uterus had been cut or ripped and that a piece of the afterbirth was still in the uterus. The women who were there stated that Mutter Mackell had cut the vaginal opening some, reached inside the mother to pull out the afterbirth, yanked on it, and then the bleeding and pain started. They signed this statement themselves, and then one of them added that Mutter Mackell had given her a little piece of flesh, telling her it was the afterbirth and that she should throw it away secretly; she had said it was not the whole afterbirth, and Mutter Mackell had told her to be quiet. Throughout all of this testimony Mutter Mackell maintained that she had been falsely accused, had gotten rid of the whole afterbirth, and had not used any unusual methods or damaged the uterus. The council found for the shoemaker, however, fined her thirty gulden, an enormous sum, and removed her from office.[130] This, again, is a single case and shows very clearly the extent to which a case had to be made against a midwife to convince the council she was actually at fault. The dangers inherent in any normal birth were recognized by everyone.

The ducal court at Württemburg does offer a few more cases, but these are really witchcraft cases in which the woman accused happened to be a midwife. In only one of them, again a very long case involving the testimony of doctors, other midwives, and women who had been in attendance, was the midwife charged with harming or killing children through physical, rather than magical, means. According to the testimony of a number of witnesses, this midwife had reached far inside women, way up to her elbows, to extract the afterbirth and had contributed to the deaths of a number of mothers and children. The unfortunate midwife was beheaded, her right hand hacked off, and both head and hand were put on a post at the marketplace to serve as a warning. Interestingly, this case includes her will and an inventory of all her property; she was extremely poor, with more debts than property, but still left some money to the needy.[131]

In general, then, I must assess the capabilities of early modern midwives positively. They knew as much about the mysteries of birth as contemporary university-trained physicians, or more, and appear to have done their job well. Later judgments of midwives as bungling, slovenly, superstitious, and inept were not shared by early modern political leaders, for they would not have been so concerned with making sure enough midwives were available had they held such views. These attacks on the quality of midwives began mostly in the eighteenth century, when male accoucheurs were attempting to gain acceptance. Whether they reflect a true decline in the midwifery system by this time, or simply an attempt to downgrade the competition, is a difficult question to answer. At any rate, they are not a valid description of sixteenth and seventeenth century midwives.

The high regard in which midwives were held can be seen from the variety of things, besides delivering babies and caring for new mothers, for which they were responsible. Their skills and experience were frequently called on.

Midwives often served as back-up medical assistants during outbreaks of the plague or other epidemics. One of the medical techniques used for treating bubonic plague was lancing the buboes, the swellings in the groin and armpits, in an attempt to draw out the poison and relieve pressure. Midwives frequently did this for female plague victims, for which they were granted special payments or given special privileges. Even midwives who had been removed from office for various reasons were called on to work in plague hospitals or pesthouses; they were promised a full reinstatement in office if they served well.[132]

Midwives were often called on to give opinions in legal cases. In 1600 a Frankfurt shoemaker complained to the council that he had been thrown out of the guild because his first child had been born too soon after his marriage, but the child was actually just several months premature. He asked that the "sworn midwives and honorable women examine the child and report their opinion." The council agreed, though the final judgment in the case is not recorded.[133]

Midwives were asked to examine any female prisoner who claimed she was pregnant. In the fifteenth century pregnant women were not tortured. Although this special treatment was gradually done away with during the sixteenth century, a milder handling was still advised, for otherwise the mothers "could become unconscious and hurt the child in their bodies."[134] Corporal punishment was still used, however. Throughout this period, a woman who claimed she was pregnant and was found not to be was dealt with more sharply. Midwives checked on nursing mothers who were in prison to be sure their children were getting enough milk and examined female corpses to see if they were pregnant or help determine the cause of death.[135]

Midwives might also be asked to examine unmarried women suspected of fornication. Although the women involved often objected to the degradation of such an examination, in at least one case it worked to the woman's advantage. Two young people in Strasbourg were accused of fornication; although they denied it, the woman was to be examined by the local midwives. The midwives were specifically not to be informed about the case in advance so that they would not be overly sympathetic, and they still found her to be "a pure virgin, just as she was when she was first born out her mother's body." The council decided the pair had been charged unjustly and fined the man who brought the charges thirty gulden and the costs of the trial, though they awarded the insulted pair no recompense other than an apology.[136]

Midwives appeared most often in court in connection with infanticide and abortion cases. As I have shown, the ordinances required them to report immediately all illegitimate children—who the parents were, whether the child was alive or dead, and where the mother was. City councils required this information not only to punish the women involved and prevent more public welfare charges but also to try to prevent the mothers from abandoning, aborting, or killing their children. They recognized that illegitimate children would be those most likely to be disposed of in some manner, as there was usually no means of public support for them. Orphanages were not to take in any children they knew were illegitimate, and public welfare funds usually went only to the wives of citizens or permanent residents whose children were legitimate.

A woman suspected of aborting or killing her child was taken into the city jail, where she was examined by a midwife to see if she had been pregnant, which generally meant only seeing if she had milk. If the suspect was from a rural area, she was often brought into the city in chains, at night or in the early morning. The midwife also questioned her, as an admission of guilt was needed for capital punishment, particularly after the institution of the *Carolina Constitutio Criminalis*, the set of legal procedures for criminal cases drawn up during the reign of Charles V and adopted by many cities in Germany during the mid-sixteenth century. Her house was searched for anything suspicious like bloody cloths or clothes, and apothecaries and neighbors were questioned as to her activities and purchases. Often the suspect was held for weeks or months while the investigation continued.[137]

The midwife and often a barber-surgeon were sent out to search for the body of the child and to examine it for signs of violence and an indication that it had been born alive.[138] This occasionally involved doing an autopsy to see if it had drawn breath: "On the report of the sworn midwives as to how they found the dead child with a piece of wood stuck in its mouth, it is recommended that the child be cut open and examined further."[139] The body was exhumed from the field, dung heap, or cow stall where it had been buried, examined, and then reburied with a simple ceremony often conducted by the midwife.[140] In one particularly gruesome case, a woman had killed the child who had been conceived in incest with her own father but had not buried it deep enough, and the body was dug up by neighborhood dogs; the midwife was dispatched to bury what was left.[141]

Occasionally the child's corpse was brought in to the mother in order to shock her into confession. One such incident, in which a child found three days after its death was shown to its mother, is dramatically retold for the city council: "And then the midwife said, 'Oh, you innocent little child, if one of us here is guilty, give us a sign!' and immediately the child raised its left arm and pointed at its mother."[142] The unfortunate mother was later executed by drowning. Using evidence from Geneva, E. William Monter has discovered that, among women, infanticide was the crime for which the accused was most likely to receive the death penalty: 25 women out of 31 charged with infanticide during the period 1595–1712 were executed as compared with 19 out of 122 charged with witchcraft.[143]

Some city councils were careful, however, to make sure the mother's actions had indeed caused the child's death, that the child had not in fact simply died of natural causes and that the mother was not confessing out of fear of torture. In cases of suspected abortion midwives were called in to give testimony as to whether the means the mother had used—either strenuous physical activity, herb mixtures, or other drugs—could in fact have caused an abortion. Women were occasionally released or given only a light sentence if the method used was not violent or strong enough to induce abortion even though the fetus had in fact died. Midwives suspected of giving advice on abortions were often treated as harshly as the mother.[144]

Midwives, or the "honorable women" who oversaw them, were often part of municipal welfare systems. They were responsible for handing out bedding, bread, and lard to needy women and making sure clean swaddling clothes and bandages were ready for the delivery. They often judged who was to receive this aid as well, each midwife or supervisor being responsible for a certain part of the city. They were also to be present at the baptism of any infant they delivered and to warn parents about any sumptuary laws which governed the baptism so that they would not spend too much money on the infant's baptism gown or invite too many people to the party afterward.[145]

As the ordinances explain, midwives performed emergency baptisms if they or the parents felt the child would not live. This created few problems before the Reformation because Catholic doctrine taught that children who had been baptized by lay people, should there be some question about the regularity of this baptism, could be rebaptized "on the condition" that they had not been baptized correctly the first time. This conditional baptism assured parents that their child had been baptized correctly and was not considered an actual rebaptism. Actual rebaptism, particularly that of adults, was punishable by death in Germany at this time, as it meant one rejected the accepted doctrine of infant baptism. Foundlings were also baptized "on condition," just in case they might already have been baptized. In 1531, however, Luther rejected as casuistry all baptisms "on condition" if it was known any baptism had already been carried out and called for a normal baptism in the case of foundlings. By 1540 most Lutheran areas were no longer baptizing "on condition," and those who still supported the practice were occasionally branded Anabaptists.[146] This made it extremely important that midwives and other lay people know how to conduct an emergency baptism correctly.

Midwives were thus examined, along with pastors, church workers, and teachers, in the visitations conducted by pastors and city leaders in many cities, and "shocking irregularities" in baptismal practice were occasionally discovered. As one (perhaps apocryphal) story tells it, a pastor found one midwife confident in her reply that, yes, she certainly baptized infants in the name of the Holy Trinity—Caspar, Melchoir, and Balthazar! During the course of the sixteenth century, most Protestant cities included a long section on emergency baptisms in their general baptismal ordinances and even gave copies of this special section to the city's midwives.[147]

In areas of Germany where Anabaptism flourished, Anabaptist midwives were charged with claiming that they had baptized babies when they really had not, so that a regular church baptism would not be required.[148] In other areas the opposite seems to have been the case. Baptism was an important social occasion and a chance for the flaunting of wealth and social position, and parents of a child who unexpectedly lived sometimes paid the midwife to conveniently forget she had baptized the child so that the whole normal church ceremony could be carried out.

These examples of the additional functions midwives carried out underline their importance in the early modern city. Their opinions and judgments in all matters regarding pregnancy and birth were taken seriously. No other group of women received more frequent consideration by the city council nor was more closely watched as to conduct, numbers, and skill.

Though there are no diaries and records from these urban midwives themselves, there are still hints that they recognized their own importance and felt a strong sense of camaraderie. Not only did they always defend against unlicensed midwives their sole right to work, but in Strasbourg they also required each new midwife to provide all the others with a "welcome meal" when she was taken on. The older midwives justified the requirement with the comment that the city council had a similar requirement for new council representatives and ambassadors, offices the older midwives maintained were certainly no more important or honorable than midwifery.[149] Natalie Davis has demonstrated the importance of such events in validating or establishing work identity and also the relative scarcity of them among women's occupational groups as compared with male guilds and trades.[150] This welcome meal is thus a clear sign of the strong occupational identity of the Strasbourg midwives. Midwives elsewhere also displayed this sense of work identity, for they were always careful to mention their occupation when appearing in court, making an appeal, or acting in any other legal or public capacity.

Die Badmeydt spricht

Ich Badmeide sich allhie allein
Mit bloffen armen / vnd weiffen bein
Auff die leut thu ich achtung haben
Oeg alet ben auff die jungen knaben
Da bin ich mit mein wasser geschwinde
Jungen vnd alt / die kleine Kindt
Den zwage ich / vnd reib sie auß
Das sie gehn sauber heim zu hauß.

Zu Nürnberg / bey Wolff
Drechsel.

*A Bath Maid. Woodcut by Wolf Drechsel, fl. 1576–1601. Published in* The German Single-Leaf Woodcut *(New York: Abaris, 1975). The verse reads: "I, a bath maid, stand here alone, / With naked arms and white legs / I take care of people / And do the same for young men / There am I with my water in a hurry / Young and old, and small children / I whip them with branches and rub them off / So that they go home clean."*

# CHAPTER THREE
# Public, Domestic, and Carnal Service

Along with health care and healing, other service occupations provided employment for many women during this period. Women served as public officials, curators of charitable endowments, and teachers for younger children. Large numbers of women worked as domestic servants, and some served as employment agents for those servants. All of these occupations were considered respectable and suitable for women at the beginning of the period, though restrictions were gradually placed on them for a variety of reasons.

Women were also involved in two service occupations viewed as somewhat disreputable: working in the public baths and prostitution. Municipal baths and brothels were accepted parts of urban life in the late Middle Ages but came under increasing attack for both health and moral reasons and were gradually closed. Illicit prostitution, often combined with petty crime, remained the only means possible for some women to support themselves.

## Officials and Teachers

Women in early modern cities had no real political voice; they did not vote in municipal or guild elections or serve on the city council or as quartermasters or mayors. This did not mean that they were totally excluded from municipal government, however, for women were often appointed as city officials. Admittedly most of the positions they held were minor ones, but there was no rejection of female officials per se.

Many of the women working in official positions were actually the wives of male officials and were also required to swear an oath of office because they often carried out the duties associated with their husband's office. In most cities the jailer, some tax collectors, those who weighed grain at the public scales, and those who opened and closed the city gates were posts to which wives were sworn with their husbands. In addition, the wives of carters, freight haulers, warehouse operators, and millers were occasionally required to swear an oath. At times the men who held these positions also had another occupation, so their wives did most of the actual work of the office. That city councils recognized the arrangement can be seen in the practice of requiring a man to step down in favor of a new couple when his wife was no longer able to work.[1] In fact, at times the city councils complained that the wives of gatekeepers and toll collectors did the job all the time, while their men worked in the fields.

Women were often allowed to continue in such occupations after their husbands had died, much like the widows of craftsmen were allowed to keep running the shop. This required a special supplication to the city council but was usually granted without much discussion, at least for a limited period of time. In many cases, the women were old and poor, and the city councils saw this as a way to give them some income and prevent them from needing public support. These requests were granted individually, with the city council refusing to set down any general principle as to whether widows were to be allowed to continue in a post or not. Indeed, arguing that other widows had previously been granted such requests might actually work against a woman, with the city council refusing her request for that very reason, unwilling to start a pattern. Supplications stressing need and poverty and appealing to the kind-heartedness and Christian charity of the city council were always much more successful than those which argued a right to continue in office. A second marriage was usually grounds to remove a widow from office, as it was assumed that the new husband would be able to support her.[2]

An interesting twist in this regard is offered by one case in Strasbourg. The widow of a toll collector who had been allowed to continue in office reported that another man wanted to marry her, as long as he could then assume the office of toll collector. She argued that he was sickly and could do no other work and that they could both live from the salary of the office. She also pointed out that a man marrying the widow of a master craftsman gained the position of master as long as the other requirements for the craft, such as an apprenticeship and masterpiece, had been met. As no special training or examination was needed to become a toll collector, why could her new husband not simply take over the office? The city council would not carry the parallel with the widows of master craftsmen that far, however, commenting that it was shocked at the idea.[3]

In addition to women who were the wives and widows of male officials, there were a number of women who held office on their own. In some cases, these were positions always held by women, but in others they were held by men or women, with no differentiation in salary or duties according to sex. Many of these were inspectors or weighers at the city marketplace. Women served as salt weighers, grain measurers, and vegetable inspectors in Munich; as milk inspectors in Memmingen; salt measurers in Koblenz; and grain weighers in Frankfurt.[4] In Memmingen and Ulm they inspected flax and linen, examining it for quality and weighing it, bringing anything found faulty to the attention of the mayor or another higher official.[5]

In Augsburg and Memmingen, and perhaps in other cities as well, women served as *Hochzeitsladerinnen* ("inviters to weddings"), inviting the guests to weddings and other festivities associated with a marriage. They either received a salary for this or were paid directly by the families involved, but in both cases they were ordered to follow all city marriage ordinances, warning the families involved if they were spending too much or carrying on too long. The Hochzeitsladerin herself was responsible if too many guests had been invited, even if the families told her to invite that many. She was to report all weddings that broke any restrictions and would be assessed a stiff fine if she did not.[6]

As cities took over the collection and distribution of public welfare from the church during the fifteenth and sixteenth centuries, women as well as men were named as curators of charitable endowments and welfare organizations. Unlike the women who served as other sorts of officials, these curators were the wives or widows of city leaders and upper-class patricians and received only a nominal salary or nothing for their work. They were actually involved in the daily operations of the endowments, however, and were not simply figureheads. They were required to make a yearly report on the financial state and operations of their organizations, and the city council often made changes acting on their reports. Some of these women remained in office for twenty to thirty years and then handed down the position to a daughter, daughter-in-law, or niece. Nuremberg offers the best example of such curators. Women were established as the overseers of three municipal charities in the late fifteenth or early sixteenth century: the girls' orphanage in 1480; the *Guldener Truncks*, which provided dowries and trousseaus for poor girls, in 1485; and the *Arme Kindbetterin Almosen* for poor expectant mothers in the 1520s. The names of the women appointed read like a who's who in early modern Nuremberg; almost all of their husbands were or had been prominent city council members or mayors.

The overseer of the girls' orphanage had the most demanding job and was accordingly paid the most for her work. She was to visit the orphanage regularly, oversee all the permanent staff there, and make sure the children and buildings were well cared for. She was to call a doctor when one was needed and pay special attention to the quality of wet nurses procured for infants, as there were frequent stories of how they abused or ignored their charges. She was occasionally given a special payment to use for any extraordinary needs of the orphanage and was to give a detailed report to the council as to how this money was spent.[7]

The Guldener Truncks ("Golden Chest"), the second endowment run by a woman, grew out of the *Jungfern Almosen* ("Maidens' Alms"), which was first endowed in 1427 by Ottilia and Hilpolt Kress. They left twelve thousand florins, the interest from which was to be used to help poor girls with their dowry and trousseau.[8] Orphan girls, serving maids, and the daughters of poverty-stricken masters could be granted funds once the curator had determined they were worthy. Memmingen and Munich also had similar funds, although in those cities the decisions about distribution were made directly by the city council without the assistance of a female official.[9]

The third charity in Nuremberg, the Arme Kindbetterin Almosen ("Alms for Poor Expectant Mothers"), was first established in 1461 and, as might be expected, received much of its funding from wealthy women. Its curator, assisted by several other women and the city's midwives, judged which expectant mothers were needy enough to warrant public support and then distributed it to them.[10] The city council often worried that women not really in need were receiving aid, often by making an agreement with their midwife to share the clothing or food to be granted on the midwife's testimony to their "poverty." The council discussed appointing more than one curator, each responsible for only one part of the city so that she would better know who really should receive support, but nothing was ever agreed upon, and only one woman remained in the position.

All three of these positions remained in existence until the city was taken over by Bavaria in 1806; the latter two were still managed solely by women into the nineteenth century. Although there is no specific mention of them, similar offices may have existed in other cities as well. In any case, women were often providing the funds for charitable endowments for poor girls and women, even if they were not the ones overseeing the distribution directly.

Thus, in many cities women carried out all kinds of official responsibilities, either along with their husbands or independently, ranging from inspecting vegetables to distributing public welfare. As with male officials, they took oaths swearing that they would carry out their job according to the regulations imposed by the council, and if they held the position independently and not as a wife, they were recorded by name in the city records. Even wives were occasionally listed by name, at least through the middle of the seventeenth century.

Studies of officials in Germany, which are exhaustive and numerous, have ignored or at least overlooked women officeholders, perhaps because they concentrate on either an earlier or a later period—the twelfth century or the eighteenth—and also because they usually focus on upper-level officials at noble courts or in the territorial states, not on middle- and lower-level officials in the cities. Even noble courts, however, such as that of the Duke of Bavaria at Munich, had female officials with independent duties and salaries, though they were often the wives of male officials. One can only wish that particularly the studies of the growth of the official class (*Beamtentum*) in late-eighteenth-century Germany had occasionally considered the reasons why women were categorically excluded from all official positions, as it is clearly not something with a long historical precedent.[11]

No doubt a great deal of the explanation for the eighteenth-century development lies in the total exclusion of women from secular higher education, a subject not really part of the present study.[12] Education in general is, however, for though women did not attend Latin gymnasia or the universities, they were active not only as students but also as teachers in private and public schools that taught reading and writing in German.

Women teachers, *Lehrfrauen*, are found as early as the fourteenth century in some cities, appearing in tax records in Speyer, Bern, Regensburg, Mainz, Zurich, and Frankfurt and shortly afterward in Augsburg and Nuremberg.[13] They taught mostly in their own homes and were often very poor, taking in spinning and sewing along with their few pupils. City councils occasionally forgave them their debts as a reward for their service as teachers or provided them with a small supplement if they thought their situation especially warranted it, as in Arnstadt when the teacher reported that her house had so deteriorated "that bugs and worms slither in and can freely creep in and out, so that the children are always screaming and terrified."[14]

Women regularly asked for and were usually granted special permission to take in pupils, usually with the limitation that they teach only girls and that they accept no boarders. These women were required to be citizens and had to have a lifestyle judged honorable by the city council. The number of pupils and their age was also often limited to make sure the women were teaching only basic reading, writing, and figuring.[15] After the Reformation the women also had to be of the religion considered proper by the city council, although female teachers are specifically mentioned in only a few of the Protestant school ordinances published during the sixteenth century.[16] If any of these requirements were missing, the woman's request was denied with no explanation.[17]

Not all female teachers were charity cases, however; occasionally one was so popular and respected that she alarmed and threatened the city's male teachers. The most celebrated of these cases was a woman in 1456 in Ueberlingen. Parents were so impressed with the instruction she was giving their daughters that they began to send their sons there as well, which caused an immediate complaint by the city schoolmaster:

> The Wartzenburgerin has been teaching girls, and some people in this city have decided to have their boys learn German as well and have sent them to her. She has understood that this has brought difficulties to me and my school. So I request that she be ordered to pay me three schillings per year for every boy that she teaches, because my own income has been diminished, and that she give this to me without stalling or objections.[18]

The city council agreed with the schoolmaster, and the woman had to pay for each pupil she "stole" away from him.

This was not the only such case, however, for from time to time in most cities the official Latin schoolmasters attempted to crack down on what they termed "*Winckleschulen*," literally, "schools set up in dark corners," that is, illegally, that were drawing pupils away from the official schools.[19] Usually these complaints were couched in religious terms to make them most effective with city councils: the women—or men—who ran these small schools were not teaching from the correct catechism, and the children were learning false doctrine. If allowed to continue teaching, the teachers often had to agree to answer questions about their beliefs to make sure they were orthodox. This was especially the case in a city like Strasbourg, which had a large number of religious refugees of all types who tried to make ends meet by teaching a few children.

It is very difficult to determine how many women were involved in teaching, as they were not organized or registered and lacked any set of regulations or instructions imposed by a city council. It is estimated that Frankfurt in 1600 had about 20 small "house schools" or "elementary schools," about half of which were taught by women. This seems a reasonable number and certainly more believable than the huge number (2,000) of pupils and teachers, both male and female, reported as having greeted Kaiser Friedrich on his entrance into Nuremberg in 1487.[20]

Particularly after the Reformation, city councils were more concerned about the moral standards and conduct of female teachers and pupils than they were about the quality of education they gave or received. In Nuremberg female teachers appear most often in the records in regard to processions and parades, which was perhaps the only time they were normally seen in public with their pupils and hence the only time the council paid much attention to them. Even before the Reformation, the teachers were ordered to watch their girls, "that they do not decorate themselves so sumptuously with gold chains and other signs of haughtiness or the council will confiscate the jewelry." Their conduct at Ascension Week dances was also questioned, and the dances were eventually forbidden; the teachers were threatened with a fine if any of their pupils were found dancing or in "extravagant or ostentatious dress."[21] After the Reformation the prohibition of dancing during Ascension Week was extended to all Ascension processions and festivities because the council thought they had not "been innocent everywhere, so the young children easily become sick through overexcitement and inflammation of the blood."[22] A fine of ten gulden was set for teachers who disobeyed, which was probably more than the average annual salary for most of these women.

Moral concerns were also uppermost in girls' education when it was handled by men. Teachers were forbidden to invite their female students to their homes for a meal, and girls who wanted to have male teachers as tutors had to ask special permission.[23] The most important qualifications for the two masters of the girls' primary schools in Memmingen was that they have an "honorable lifestyle" and a "good reputation."[24] Propriety was also given as the reason why girls and boys were never to be taught together, by either male or female teachers.

The goals of education for girls can be seen in a number of treatises written by prominent humanists—Erasmus, More, Juan Vives, Thomas Elyot—but also somewhat less esoterically in the ordinances for the girls' schools in Memmingen, first promulgated in 1587. Each year the best student was chosen as "queen" and honored with a small ceremony by the schoolmasters. What made her the best? "Great diligence and application in learning her catechism, modesty, obedience, and excellent penmanship."[25] The other girls were allowed to congratulate her on the honor, but there were no parties or dances held to celebrate lest she become too proud of her own achievements.

As the 1643 version of this ordinance reads, "The main thing is for the girls to learn Christian teachings and religion, together with the explanation of these as it is given in the Christian catechism, and to recite this obediently not only in school, but also in church or wherever else it is requested of them." They should always be obedient to every older person and not call each other names, "but live with each other peacefully and in friendship." They were to report any bad activities of other girls to the schoolmaster and to take any punishment he gave them patiently and willingly, or they could be called before the city council for being "rebellious, disobedient, and obstinate."[26]

Memmingen is unusual in that it set up primary schools for girls which had roughly the same structure and regulations as those it set up for boys. During the period 1556–1600 there were two girls' schools and two boys' schools, each headed by a schoolmaster paid by the city and by his pupils. Girls who could not afford the fees required were even granted scholarships by wealthy citizens, in the same way a poor boy might be given one to a Latin gymnasium or a university.[27] The boys' schoolmasters were paid more, however, and "the girls' schoolmasters are always under their supervision"; when a master of one of the boys' schools left or died, one from the girls' schools usually moved up, and the girls received an inexperienced teacher.[28]

This is more than most cities did, however, for despite the recommendations of Philip Melanchton, Luther's close associate and strong advocate of education for both boys and girls, very few cities, either Protestant or Catholic, set up any schools for girls at all. One was established in Stuttgart by 1563 with the odd name of Magdalene School, a name usually reserved for houses for former prostitutes. It was especially unusual in that the teachers were female, paid by the city, and even called "mistresses." Unfortunately, that is about all one can learn about the school because all its records were destroyed in World War II, as were those of a late-seventeenth-century girls' school in Stuttgart, also with female teachers and supported by the city.[29]

Even when schools were available, parents did not want to send their daughters for very long. As a 1599 report to the Augsburg city council reads, "The children must be soon sent out to work, especially the daughters, who can expect only very little time in school . . . they must also learn sewing and be used in running the household."[30] Sewing was considered a much more useful skill for any girl than reading; the scholarships set up for girls read: "to be sent to school, and especially to learn to sew."[31] This probably worked to the advantage of female teachers, however, who could teach the young girls they had in their homes not only a little reading, writing, and figuring and a few Bible verses and hymns but also sewing and other domestic skills.

Teaching, then, offered a few women in most cities an opportunity to make a little extra money and maintain themselves in their own homes when they could not carry out more physically taxing work. It is difficult to assess how much education they gave their pupils, but judging from the quite high level of basic literacy—at least the ability to write their own names—among city women during this period, someone, whether a parent or teacher, was taking the time to teach girls.

## DOMESTIC SERVICE

Most women who worked outside their own homes worked as domestic servants. Service was a stage in life for many women, until they had reached the age they could marry and had earned a small dowry. It was also a permanent "career" for many, who worked their way up in a large household from goosegirl to children's maid to serving maid to cook, or who more likely remained with a family as its single servant for twenty, thirty, or forty years. They rarely received much more than room and board as their wages, and inventories taken at the death of maids indicate they usually owned no more than the clothes in which they were buried. Only the top level of servants in wealthy, large households could hope to earn enough to enable them to leave and perhaps set up a small business. For many women, however, there was no other possible means of support, either until they were married and could set up their own households or after the death of a husband left them penniless.

Because of the large number of women and men involved, some cities saw the need for some kind of organized means to facilitate the hiring of servants. They thus set up a system of employment agents, to whom a girl or boy coming in from the countryside could go if they had no relatives or personal contacts in the city. This was easier than simply knocking door-to-door for work and also enabled cities to have some control over how domestic servants were hired.

The earliest mention of such agents is in Nuremberg in 1421, when both men and women are listed; but by the sixteenth century this was strictly a female occupation. The wording of their appointment in the Nuremberg city council minutes is exactly the same as a master of a craft or a minor city official. They first received a comprehensive ordinance in Nuremberg in 1521, in Strasbourg in 1557, and in Munich in 1580, although it is clear in all these cities that the system was already in operation before the ordinance was drafted. The ordinances were usually issued to clear up disagreements and solve problems the city councils saw in their handling of maids and servants. The ordinances differ somewhat in that they respond to particular problems in each city, but many of the clauses are repeated in all of them.[32]

The number of official employment agents was limited, to eight in Nuremberg and Munich and to five in Strasbourg, although other people were specifically allowed to find positions for their friends and relatives as long as they took no pay for doing so. Employment agents were all to hang out a sign in front of their houses so that people coming in from the countryside would know where to locate them. Servants were to be sent out to all households, rich and poor, without favoritism, unless the agent knew the employer had a history of mistreating servants.[33]

City councils were of the opinion that servants were changing positions much too frequently, so they ordered the agents not to find a new position for anyone who had not worked at least six months. Indeed, any servant who had left a household without just cause for doing so—like the death of an employer—was suspect and was to be investigated before being sent to a new position. The agents were also not to lure anyone from a household with a promise of better pay or gifts or house any servant for longer than one night between positions. In Munich and Strasbourg two special days, six months apart, were set as the two times a year at which servants could change jobs; in Nuremberg servants were only to change positions once a year.[34]

The agents were paid by both the employer and the servant whenever they placed someone, with the employer paying about twice as much. The amount the servants paid varied according to rank, with cooks and other higher level servants paying two to three times what a children's maid or scullery girl paid. The rates the agents could charge were set in the ordinances, although they could charge a special fee for extra work, for "much running back and forth." They were always forbidden to accept any presents, however, and threatened with a stiff fine and possible loss of office if they did.[35]

These ordinances were often reissued, with additional clauses added as new problems developed. The employment agents were not to praise or denigrate any master in front of the maids, lest any false rumors be spread. They were not to offer any new jobs to any servants, "because no one can keep servants these days—who would otherwise gladly stay—as the agents run after them with promises of a better position."[36] They were not to house any servants themselves and to report anyone who was housing servants illegally, for this allowed maids to "walk up and down freely whenever they want to, and is a source of great annoyance."[37] As I explained in chapter 1, unmarried women who lived on their own and not under the supervision of a male head-of-household were always regarded with suspicion by city councils. Employment agents were also not to keep the trunk or goods of any servant, first, because this would enable the servant to leave a place of employment more easily, and second, because the trunks could contain stolen goods. Strasbourg specifically ordered its employment agents not to be a part of any stealing ring or accept any goods they felt might have been stolen "because they, as the holder, give the stealer the opportunity and cause to do such a deed."[38]

Apparently women other than the sworn employment agents were frequently acting as such, for later sixteenth- and seventeenth-century ordinances specifically forbade all others to do such work and set quite high fines and a period of time in jail for those who did. In Munich those attached to the ducal court were frequently and pointedly ordered not to act as employment agents, as the city wanted to make sure only citizens held that position. The employment agents were required to do all the work themselves, without the aid of a maid; if they could not, they were to step down from office.[39] The work included bringing all new maids to their employers personally.

Most of the women who acted as employment agents operated out of their own homes, with a sign hung out in front just like any other occupation, although some had small stands at the marketplace.[40] They were not to combine their work with selling any merchandise, a restriction probably introduced to prevent their selling things which might have been stolen from employers. They were generally the wives or widows of craftsmen or minor officials—glassmakers, clerks, masons, goldsmiths, combmakers, church wardens. To get their appointments they had applied to the city council when an employment agent had died; the council had then checked into the reputation, lifestyle, and need of each applicant before making a decision.

The recommendations of former employers were often added to a woman's application for the position, along with pleas stressing her great need and poverty. Widows with no other means of support were the favored candidates, as were the daughters of former employment agents and women whose husbands had performed special services for the city.[41] Although appointment as an agent was thus a kind of charity position, it was still a highly desired post; in Nuremberg in 1530 an agent made a contract with another woman to be paid two pence a week if she allowed her to take over her post. The second woman was then to be made an agent in her own right after the first one's death.[42]

It is evident from the frequency with which the ordinances were repeated that the employment agents were not following them to the satisfaction of the city councils. The register of agents in Nuremberg is accompanied year after year with *streffliche Rede*, admonitions for one abuse or another: they were hiring out maids they knew were irresponsible, demanding too much payment, or allowing maids to stay with them between jobs. At one point, six agents were removed from office within one year for placing maids who had already run away from a position.[43] In 1579 the female agents in Nuremberg were forbidden to find positions for male servants anymore; although this prohibition does not appear explicitly in other cities, by the end of the sixteenth century, female employment agents everywhere were handling only female servants.[44]

Not only did cities try to regulate the hiring of servants but also their activities once they were hired. Many cities, including those without an organized system of employment agents, began to pass ordinances in the sixteenth century regulating the salaries, conduct, and social activities of the maids, justifying the regulation on a variety of economic and moral grounds. Maids were to follow all regulations even when not hired through an agent. The friend or neighbor who had found them the job was not, however, responsible for their later conduct the way an agent was.

Nuremberg was the first city to pass regulatory ordinances. In 1499 maids were not allowed into any dances at the city hall without their mistresses and were always to be seated behind them if they did attend, for the council thought their conduct did not always show the proper deference. A later attempt to forbid them to attend dances altogether failed because enough women complained; the maids were again allowed to accompany their mistresses but now had to stay in a separate, locked room until they were needed.[45] If a woman wanted her maid, she could send a message and the maid would be brought to her. The conduct of maids at dances was also seen as a problem in Frankfurt, where the city council discussed canceling all dances "because maids seduce other servants and cause them not only to do questionable acts but also to stay away from their work longer than is proper."[46]

The first ordinance for employment agents in Nuremberg also includes paragraphs dealing with the duties of maids and servants.[47] As I have said, they were required to stay at a job at least six months, and later at least one year, unless gross misconduct by the employer could be proven. Breaking this rule, even to go to another post, could bring punishment of up to a three-year banishment from the entire Nuremberg area, not just the city itself, which meant staying at least 37 kilometers away. The guilty maid could never be hired again in the city, or both she and the agent who found her the position would be liable to a stiff fine. No one, including her parents, was to give a runaway shelter or aid. Even if a maid was simply between posts and had been let go for legitimate reasons by her former employer, or that employer had died, she was not to be housed in an inn but was to go immediately to an agent to find a new post. One wonders how the agents could find new positions for maids within a day, as they were only allowed to house them one night. This is another example of the city councils' attempts to prevent women from living on their own.

The councils regulated the conduct of employers as well. No one could coax a maid or servant away from her first master with "more pay, tips, beer, money or other devices"—as long as the first master provided well enough—under penalty of a fine of ten gulden. Promises of marriage were not to be used, unless they were legitimate and did not first involve a period of employment in the future husband's home.[48] In an attempt to make sure all native girls had employment, the Nuremberg city council forbade people to hire foreigners, even if they were relatives, without first receiving special permission from the council. This was almost impossible to enforce, however, because people simply argued that the girls were just staying with them and were not really maids.[49]

During the middle of the sixteenth century, a number of other areas passed ordinances regulating relations between employers and maids, mainly because it was held that wages had gotten too high. Strasbourg limited the wages a normal maid could be paid to six gulden a year, "although one may certainly pas less"; employers were not responsible to pay maids anything if they found them unsuitable or if the maids left without cause. Its ordinance did give the maids a little protection vis-à-vis their employers; though the maids could be let go at any time, the employers were supposed to give them several weeks' notice so they could find another position.[50] The following year a second and sterner notice was issued because the council had heard that servants were even demanding gifts of their employers and were in general behaving in a "disobedient, contrary, untrue, and otherwise inappropriate manner."[51] In addition to their regular salary, only servants who had served "obediently, truly, and industriously" for a long time were to be rewarded with anything extra, and this was to be done only once.[52] A special court was set up to hear cases between employers and servants, and it was to rule on any other breaking of the regulations. In an attempt to control the extravagance of maids, those who did not own at least one hundred gulden worth of property themselves were not allowed to wear silk or satin, a property limit which probably excluded all maids. This restriction even applied to clothing they had inherited or been given by a generous mistress.[53]

The ordinance passed at the same time in the Duchy of Württemburg was stricter than those in Nuremberg or Strasbourg. Servants were specifically charged with causing the general inflation, as they now demanded a salary along with their room and board, so that salary was to be strictly limited.[54] No one was to be taken on as a maid unless she had proof of her conduct and honorable dismissal from her last position. No employer was to give a maid more than one glass of wine a day, even on festive occasions, and parents were forbidden to take their children out of one place of employment and put them in another. Maids who convinced others to leave their positions were to be immediately thrown into the city jail in Stuttgart.[55]

In the later sixteenth century, regulations became harsher and more hostile to servants. The Munich ordinance from 1580 forbade anyone to coax servants away from their masters, not only with promises of gifts or money, but also with promises of "more freedom." Everyone was forbidden to rent rooms to single women or men who were not in service somewhere or keep their trunks and possessions. All unmarried male or female servants who would not take positions, but tried to live on their own as day laborers, were to be banished, as were people, including public innkeepers, who housed them. Servants who married and set up their own households but were then not able to find enough work to support themselves and their families were also to be banished, "so that such young people will first think over how they will support themselves and their children before they get married."[56]

This ordinance reflects a great amount of distrust between employer and servant. Servants were not to leave the house for any reason without the knowledge of their employer. They were to take no food out of the house at any time and had to open their chests and trunks if the employer suspected them of having taken something. If they pretended to be ill to get out of work, the servants were to be banished; but if they really were ill and the employer did not want them around, they could go to some unspecified "honorable place" until they were healthy again. Servants who spoke against their masters were to be punished, but employers who were found to be "entirely too strict and harsh" were to be as well. Hostility between servants was also to be avoided; upper-level maids were specifically ordered not to treat those under them too harshly.[57]

Seventeenth-century ordinances read much the same, with maids continually charged with demanding too much salary to pay for expensive clothing, speaking against their employers, refusing to go into service but instead working as day laborers, and general "disobedience and pride." The salaries allowed were higher than those of the sixteenth century but certainly not enough to make up for the inflation in most areas.[58]

The 1665 Strasbourg ordinance also adds a completely new clause, which points out how far the city would go in controlling the activities of its young women:

> Numerous complaints have been made that some widows living here have two, three, or more daughters living with them at their expense. These girls go into service during the winter but during the summer return to their mothers, partly because they want to wear more expensive clothes than servants are normally allowed to and partly because they want to have more freedom to walk around, to saunter back and forth whenever they want to. It is our experience that this causes nothing but shame, immodesty, wantonness, and immorality, so that a watchful eye should be kept on this, and if it is discovered, the parents as well as the daughters should be punished with a fine, a jail sentence, or even banishment from the city in order to serve as an example to others.[59]

Not only were young women to be prevented from living alone but also from living with their own mothers if they were not needed in the household, as the council believed the mothers could not control them as well as an employer could. Thus even the family itself was not as important as propriety and decorum in the city, at least in this case.

In addition to all these city ordinances, the guilds and sworn crafts in each city regulated the activities of maids as well. Particularly in areas with a large textile industry, most of the maids in a household spent their time carding, spinning, and preparing thread for the master rather than doing domestic tasks. The borders between domestic service and craft production were very fluid; Olwen Hufton would even call such maids "resident industrial employees."[60] During the sixteenth century, however, some crafts began to feel that masters were using their maids to do tasks that rightfully belonged to apprentices and journeymen, and so they restricted work by maids. In many crafts maids could be used to do no work at all, or only polishing, cleaning, and packing the finished product. Often only one maid in each household was allowed to do specific work—like pulling brass or copper cable or putting together chain mail—while all other maids were limited to housework.[61] These regulations were very difficult to enforce, and breaking them resulted in a fine or punishment for the employer only, not the maid, as it was recognized that maids had little control over what they did in a household.

These regulations paint a rather grim picture, but they are designed to cover every possible problem no matter how rarely it occurred. As city council minutes and court records point out, relations between employers and servants, or between servants themselves, were not always peaceful, although there are fewer serious cases than one might imagine given the number of servants in any city. Most of the cases involving servants had to do with minor theft of some kind—a cook was ordered to return silver goblets she had stolen; another was banished for stealing chickens; maids were charged with stealing clothing or household goods or with simple neglect of duty.[62]

Employers in turn were accused by their maids of holding their clothing or trunks illegally after the maids had left the household, with the employers answering that the maids had left before the allowed time and thus had no claim to their property. Servants also took their employers to court to get wages they claimed were due them, especially as it was quite common not to pay a servant anything until he or she left one's service.[63] In addition, servants appeared very frequently as plaintiffs or defendants in slander cases involving either their employer or another servant.[64] Name calling and cursing are common outlets for the frustrations of those who have no real power, as students of witchcraft in any culture well know.

Occasionally maids were involved in more serious cases, again either as plaintiffs or defendants. They accused their employers of beating them, starving them, or most commonly, raping them.[65] A woman in Munich accused her employer of giving her such a bad case of syphilis that she had become unable to work and was now deep in debt; the employer and other servants answered that it was the other way around, that she had given him the disease, and the court in this case found for the employer.[66]

In general, courts were objective in their handling of master–servant disputes. For example, a man in Memmingen accused his maid of stealing, trying to burn down his house, and then trying to smother him. She answered that he had promised to marry her, "taken her honor," and then jeered at her, and the court in this case found for the woman, forcing him to pay damages.[67] Maids found guilty of serious crimes against their employers were treated especially harshly. In Nuremberg a maid who set fire to her employer's barn was decapitated, her body burned, and her head stuck on a pole as an example to other maids.[68] In Frankfurt, two maids, more than a century apart, were buried alive in the same gruesome manner for killing their employers; each was led out to a hole lined with thorn branches, and then thorns, earth, and nettles were thrown down on top of her until she was covered. The city executioner then stuck an oak spike through her so that she was held to the ground.[69] Killing one's employer was a serious crime not only against God's law but also against the established social order, and so it had to be dealt with more sharply than simple murder.

Private household journals and accounts give a more balanced and peaceful picture of employer–employee relations, however, and demonstrate that the cases given above were the exceptions, not the rule. Wet nurses and maids were made special guardians for children and were granted substantial sums on the death of their master or mistress.[70] Wealthy people often set up funds to provide small dowries and hope chests for maids who left their service to get married. A fortunate maid might even marry her employer when his first wife died.

Cities themselves, as well as more generous employers, rewarded maids for long periods of loyal service. It was often the practice, once maids had served a certain period of employment in the city with one employer, to grant them citizenship without the fee normally required of new citizens. At first citizenship was granted freely and was quite a benefit for maids, for they could then offer citizenship through marriage to prospective husbands who were not citizens. As the sixteenth century progressed, however, and cities began to worry about too many foreigners coming in, maids were often granted citizenship with the limitation that they could only marry a citizen. The length of time required before a maid was granted citizenship was also increased, perhaps to ensure that she would be beyond marrying age when she finally became a citizen.[71]

Along with grants of citizenship, maids in some cities were given a monetary payment as a reward for long service, a sort of dowry which would enable them to get married. Munich had the most elaborate system. Maids could apply once a year and were required to accompany their applications with letters of recommendation from employers and notes on how long they had served. The city council then voted on which of the applicants were to receive the "maidens' money" (*Jungfrau Gelt*), which was to go toward their dowries. The qualifications in some ways worked against the purpose of the fund, as some of the maids had been in service for more than twenty-five years and would certainly have had some difficulty finding husbands.[72] In fact, in one case, a maid reported she had been given the grant but had not been able to find a husband and was now so old and weak she needed the money to support herself. The council decided to allow her to have the money anyway, without marriage.[73]

Thus, as might be expected, the situation of maids and servants varied tremendously from city to city and from employer to employer. Though their actual money wages were low—and were always lower than male servants' with similar responsibilities in the same household—the fact that room and board were provided meant that their situation was more secure than that of pieceworkers or day laborers.[74] Even on the very low salary, some women were able to save enough to build a dowry or make small investments or play city lotteries.[75] Women who had been servants often married late and had more freedom in choosing their own spouses and a more active role in the courtship and marriage process.[76]

No matter what the conditions of service were, for most women there were few other choices open. The proportion of the urban population, both male and female, who were servants seems to have been about 15–20 percent, with larger and more commercial cities having a higher percentage than smaller and more agrarian ones.[77] More than one out of every three households in late-fifteenth-century Nuremburg had at least one maid, even when all the single-person households are included in the figures. As opportunities for women to work in other occupations decreased, opportunities in domestic service remained the same or increased as larger household staffs became more fashionable. By the seventeenth century a greater share of the women who worked outside their own homes worked as servants in the homes of others.[78]

## DAY LABORERS

It is very difficult to estimate even rough numbers, but numerous women did find employment throughout the entire period as day laborers, either working in agriculture on the land surrounding the city or finding odd jobs in the city itself. Not only did rural women come into the cities to look for work or to sell agricultural products, but city women migrated seasonally to the countryside for certain types of work, especially harvesting and care of vineyards.[79] Many cities felt responsible for regulating the wages of the laborers who worked that land outside the city walls which was under the city's control. Later their hours and the amount and kinds of food they were to receive were regulated as well. These regulations give some idea of the situation in which such women found themselves.

As a general rule, female agricultural workers received half of what men did. In a few cases, this wage differential was justified by describing the work men were doing (mowing and reaping) as the hardest tasks physically and that which the women were doing (gathering, weeding, or gleaning) as easier. Most often the ordinances simply state: "For agricultural work, men, four and one-half schillings a day; women, two schillings," or something similar.[80] Boys who were just learning were to be paid the same as women.

The food male and female agricultural workers were to be given was also different. Female vineyard workers were to receive soup and vegetable for their morning meal, "but no wine"; milk and bread for their midday meal; and nothing in the evening. According to the same ordi-

nance, men were to be fed soup and wine for breakfast; beer, vegetables, and meat at midday; and vegetables and wine at night, as well
as receiving twice the salary.[81] Thus the women got less food, decidedly less protein, and no alcohol, while the men had alcohol with
every meal, including breakfast.

There was some differentiation among female workers according to
the kind of work they did. Those who weeded or gleaned were paid
slightly less than those who worked with sickles, hoes, or other tools.
Women who dug postholes or hauled manure were paid more, as it
was recognized this was extremely hard work, and women who could
do such work were as strong as men.[82] Michael Roberts would take
this even further, commenting that agricultural wage differentials in
Britain were based more on strength than on sex, and women who
could do men's tasks did. Whether this meant they were also paid the
same as men is not clear, however. What is clear from Roberts's research is that the gradual adoption of the scythe instead of the sickle
for harvesting increased the wage difference between men and women
in agriculture. Women rarely mowed with a scythe, except during
times of labor shortage such as after a plague or war, for the scythe
requires long arms and great physical strength. As he notes, "the
physical qualifications for mowing probably helped those eager to dismiss the female as 'the weaker vessel.'"[83] The use of a scythe by men
also meant that women had less opportunities for the more highly
paid tasks, like cutting with a sickle, and were relegated to the lowest
paid, like gleaning and gathering. Luckily for women working in agriculture, the scythe was adopted slowly because its use resulted in
much greater loss of grain than the use of a sickle did.[84]

Only in one instance in the cities studied were women paid as much
as men, and this was only if they did men's work. In 1633 Strasbourg
was repairing its fortifications during the Thirty Years' War and specifically allowed soldiers and "foreign men and women" to be hired
so that there would be enough laborers. The men were to be given
5 batzen a day, and the women 3, "except that strong women may
work at men's work and be paid like a man. The weak young girls and
young boys are not to be used at men's work, however."[85]

For day laborers in the city as well, the wages for women were
roughly half those for men, as was the case with domestic servants.
Seamstresses, laundresses, or women hired for other housework received only a few pennies if they were given their meals, or little more
than enough to buy a loaf of bread and a few herrings if they were
not.[86] I cannot determine how such women (or male day-laborers for
that matter) were hired, for strangely enough, the city councils did
not regulate this. There was probably a designated place in the city
where they met those who needed workers, perhaps a corner of the

market. The regulations imposed on laundresses in Nuremberg do, however, reveal a bit about the conditions of their work. The ordinance for laundresses was short and simple:

> From now on no laundress who washes for pay should wash on a stone if the clothing the people are having them wash would be hurt by this. Those who wash for pay should wash on a table or other wooden structure and should not use lime, woad ashes, or other dangerous things. Those who do this will be punished as advised.
> They should also wash everything that they receive faithfully and give it back without deceit.[87]

The council listed the laundresses by name and required them to swear to the bailiff that they would abide by this ordinance. There are 18 listed in 1417, the year they first appear in the Nuremberg records, with the number increasing steadily to 47 in 1562, the last year the city made such a list.[88]

The laundresses themselves were usually required to pick up and deliver the articles to be washed, including heavy household linens, and were held responsible if anything was lost or destroyed. Along one of the streams flowing through the city, they had small washhouses in which they could work and hang drying clothes. With a stone chute they diverted a small amount of water from the stream flowing by so that dirty rinse water could be carried away immediately. Many cleaning agents were quite strong, so the water coming out was often quite polluted. In 1545, in fact, the laundresses were not allowed to dump ashes or other "uncleanness" into the stream, which was viewed as common property and the neighbors complained so much. The fine was set at four gulden, impossible for these women to pay, so the council was obviously intent on maintaining the brook's cleanliness.[89] No mention is made of where these women could dump their refuse, however. Similar restrictions were placed on laundresses in other cities as well.[90]

These washhouses were in parts of the city removed from other shops and businesses because of the smell and the need for water, but this isolation could also lead to problems. In 1552 in Nuremberg, for example, the houses were all ordered locked at night so that "the laundresses have no place for their indecent behavior."[91] In 1603 in Munich a laundress was charged with procuring and wanton behavior and was told to close her washhouse.[92] Iwan Bloch reports that in many German cities laundresses augmented their often meager incomes with prostitution; although these two cases do not specifically state this, the phrase used in the councils' orders—*unzuchtige leben*—imply it.[93]

The women hired as day laborers were of all ages and all marital statuses; young girls, unmarried women, and widows made up a large share, but women whose husbands were not able to support the family alone often picked up this kind of work as well.[94] This was especially the case with the wives of soldiers stationed in or near a town; they often came into the city by day, in search of work as laundresses, cooks, or seamstresses.[95] The cities objected because they thought the women might bring in disease and "dangerous ideas" and also because the women were considered to be taking work away from native women.[96] Attempts to forbid such "unruly, disreputable soldiers' wives" to enter the city were usually ineffective, however.[97]

## PUBLIC BATHS

Every medieval city had public baths at which women were employed in a variety of functions. They helped people coming to the baths undress or held their clothes for them; they rubbed them, beat them with switches, washed their hair, or scratched them with their fingernails to increase circulation; they shaved them, dried them, and oiled their bodies—in all cases handling both male and female customers. Male bath employees usually heated the water and did bloodletting, although in some cases the bath maids also let blood. During times of plague, the bath maids, who were considered to have a bit more medical experience than the average woman, were also asked to nurse the sick.[98]

The public bath as an institution was a necessary part of urban life in earlier times. Although general standards of hygiene were low, an occasional or even weekly bath was regarded as necessary and normal. Workmen's weekly wages often included a specific sum as "bath money," and servants accompanied their employers into the baths, with the employer paying the fee.[99] Baths served social as well as hygienic purposes. Entrance into a guild, engagement, the closing of a business contract, or the birth of an heir might well be celebrated not only with a festive meal but also with a special bath in which all parties concerned bathed together. The bathers often stayed in the tub for several hours and were served drinks and small meals by the bath maids. Both Catholic and Protestant preachers attacked the practice, but with little success.[100]

Many cities had as many as ten or fifteen public baths, some of them located within the city walls, others outside at places with natural springs thought to have healing qualities. Each was supervised by a bath master or bath mistress, all of whom were often joined together in a guildlike structure.[101] In a common bath ordinance agreed upon in 1421 by Frankfurt, Mainz, Worms, and Speyer, all of the bath personnel, from master or mistress to maids, had to pay an entrance fee and weekly tax and swear to an oath.[102] Similar clauses were included in a 1487 ordinance from Strasbourg, which also provided that the female rubbers, beaters, and clothing watchers were specifically allowed eight days vacation if they were ill or had a child; those who had a child were also to be freed from paying the weekly tax, as long as the child was legitimate. Fighting, playing cards, drinking out of a pitcher, and shooting dice were also forbidden in the bathhouse; the Strasbourg city council wanted to prevent all "unseemly conduct" there.[103]

This ordinance forbade any bath master or mistress to take on any woman as a bath maid who had previously been a prostitute "unless she has changed her ways and come back to a pious life."[104] The wife of the bath master was often given the task of investigating the background of each prospective bath maid, the thinking being that she might get more accurate information than her husband would. Cities attempted to keep prostitution out of the public baths, although they were never very successful. As both bath maid and customer were dressed only in a short white garment which left arms and legs free, the opportunities for intimacy were rather great. "Bath whore" was a frequent term of derision, although not warranted in all cases, as many bath maids were older women hired for their skills at massaging, not their erotic attractions.[105]

Because of this association with prostitution, and because of the servile nature of the work, the bath master and bath maids in some cities were considered "dishonorable" (*unehrlich*), a specific legal designation which also applied to the city executioner, gravediggers, and latrine cleaners and which meant they could not be buried in the normal cemetery, nor could their children be accepted into guilds. This was not true everywhere; in cities where the bath master and barber-surgeons were members of one guild, none of the bath personnel was considered dishonorable.

The baths began to decline in popularity during the first part of the sixteenth century, and the number of public baths in most cities decreased accordingly—in Frankfurt from 15 in 1500 to 2 in 1550—although they never disappeared completely. Their decline was due in part to the spread of syphilis, for the warm, moist air of the bath was seen as particularly conducive to the breeding of "miasmas," the small bodies which were believed to spread the disease. It was also the result of an increase in the price of firewood, which forced the price of baths up so much that many people could no longer afford them.[106]

During the seventeenth century city councils generally forbade men and women to bathe together and required baths either to have separate rooms for male and female customers or to limit themselves to one sex if they had only one room.[107] In Strasbourg the bath masters complained that this hurt them immeasurably, as now even fewer people would take baths, but the city council replied that "public decency" demanded it.[108] By this time, baths had generally gone out of fashion and were used by only the poorest segment of society or by those seeking relief from certain specific illnesses. The few baths that remained probably continued to employ a few women, although the title "bath maid" disappears totally from the records.

## PROSTITUTION

One of the most visible female occupations in any early modern city was prostitution. In his listing of occupations found in the city of Frankfurt, Karl Bücher finds some sixteen different names for prostitutes, more than for any other occupation, male or female. By the fifteenth century nearly every major city in Germany and most of the smaller ones had an official house of prostitution (*Frauenhaus*).[109] Many, such as one in Frankfurt and one in Mainz, actually belonged to bishops or religious houses; the bishop of Mainz complained at one point that the house was not getting enough business.[110] Such houses became increasingly controversial, and by the early seventeenth century most of them were closed, but illicit prostitution still thrived.

Prostitution can generally be divided into two sorts, that which occurred with the sanctions and regulations of city councils in official houses, and illegal prostitution, which often led to arrest and banishment. In both cases, however, prostitutes were often involved in petty crimes and violence, and their lives cannot be romanticized. I discuss the two separately, however, because they were regarded as quite different things by city governments and the population as a whole during this period.

Although the founding of a municipal brothel was not usually announced publicly, Frankfurt had opened one by 1396, Nuremberg by 1400, Munich by 1433, Memmingen by 1454, and Strasbourg by 1469.[111] They were generally first mentioned in statements in city council records or in law codes which ordered all prostitutes in the city to either leave or move into this house (or houses). Often they were set up right inside one of the city's gates, on a small street away from the general flow of traffic, so that people were not constantly reminded of their presence.

During the course of the fifteenth century, many cities set down strict rules for the male managers of these houses (*Frauenwirte*) and the residents.[112] Only women who had been prostitutes elsewhere were supposed to be taken in (a rule obviously not always followed, else no women would have been eligible), and no daughter of a citizen

97

was to live in the bordello. In 1548 in Nuremberg, a citizen's daughter was found; the Frauenwirt was given a light fine, but the poor citizen's daughter was held in the city jail for five years.[113] Virgins and married women were usually forbidden to engage in prostitution, although how their status was to be determined beforehand is never explained.

The women were to pay the Frauenwirt a designated amount per customer, usually more if the man stayed all night; the amount the customers were to give the women is not mentioned in any of the regulations, however. The women were to receive two or three meals a day in the house and were not required to pay any rent when they did not have customers. If a woman owed money to the Frauenwirt or he felt she was not giving him his fair share, he could seize her clothing and personal effects until the case was brought to trial, but he could not force her to stay in the house.

The women were to be allowed out of the house whenever they wanted to go to church and were not to be forced to work at any time: "The Frauenwirt, his wife, or his servants shall not force, coerce, or compel in any way any woman who lives in his house to care for a man when she is pregnant or menstruating [*mit weiblichen Rechten beladen*] or in any other way unfit or wants to hold back from bodily work."[114] In Munich menstruating women were to have their normal meals augmented by a couple of eggs, as this was believed to ease any pains accompanying a menstrual period.[115] Most cities made some attempt to guard the cleanliness and health of the women in the Frauenhaus. They were to be allowed at least one bath a week, and some cities had a special separate bathing room for them at the public baths. In Ulm a midwife regularly conducted examinations of all prostitutes, both to check if they were pregnant and to make sure they were "fit, clean, and healthy women."[116]

In several other ways as well, Ulm had the most sensible and humane ordinance. All of the money the women made went into a common box and was then distributed each week by a woman who was not herself a prostitute, according to the needs of each woman. This box had three separate locks, with one key held by the Frauenwirt, one by one of the prostitutes, and the third by this outside woman, so that no one could get money from it illegally. Ulm also had a second fund, into which all prostitutes and the Frauenwirt paid a portion of their incomes, that went to support prostitutes who were too old and sick to work any more.[117] In return for this old-age pension, recipients were required to spin two spindles of yarn every day for the Frauenwirt. They did spinning as well in other cities, but the amounts and purposes were never specified.

Women were not required to accept any man that wanted them, although in Nuremberg the council also forbade women to have favorite customers, for it felt this brought "clamour, indignation, discord, and displeasure" and could lead to fights.[118] The ordinances usually included a clause stating that a man could be charged with rape for trying to force himself on a prostitute, although criminal records reveal no such cases.

Most of these ordinances were first promulgated to protect the women involved, and from their clauses suggest how awful the situation actually was before the ordinances. All of them forbade parents and other people to place women in a brothel if they owed the Frauenwirt a debt; later editions repeat and strengthen these clauses, a clear indication that this was occurring. The Frauenwirt also freely traded women who had become indebted to him after coming into the house; the 1488 Munich ordinance forbade a Frauenwirt to trade away a woman for more than the debts she owed him, and later ordinances from Strasbourg, Nuremberg, and Frankfurt forbade him to sell or trade away any woman no matter how much she owed him. They attempted to take away all temptation to do so by forbidding him to loan the women more than a small amount at any one time. The Frauenwirt was forbidden to force women into the house as well, though the burden of proof in such cases was on the woman, not on him.[119]

Usually the minimum age for women in the Frauenhaus was fourteen, although the treatment of girls found to be too young was hardly gentle: "Whichever daughters are found whose bodies are not yet ready for such work, that is, who have neither breasts nor the other things which are necessary for this, should be driven out of the city with blows and are to stay out under threat of bodily punishment until they reach the proper age."[120] Apparently the city council saw no contradiction in its judgment that these girls were too young to be prostitutes but old enough to be banished out of the city on their own.

The Frauenwirt himself was often a very disreputable character. His occupation, like that of gravedigger or city executioner, was considered "dishonorable," so he could never be a citizen. He was allowed to own the Frauenhaus outright, however, a privilege not usually granted a noncitizen. He often overcharged the women and, on two occasions in Nuremberg, was charged with murdering a man in the Frauenhaus.[121] If he decided to sell the Frauenhaus, he was usually required to leave the city.[122]

The position of the Frauenwirt could be very lucrative, however. The *Register des Gemeinen Pfennig* in Nuremberg in 1497, a special head tax to be paid by all according to their wealth, found him owning more than 1,000 gulden, which put him in the upper 1 percent of the population. The census for the head tax found twenty-six people living in the Frauenhaus, which made it the largest household in Nuremberg. As is to be expected, none of the women had any great wealth, and all paid the basic tax of 10 pfennige. The Frauenwirt and others in his tax bracket were charged twenty-four times that, or 1 gulden.[123]

The same was true in Frankfurt. The prostitutes there, who lived in two separate houses, were all under the protection of a *Stocker* (bailiff), who lived near but not in the houses. He received an annual income of 40 gulden from the houses and also a payment of 1 schilling a week from the prostitutes who lived outside the houses. In addition, he was to be paid 1 gulden per fair from the women who came into the city to work only at fair times, or even more if they wanted to work all over the city and not just in the area near the two houses. Most of this money was his to keep, as he only paid minimal taxes and the rent on the two houses.[124] The prostitutes themselves also had to pay city head taxes, but they were charged the smallest amount, as they had so little personal property.

For this reason, and despite the dishonorable nature of the occupation, whenever a position as Frauenwirt was vacant, there were a large number of applicants. When the Munich Frauenwirt was dismissed from his position for misconduct, not only did several men from neighboring cities apply for the job but also one woman from Ingolstadt! The job finally went, however, after much discussion, to the man who had been the Frauenwirt in Nordlingen.[125]

Throughout the fifteenth century the prostitutes themselves were an accepted group and appeared often in public. A chronicle from 1471 reports on the stay of Emperor Friedrich III in Nuremberg: "[The emperor] rode behind the grain houses and looked at the weapons and the grain, and while he was leaving the grain houses, two whores caught him with a silver chain and said, 'Your Grace must be captured.' He said, 'We haven't been captured yet and would rather be released' and gave them one gulden. Then he rode to the Frauenhaus, where another four were waiting, and he gave them another gulden."[126] Although chroniclers often exaggerate, this may not have been far from the truth. Prostitutes were allowed to come to dances at the city hall whenever they wished for another twenty-five years.

In Frankfurt prostitutes brought flowers to the city council at their yearly festive meal and were then allowed to eat with the council until 1529, after which they still received from the council a free dinner brought to them in the Frauenhaus. The Würzburg fire ordinances required prostitutes to help put out fires which broke out in the city until 1528, and in Frankfurt prostitutes gave flowers and congratulations to newly married couples.[127] In Memmingen they, along with the city's midwives, were given a special New Year's gift every year.[128] Although only in Lübeck were they organized into an actual guild, with an elected head and a yearly procession, they were viewed in most cities as a guildlike group with the right to defend their interests against outsiders.

Attempts were made, however, to draw women out of the Frauenhaus to more honorable callings. In many cities anyone who married a prostitute was given free citizenship, as long as the couple maintained an "honorable way of life." In Nuremberg an endowed fund was set up by Dr. Conrad Khunhof to provide support each year for four women who wanted to leave the Frauenhaus and join the sisters at the nearby convent at Pillenreuth. After the Reformation, when the convent at Pillenreuth was forbidden to take in any new women, the city council decided to continue support for the women who were already there but to look into other ways to use the money in future which would correspond with Dr. Khunhof's aims. Two years later it finally decided to provide annually dowries of twenty gulden each to four women from the Frauenhaus who had worked two years in the city's main hospital. The council also used some of Khunhof's money for a quite different purpose, setting up a stipend fund of fifty-two gulden a year for university students.[129]

The same kind of opportunities were offered in other cities by "Magdalene houses," small houses specifically set up to provide homes for prostitutes who had decided to give up their former lives or else were too old to work. Most of these were similar to Beguinages, so that the women did not take actual vows, and many of them were endowed by women who considered this a particularly appropriate form of charity for a woman. Eventually the "Magdalene houses" in Germany would take in any woman who wanted to get in, without the necessity of a previous career as a prostitute.[130]

During the fifteenth century most cities attempted to control what went on in the municipal brothels by restricting the conduct of the customers, not the women. The innkeepers in the area around the houses in Nuremberg were limited in the amount of wine that they could sell either to the women or their customers.[131] In 1478 the Frankfurt city council put two iron bands in the Frauenhaus for imprisoning men who got out of hand and specifically allowed the Frauenwirt to carry a knife to defend himself or the women. Men who had beaten up or injured prostitutes were to be given longer jail sentences than those given for a normal assault.[132]

Priests, Jews, and married men were not supposed to be admitted to a Frauenhaus at all, although this appears to have been enforced only in the case of Jews. In Nuremberg some attempts were made to control the presence of married men—they could be thrown into a stream which doubled as the area's sewer or sent before one of the city's courts—but these were sporadic and of doubtful effectiveness.

All men were to be out of the Frauenhaus by eleven unless they had agreed to stay with one woman all night, and no one was to be admitted at all on Sundays, holidays, or during Holy Week.[133] Again, one wonders about the degree of enforcement of such rules.

Restrictions on the conduct of the women themselves began during the late fifteenth and early sixteenth centuries in most cities, although the timing and level of restrictions varied considerably. I was able to trace this process quite well in several cities and see how it reflects changes in attitude toward prostitution in general. For instance, in Nuremberg the first restrictions came in 1508, when the Frauenwirt was ordered to keep all women off the streets in their "whore's clothing"; if they went to church or elsewhere, they were to wear a coat or veil. Later the Frauenhaus was closed until noon every day and at sunset on Saturday night and the eves of holidays. In 1544 on a complaint of the neighbors, the council ordered a special door to be built on the Frauenhaus so that no one could see inside and held the Frauenwirt responsible to make sure it was always shut. Two years later, prostitutes were no longer to be allowed at public dances or at the wine market; if a number were found out of the house, the Frauenwirt was to be thrown in jail. The neighbors grumbled again that they had to walk by and "bear their [the prostitutes'] annoying and unsightly presence," so the door was ordered locked shut during the day. It was to be opened only at night so city officials could go in easily if there was a problem.[134]

In Frankfurt the process began somewhat earlier, in 1472 and 1478, when prostitutes were ordered not to sit at the door of their house and call out to prospective customers. Here the lead was taken by the guilds rather than the city council, however, as in 1521 all masters and journeymen were forbidden to dance with prostitutes or other "dishonorable" women or even to stand next to them in a public place. Similar clauses were added to many guild and journeymen's ordinances throughout Germany beginning about this time. The fustian weavers went one step further, forbidding their members to dance with or give drinks to women who were simply suspected of being dishonorable. By 1546 the city council in Frankfurt had agreed to forbid the burial of prostitutes in hallowed ground; a special cemetery was opened for them near the city's gallows.[135]

In Strasbourg the prostitutes were a continual subject of discussion for the city council, which attempted over and over to control their behavior. In 1469 prostitutes were found to be living throughout the city, to the dismay of "decent and honorable people"; the council gave them a week to move into the section of the city in which "women such as these have always lived."[136] It also took a survey of the women, finding 8 to be living in the official brothel with the Frauenwirt and 14 others noted as "living alone" or "living with two, three, or four others," which makes one suspect that these were women who ran small, unofficial houses. In addition, there is a list of 16 names with the note "These do not want to be considered public prostitutes [*offen huren*]." Several members of the city council were sent out to examine the houses where these women were living, to make sure they were "appropriate for such use," and reported that at least twenty-five or thirty houses in the approved area of the city could be used by prostitutes, along with the official Frauenhaus.[137] Apparently this was not enough, or at any rate the women did not want to move into these houses, for the council repeated its warning that they were not to live among "honorable people," but only in one area of the city. It increased the fines and threats of punishment in 1471, 1493, 1496, 1501, and on into the sixteenth century.[138]

The city council also attempted to control the behavior of prostitutes and to make them instantly recognizable. They were not to sit directly in front of the altar at church, for they often spent the time talking or turning around so their faces were visible to those behind them. If they were found to be there, they were to be followed when leaving the cathedral, their coats or shawls taken from them, pawned, and the money given to the poor; the council recognized that they were probably too poor to pay a fine outright. They were to wear a shorter coat than was customary, so that they could be easily distinguished from other women.[139] In addition, they could not wear elaborate jewelry, have silk or fur trim on anything, or leave their hair uncovered the way other young unmarried women could.

In 1493 all these restrictions were repeated and further extended in a comprehensive ordinance for prostitutes. They were forbidden to come to dances where honorable women were present, with the additional proviso that there would be no punishment for anyone who attacked the prostitute or the person who brought her, unless it led to a serious wounding or death. In addition to wearing a shorter coat than normal, prostitutes were also to wear a yellow band of cloth somewhere on their clothing where it could be seen easily.[140] Yellow bands or veils were the normal way of identifying prostitutes; in one of his sermons, Geiler of Kaisersberg compared the color to the flames of hell.[141] A 1501 addition to this ordinance forbade prostitutes to have a maid servant accompanying them when they went out; if two went somewhere together, they were ordered to walk side by side, not one behind the other, lest people even think one were a maid.[142]

The city council was also troubled by women who made their living in a "dishonorable" way yet claimed they were not really prostitutes but had another occupation or craft. These women as well were to move to the approved area of the city "and not protect themselves with the argument that they do not carry out such sinful work in their houses." Not only admitted prostitutes but also any woman "who serve[d] a priest or layman and live[d] with him publicly without marriage" was to wear the short coat and yellow band identifying her as dishonorable. No excuses that she was simply a housekeeper, or really had another craft, were to be tolerated as long as it was "widely known and recognized" that she was really that sort of woman.[143]

All of these restrictions, and there were similar ones in most other cities, culminated in the middle of the sixteenth century with a closing of the official brothels. Augsburg led the way in 1532 (it had always had the most stringent limitations on the conduct of prostitutes), with Basel following in 1534, Nordlingen in 1536, Ulm in 1537, Regensburg in 1553, and Frankfurt in 1560.[144] No provision was made for the women or the Frauenwirt; indeed, the Augsburg Frauenwirt asked the city council where he should go now with the women, so that they would have a place to live, but received no answer.

It is easiest to trace the arguments for and against the closing of a city's Frauenhaus in Nuremberg, which was always cautious about doing anything which might bring more harm than good. Not until 1562 did the city council begin to ask for opinions as to whether the house should be closed "or if it were closed, if other dangers and still more evil would possibly be the result."[145] The discussion among the jurists and theologians is very interesting. Augsburg had reported an increase and spread in unchastity after it closed its Frauenhaus, so the Nuremberg jurists asserted that the closing could cause journeymen and foreign workers to turn to their masters' or landlords' wives and daughters. The theologians urged the council to think of Nuremberg's reputation as the leading free imperial city and not allow it to break "the word of God" just because of the possible complaints of foreigners who visited or lived in Nuremberg should the house be closed. One argued that the Frauenhaus caused young men to have impure thoughts about women; if they had no opportunity and were never introduced to sex, they would not chase other women.[146]

The spread of syphilis was also given as a reason for closing the house: "If the house is not closed in a short time, then it will be necessary to build three syphilis clinics instead of just one."[147] The council had recognized early that women in the Frauenhaus were more likely than the population as a whole to get syphilis and to pass it on to other people; it usually attributed this to moral, rather than medical, reasons. When syphilis first swept through the city in 1496, a special clinic was set up for syphilitics, and prostitutes were readily taken in, though other noncitizens were not.[148] Other cities were not so enlightened. In 1498 in Munich, journeymen stormed the Frauenhaus and tried to kill the Frauenwirt because they were angry about the intro-

duction of syphilis. Thirty-five armed men had to watch the Frauenhaus day and night for a month and a half before things quieted
down again.[149]

The Nuremberg council wanted an exact report from Augsburg of
the number of illegitimate children before and after the closing of the
Frauenhaus, to see if the number had actually increased. One council
member argued that men did good deeds when they married prostitutes, and closing the house would take away this opportunity;
another rejected that argument, stating that closing the house would
also "pull the women out of the devil's jaws." Another jurist realisti-
cally noted that since there were only ten to twelve women in the
house, they could not possibly be taking care of the sexual needs of all
the city's unmarried men, so the closing would not make that much
difference.[150]

Those arguing for the closing were more persuasive, and the council decided to follow the example of Augsburg and others:

> On the recommendation written and read by the high honorable
> theologians and jurists, why the men of the council are authorized
> and obliged to close the common Frauenhaus, it has been decided by
> the whole council to follow the same recommendation and from this
> hour on forbid all activity in that house, to post a guard in the house
> and let no man enter it any more. Also to send for the Frauenwirt and
> say to him that he is to send all women that he has out of the house
> and never take them in again. From this time on he is to act so
> blamelessly and unsuspiciously that the council has no cause to pun-
> ish him. When this has been completed, the preachers should be told
> to admonish the young people to guard themselves from such de-
> pravity and to keep their children and servants from it and to lead
> such an irreproachable life that the council has no cause to punish
> anyone for this vice.[151]

Unfortunately for the council, its final words were not heeded. The
house was closed, but a short time later the council found that "adultery, prostitution, fornication, and rape have taken over forcibly here
in the city and in the countryside" and wondered whether its move
had been a wise one.[152]

Many city brothels had already been declining before their final
closing, however. In 1546 the Frauenhaus in Frankfurt had fallen into
such disrepair that the city building inspector was sent out to decide
what to do with it and to determine if it posed a danger to its inhabitants or neighbors. Because of the connection made between the brothels and syphilis, the number of customers was declining, and the
council had difficulty finding a Frauenwirt if one left.[153] When Munich
finally closed its Frauenhaus in 1585, it found nothing in the house of

any value, and the Frauenwirt himself owned so little that an inventory of his goods was not considered necessary.[154] Thus even without the moral justification provided by reforming Protestant and Catholic preachers and theologians, official city brothels may have closed their doors anyway about this time.

## ILLICIT PROSTITUTION AND CRIME

Along with official city brothels, illicit prostitution was evident throughout the period, although it is very difficult to judge its extent. If we were to believe the reports of preachers and moralists and also city officials trying to point out how bad things were, nearly every woman who lived by herself was a prostitute, or at least made some of her income that way. Several members of the Strasbourg city council reported 57 secret "nests of whores" in the city in 1490, and in 1529 Lucerne, with a population of 4,000, found 200 prostitutes working in the city.[155]

Although these numbers are difficult to believe, the number of women was probably quite large, particularly in cities with major markets or fairs. As the "freedom of the fair" (*Messefreiheit*) in Frankfurt, for example, extended to all occupations, women came in from Mainz, Worms, and a number of other cities, often in groups with a madame or procurer along with them. They were even allowed to carry out their trade on the streets as long as they did not make too much of a disturbance. They moved into areas with the lowest rents and were very difficult to get rid of once the fair was over.[156] The problem was seen as so acute that in 1501 Claus Stahlberg, a member of the city council, gave two hundred gulden to build an additional large Frauenhaus so that all these women could be put into it and thus controlled by the council. His will read: "Since dishonorable women are now living in all parts of the city and serving as a bad example for many women and girls, that they too are tempted to take up an impure life, so it is my will that if the council will set up one house and drive all these women into it, my agents and heirs will give them two hundred gulden for this purpose."[157] Stahlberg's will was never acted upon, however, and four years later the Frauenwirt reported that the official prostitutes could not make a living because of the large number of unofficial ones.[158]

The number of women making a living this way increased not only during fair times but also during times of war, whenever there was an army in the area, or even if the rumor spread that one was likely to assemble. In 1570 military officers reported to the Frankfurt city council that the number of prostitutes and other women who had gathered on the field around the small group of soldiers threatened to engulf them and made all movement difficult. The council sent several officers out to order all women to disperse, even those who claimed to be wives of soldiers, but with little effect.[159] The Strasbourg city council in 1684 ordered that all unmarried women staying in the city who were not domestic servants be registered "because so many immoral and indecent female persons have crept into the city and upset honorable citizens with their scandalous and animal-like lifestyle and have created noticeable problems among the king's garrison stationed here."[160] Innkeepers were ordered not to allow prostitutes to stay—or often even drink or eat—in their establishments and could be arrested and punished if such women were found. They often argued in such cases that they had no idea what the women were doing or how they made their living but were found at times to be taking a cut of the women's income and acting as pimps as well.[161]

As long as the official houses of prostitution were open, women found guilty of working on their own were usually first ordered to move into the Frauenhaus. The house residents themselves were given permission to drag women into the house or allowed to break up—often physically, brick by brick—illegal brothels. Indeed the residents of the official Frauenhaus were often the ones who complained to the council first about women working illegally.[162] After the official brothels were closed, and even before for repeat offenders or those who refused to move into the house, women found guilty of prostitution were banished. This often occurred after a period of time in jail or in the stocks and was often carried out forcefully, the women literally driven out of the town with blows.[163]

Interestingly, despite the dishonorable and disreputable character these women were supposed to have, they were all required to swear an oath that they would not come back into the city again, and if they were discovered to have returned, they were judged more harshly for their perjury than for their prostitution.[164] Usually these women did not go very far away. In Nuremberg, for example, once the Frauenhaus was closed, prostitutes were often referred to as "New Forest whores" because they lived directly outside the city walls in an area called the New Forest.[165]

It is impossible to gauge accurately the extent of prostitution in any of these cities or to see what real effect the closing of the official brothels had on it. Times of war and disturbance increased the number of women who were forced to make their living this way, and the number who combined occasional prostitution with work as a pieceworker or day laborer was undoubtedly very high. Although one can view the period of official city brothels as an unusually positive one for prostitutes, the period in which they were seen as worthwhile members of the community was very short—from the first ordinances which protected them from being sold or pawned, to those which set them clearly apart from honorable women—a period of, at most, one hundred years. Even during this period the majority of women who made their living by prostitution did so illicitly, without city or community approval, and were never regarded as more than the "common, base, lewd whores" they are referred to as in their sentences. Indeed, many of their sentences do not even include a first name, much less a last one or any identifying characteristics. The women were often victims of crimes as well. Despite threats of punishment, murders and beatings of prostitutes were common, either inside the Frauenhaus or along streets and alleyways.[166] Prostitution was truly an occupation of last resort.

This was also the case with women who went beyond prostitution to become involved in crimes of various sorts. Although it may seem peculiar to consider crime when examining women's work, for a few women, crime was an occupation. They worked at it regularly and made their living from it in the same way other women did from spinning or working in the fields. Women were involved in every kind of crime and appear continually before municipal criminal courts. Most of these crimes—arson, murder, fornication, adultery, slander, maintaining a "dishonorable" lifestyle, witchcraft—cannot really be considered occupations, but it is interesting to note that women were questioned just as severely, often with torture, and punished just as harshly as men. Theft, however, was an occupation for some women, often combined with prostitution. Although most early modern cities probably did not have the organized criminal world reported—or invented—for London, women were members of stealing rings and fencing operations, as either the actual thieves or the receivers of stolen goods.[167]

Women usually stole from households or stores, not directly from people. Only very rarely did their thefts involve an attack on a person, but they often took advantage of opportunities for theft when they were helping other people who were sick or moving or during short-term employment. Theft in some cases was a family occupation, with husband and wife or mother and daughter acting together; in such cases, both usually received the same punishment once caught.[168] In an interesting case in Stuttgart, a husband and wife and their two daughters were charged with repeated theft and arson. The mother's confession gave a long story of how she had been forced into each action by her husband at knife point and how the two daughters were not involved at all "but have warned us often and repeatedly, as their dear mother and father, not to do such bad things." The court did not believe her first claim, and both parents were executed, but it apparently did believe her second one, as the daughters were let off with a warning.[169]

Of course most women who stole did so out of great desperation and stole things they or their families could use immediately, such as lard, bread, or clothing. City courts took this into consideration and often gave a fairly light sentence to women who pleaded that they had stolen solely because of "unimaginable and incontestable poverty."[170] Poverty was usually the only grounds for giving a milder sentence, as women who were pregnant were regularly banished or punished corporally, as were mothers of small children. In the latter cases, city courts had to decide what to do with the children and usually attempted to find a relative to care for them when the mother was banished, but at times they were simply sent out of town with the mother. This was also a problem for courts when women were executed for more serious crimes like murder or counterfeiting, but the presence of small children never served as a deterrent to an execution.[171]

Repeat offenders were handled very harshly, often being beaten, branded, mutilated by having their fingers or ears chopped off, and then banished.[172] Cases like the following in Nuremberg show how desperate some of these women could become:

> Barbara Wissnerin, a very base, lewd whore, who due to great unchastity, multiple theft, and breaking and entering has already been in jail eight times. She was banished many times and has perjured herself [i.e., and come back into Nuremberg] and was beaten in the jail. She was publicly burned through the cheeks, and her first two fingers were chopped off. But all warnings have not helped. When she was recently arrested again, she made herself a large belly out of rags, as if she were pregnant, so that the officials would hold back and not use the necessary severity. She was let out of the city after swearing an oath and warned under penalty of death not to come into the city again. Whereupon she came in again and was caught at theft. Now, on her own confession, her day of execution is set for Thursday, the first of March. For the said punishment she will be drowned.[173]

The physical mutilation had made it impossible for this woman to do anything but steal or carry out other kinds of crime because no one would have hired her to do anything else. The effect of marking people as thieves was to insure that they would always remain such.

*Market Woman Selling a Variety of Merchandise.* Woodcut from Cicero's De Officiis
(*Augsburg: Steyner, 1531*).

# CHAPTER FOUR
## The Sale and Trade of Life's Necessities

The center of economic life within any early modern city was the city marketplace. Whether the goods came from far away or were produced at home, they were usually bought, sold, or traded at the market, often directly in front of the city's cathedral or major church. As one might expect, the business that went on at this market was conducted primarily by women. Women were responsible for nearly all retail distribution of food, used clothing, household articles, liquor, and other things which made up the major share of most family budgets.[1] This has often been termed the "subeconomy" of a city by economic historians, who prefer to concentrate on long-distance wholesale trade; but it was this subeconomy which was of greatest concern to contemporaries, both city councils and private citizens.[2] Conditions in this subeconomy determined whether the people of the city would be able to afford to buy food or clothing and what the quality of those products would be once they bought them.

In addition, the marketplace served as a gathering place for women, who were the majority of the customers as well as the vendors. As Alice Clark notes, "While the market was frequented by all the women of the neighborhood it must certainly have favored the formation of a feminine public opinion on current events, which prevented individual women from relying exclusively upon their husbands for information and advice."[3] At times, city governments worried about this, particularly when the "current events" included religion, as, for example, the Memmingen city council, which ordered maids and other women not to discuss religion when drawing water at the neighborhood wells.[4]

Recognizing the importance of a well-ordered and smoothly running market, city councils set up ordinances and regulations for all types of sales. These dealt with a wide variety of issues: cleanliness and hygiene, proper locations and size of booths and shops, market hours, fair prices, product quality and purity. Supplying even a small city was a complicated process, and an examination of the women involved in the process gives insight into the day-to-day economic life of a sixteenth-century city.

Every type of item had its particular location at the marketplace, which made price and quality control and maintenance of cleanliness standards easier. Each woman was generally allowed only one sort of merchandise and permitted to operate only one stand at a time; nor could she hire a maid or use her daughter to sell from another one for her.[5] The stands were very small, often little more than a bench or table, with a small pot filled with coals for warmth in the winter. A woman needed very little capital to set up such a business. Her wares were made or gathered by herself and her family or else purchased on credit from a wholesale distributor, with perhaps some household goods as collateral. Her bench, pots, jugs, jars, baskets, or whatever else was needed were brought from home, so she operated with almost no overhead.

Interestingly, there are no statements about unfitness of women for sales. Various groups were admonished for unfair business practices, selling bad products, or raising prices unfairly, but the fact that they were women was never even mentioned.[6] In occupations like selling game, fish, or poultry in which both women and men were active, the regulations were simply addressed to both sexes.

Although city councils attempted to divide these women sharply by what they were selling, the distinctions become somewhat blurred when looked at from a distance of five hundred years. It is still possible to discern three basic groups: first, those who sold food and liquor, which was often the largest part of any family budget; second, those who sold other things which they had made or gathered; and third, those who were licensed to sell used clothing and other items and who often did appraisals as well.

## MEAT

In most cities the butchers' guild was one of the earliest guilds formed and one of the strongest. Butchers were ready and able to defend their rights against foreigners who wanted to sell meat in a city, innkeepers who wanted to do their own slaughtering, or anyone else they perceived as encroaching on their legitimate sphere of action. Although records indicate no women joined the guild on their own, the wives and daughters of butchers did much of the actual work and were just as strong as their husbands or fathers, in physical strength— for the women slaughtered pigs, sheep, and cattle themselves—and in work identity. This involvement was recognized by city councils, for wives as well as husbands had to abide by the butchers' ordinances and could be fined, jailed, or have their right to work taken away from them for infractions.[7]

Occasionally wives were forbidden to sell meat at the same time their husbands were selling, but this was done so that only one person at a time would be operating the scale and there would be less chance of cheating customers. When the husband was unable to sell for some reason or was away, his wife could then sell freely. A widow was usually given the right to continue operating the shop after her husband's death, and in some cases a butcher's daughter could work as a butcher herself even if her husband belonged to another trade, as long as she paid the normal guild fees.[8]

As might be expected, cities had very strict regulations about the handling and sale of meat. All meat except beef had to be sold on the day the animal was slaughtered; the origin of the animal had to be known; various types of meat had to be kept separate from each other; and butchers had to allow regular inspection of their stock and scales to make sure everything was in order so that customers were not cheated in any way. As also might be expected, all of these regulations were broken from time to time, as butchers or their wives saw the opportunity to increase sales. In fact, 90 percent of the cases brought before the Munich *Bussamt* (the court which handled market regulations) involved butchers or bakers, with wives and widows fined just as much as their husbands for similar offenses.[9]

Actually, butchers' wives were more often charged with breaking regulations than the butchers themselves. One in Memmingen was found to be selling meat to people during Lent without the required approval of religious authorities; two in Munich to be requiring that their customers buy less desirable cuts of meat before they would sell them what they wanted; several others in Munich to be setting their scales falsely or adding a weight to the meat so that customers were short-changed.[10] One woman in Strasbourg refused to allow her meat to be inspected and then answered the inspectors with "totally inappropriate and shameful language."[11] The most common offense was selling house to house, not at the public market, for then, according to the city councils, all kinds of "questionable and suspicious" meat could be sold. Butchers' wives apparently took the chance that they would not be caught selling suspect meat house-to-house, whereas they would be if they or their husbands sold it at the public market.

Occasionally the city council did make an exception to this rule, allowing butchers' widows who were extremely poor to do some peddling, but only as long as they did it with "modesty and decorum," not hawking their wares too loudly.[12]

Modesty and decorum were not qualities very often found among butchers' wives and widows, as two cases in Frankfurt demonstrate. In 1648 a butcher's widow complained that she had been denied her right to work, "which widows usually have, solely because of their [the other butchers' and their wives'] irresponsibly practiced wickedness and insults, which they did solely out of envy and vengeful spite."[13] She wanted to be reinstated, and the city council agreed, also ordering those who had insulted her to make a formal apology so that she got her "honor" back. The council had to repeat this last order several times before all the butchers' wives would apologize, although the butchers themselves appear to have done so readily.

Six years later another widow brought a similar case, stating that she had been thrown out of the guild, ostensibly because she had not sold all her meat on the day the animal was killed, but really because of the "misunderstanding, error, stupidity, and jealousy" of the other butchers. This time the council did not agree so easily, and she repeated her request three times before any action was taken, each time stressing her poverty and the hardship this was bringing to her many innocent children. In the final request, she stated that if she had done something wrong, it was solely out of "feminine stupidity" and therefore she was not to be judged or punished too harshly. Besides, she also mentioned, the butchers really did not have the power to exclude someone for as long as they had excluded her; that power rested solely with the city council. One or both of these arguments was apparently effective—a good example of her "feminine stupidity"—because the council ordered the butchers to reinstate her.[14]

Butchers' widows and other women were more likely to receive permission to make sausages and headcheese than they were to slaughter or sell fresh meat. Sausage making had long been a female occupation, and in some cities it remained so.[15] Butchers in Stuttgart in 1512 were expressly forbidden to make bratwurst because this was the special province of female *Sulzerinnen* (sausage and headcheese makers), who had a separate ordinance and an oath they had to swear to whenever the butchers took their oath.[16] In Memmingen as well, women prepared and sold special Christmas sausages the butchers were prohibited from making. Even butchers' widows in Memmingen had to choose between making sausage and handling fresh meat; they were not allowed to do both.[17]

Besides making sausage, women cleaned and sold innards and tripe, a rather unpleasant occupation usually separated from butchering. They got the innards fresh each day from a butcher and then washed and prepared them to be used as sausage casings or food. These "innards-washers" (*Khudlwescherin*) had their own ordinances in Memmingen, Munich, and Strasbourg, and these usually referred only to women in the occupation.[18]

In 1614 in Strasbourg one of these women became involved in a long dispute with the butchers, during the course of which a number of interesting things emerged. She was the widow of a butcher but was now married again to someone who was not associated with the butchers' guild, so she was forbidden to sell innards.[19] She was selling them anyway in clear defiance of an order from the butchers, indeed had answered their order with a letter containing "shameful things," according to their complaint to the city council. She also said she had a special letter from the council which allowed her to sell, so she did not care what the butchers said, as the council had been "so gracious in its permission."[20] The council responded to her flattery and allowed her to work, so the butchers brought in six other innards-washers, all widows, who said they wanted this woman forbidden to work because she had stolen some things from them and was giving them a bad name. They also argued that she had older children and a husband who could work so did not need the money as much as they, as poor widows, did.[21] At this, the council changed its mind and forbade her to work; she then reappeared with two small children in tow, arguing that there were other married women who were working, even making sausage as well as preparing innards (in Strasbourg the right to do the former rested with the butchers), so that what she did should not upset anyone. Besides, her husband was ill, and her work was the only thing that kept the family going.[22] The butchers answered that her working would bring "disunity and bad consequences"; anyway, her husband was not really sick but was "always picking fights . . . and a lazy louse that doesn't want to work, and it is her fault that she has attached herself to someone like that." This last argument was effective with the city council, as it took back its permission and refused to allow her to work.[23]

In all these disputes the female supplicant attempted to play on the city council's jealousy and resentment of the power of the butchers' guild. In the Frankfurt cases the women were successful; in the Strasbourg case, the woman was not. Bringing the six women in to argue against her was an effective move by the butchers, a tactic used by other occupational groups as well.

Bakers were another strong guild in most early modern cities, and in many ways the situation was similar to that of butchers: Women worked as regular bread bakers when they were the wives, daughters, or widows of bakers. Women also made small cakes, pretzels, and cookies at certain times of the year or when they had no other means of support.

Bakers' wives usually handled the sales in a shop. Most debts to bakers listed in inventories read "to the baker's wife," not to the baker himself.[24] Unlike butchers' wives, they were never prohibited from selling alongside their husbands, as they did not use a scale but simply sold bread of standard sizes. When the bread was found to be too small or too light, it was often the baker's wife that was fined, not the baker, because she was the one who had sold it for more than its actual worth. If the offense was repeated, women were put in jail for short periods despite apologies and promises that it would never happen again. Bakers' wives also bought the grain, yeast, and other raw materials needed for bread and were often responsible for getting the grain milled into flour.[25]

Bakers' widows who did the baking themselves were also fined for bread of poor quality (bread that was "too rough on the tongue and not baked long enough" for example) or for bread of other than the allowable sizes.[26] In general, bakers' widows were allowed to continue baking as long as they did not remarry and paid normal guild fees.[27] Only if they were unusually successful was there any opposition—as, for example, a Frankfurt widow who wanted to expand her shop but was instead forbidden to work.[28]

Like butchers' widows, bakers' widows were not at all reticent about bringing complaints when they thought their rights had been violated. In 1626 a baker's widow in Strasbourg asked that baker who had recently moved to her street be forbidden to bake on the day she did "so that she could keep the advantage in her hand."[29] He answered that she had changed her baking day to take away his customers "and has said that she would spend 200 gulden to bring him to ruin . . . if only he could get away from this terrible neighborhood, especially from this widow, who was a horrible annoyance." The city council grew weary of the case, as did the baker's guild, which ordered the two to make peace or it would forbid both of them to bake.[30]

Bakers' widows often quit baking bread and other "large goods" and concentrated instead on making small yeast cakes and rolls.[31] In addition, other women occasionally received permission to bake certain kinds of small items. The things that women were allowed to bake varied from city to city and from time to time, depending on how threatened the bakers' guilds felt by this activity. For example, in most cities women were allowed to bake and sell Lebkuchen, the dark, spicy Christmas cookie known throughout south Germany.[32] In Nuremberg, however, only members of the bakers' guild could bake Lebkuchen. Those bakers who specialized in Lebkuchen appealed to the city council to become an independent guild on several occasions, but the request was denied; any baker was essentially allowed to make Lebkuchen, although only certain ones actually did.[33] Although frustrated in this attempt, the Nuremberg bakers were successful at keeping women from baking; Nuremberg had no female Lebkuchen bakers, despite a very high level of Lebkuchen production. (This of course does not mean that women did not bake Lebkuchen at home for private use. A sixteenth-century cookbook printed in Nuremberg includes many recipes for baked goods; it was written by Susanna Harsdorff and dedicated to "my dear children with the best." It includes a recipe for Lebkuchen, although, like all early recipes, not a very specific one: "Use what spices are needed for 180 sugar Lebkuchen, especially cinnamon, nutmeg, ginger and cloves.")[34]

Usually women who were especially needy and who had no other means of support were allowed to bake, with city councils making it clear that these were exceptions. They were allowed to bake only for fairs or market days or at those times during the year when the ingredients, like lard, eggs, or honey, were in abundance so the women could use them without driving up the price. They were often forbidden to sell house to house, as it would then be difficult to control what they were selling, but could sell only from their homes or from small stands at the public market.[35]

During times of war or general unrest, the number of women who had to support themselves in this way increased, especially in cities experiencing an influx of refugees. In 1632 a woman appealed to the Strasbourg city council for permission to bake egg pretzels (*Ayerwecken*). She and her husband had been driven out of the Palatinate, and then he had ridden off to fight in the battle of White Mountain in the Thirty Years' War and had "remained there along the way." Despite objections by the bakers that there were already too many people making pretzels and selling them all over the city without the proper taxes, the city council allowed her to bake.[36] Two years later it granted permission to a number of other women as well, "because all of the supplicants are poor people that are particularly hard pressed in these difficult times."[37]

City councils stepped back, however, when they feared a bad precedent would be set, despite the poverty and need of the particular woman involved. In 1603 a widow in Nuremberg asked permission to sell bread and rolls house to house. Others had also asked, and the council wanted a reexamination of the law to see if she should be granted permission or whether, "to prevent a bad thing from starting, the applicant should be denied permission, and should be given a penny from the general welfare fund because she complains so loudly about her poverty." [38] The second alternative was chosen in this case. In 1616 the widow of a pastry baker in Strasbourg asked for permission to bake "egg bread with yeast." [39] The bakers replied that only regular bakers were to use yeast, a regulation which she well knew, and that she could only use sourdough. She pled her poverty, weakness, many children, and recalcitrant eldest son and noted that her wares were tasty and popular; despite all this, she was forbidden to bake on the grounds that "others would take this as an example, and great disorder would be the result." [40]

Oftentimes the request for a legal stand or for permission to sell house to house led to a crackdown on those operating without council permission. Rather than allowing a supplicant to bake "as so many others are doing," city councils instead ordered everyone else to stop as well. [41] This was particularly true if they found that foreign women were baking and selling things, for this was then "taking the bread out of the mouths of our children." [42]

If, despite all her pleas for Christian charity and mercy, a woman's own request was not granted, she could then turn to someone else to write a request for her, preferably someone whose voice would be heeded. In 1636, for example, a widow wrote to Maximilian, the duke of Bavaria, asking him to write to the Munich city council on her behalf, as she wanted permission to bake sweet cakes. Her letter to him is a model of the cringing humility seen as necessary in such supplications: "During my whole life I have prayed to God with my poor, simple, and unworthy daily prayers for your beneficent grace's health and happiness, and now with most humble thankfulness I turn to your beneficent Grace, in all obedience and humility, and wait for your gracious answer." [43]

She was successful, both in convincing Maximilian to write for her and in receiving permission to bake. The language of the letter should not deceive; her humility obviously did not prevent her from writing to Maximilian in the first place. Other women as well made similar requests to nobles and churchmen, for city council minutes frequently mention letters from highly placed individuals requesting favors for local women. Even women who were in jail asked influential people to write in their behalf.

Fish handling was an occupation often shared by husband and wife. He caught local lake and river fish, and she prepared and sold them. Women also acted alone, buying fish from rural fishermen and handling salted sea fish shipped from the North Sea.[44] Particularly before the Reformation, a constant supply of fish was needed, and fishmongers were always present on the city streets and in the market. An ordinance from 1491 in Nuremberg forbade the herring sellers to begin their "fish calling" before six in the morning, which means they were still out selling before dawn in winter. Frankfurt was even stricter, forbidding its fishmongers to sell or buy any fish before ten in the morning, despite their frequent pleas for a relaxation of this provision.[45]

The types of dried and salted fish (*Stockfische*) which could be brought into the city were limited, both to assure that the source was known and to protect the local industry from too much competition from foreign preserved fish. From time to time women were admonished or fined for bringing in forbidden fish or for selling fish which had not been inspected.[46] Like the butchers' wives, they were occasionally charged with forcing people to buy less desirable fish before they would sell them what they wanted. Salted or dried fish that had come into the city illegally was not destroyed the way illegal meat was, as there was little danger of its being tainted; instead the cities simply confiscated it and gave it to the city hospital or distributed it among the poor.

Under unusual circumstances, women were allowed to sell fish that was normally forbidden. For example, the wife of a shipper in Strasbourg asked for permission to sell two barrels of herring her husband had received in Mainz as payment for a debt. The fish was "still completely fresh and of good merchants' quality [*Kaufmannsgut*] and has been checked by the inspectors and judged to be good." She was granted permission "as long as she will swear an oath that she is telling the truth about this," the same thing that would be required of any male fishmonger bringing such a request.[47]

City councils set restrictions on the women who handled fish in order to maintain the cleanliness of the marketplace and the quality of water flowing through the city. Fishmongers were set off in a far corner of the marketplace, for the stench must have been considerable, and they could be fined if they set up a stand elsewhere. In Nuremberg the women who salted and pickled fish were ordered not to use the water going into the city hospital for their purposes, but only the water by the butchers' stalls.[48] The fine was set very high to ensure that the hospital did not end up with fish heads and entrails floating in its drinking water.

The sale of game and poultry was also an occupation often shared by husband and wife, although women acted alone in this as well. Only Nuremberg had a specific ordinance for these people, which simply stated that all tame animals—chickens, ducks, rabbits, and such—had to be sold live and that for all wild ones, the source had to be known. The approved way to prepare geese and ducks for sale was spelled out in a section directed only to female game dealers, which implies that women handled the slaughter, plucking, and cleaning of birds. In fact, after 1520 only women were listed among the registered game dealers, so they apparently bought their game from area hunters rather than getting it from their husbands.[49] In Strasbourg and Frankfurt the wife or widow of the city *Vogler*, the man who tended the meadow where geese and ducks were kept, actually did most of the work.[50]

Game handlers in Nuremberg were forbidden to make agreements setting prices and on more than one occasion were ordered to take their "dead goose-bellies" out of the city because no one believed they had been killed recently and were still fit to eat.[51] Game handlers were a constant source of annoyance to their neighbors, who complained of the smell and that sales went on at the wrong times and places. They were also occasionally accused of hoarding, of buying up all the available poultry in order to charge a higher price. The game dealers themselves were quick to complain if they felt their rights and privileges were being violated, particularly if foreigners were selling game either within the city or too close to it.[52]

## FRUIT, VEGETABLES, AND HERBS

Retail sales of fresh fruits and vegetables were handled in all early modern cities by women operating small stands at the public market.[53] Fruit was either raised locally, in the gardens surrounding the city, or by nearby farmers or was brought in from the Mediterranean by long-distance traders if it was especially prized and relatively easy to transport. Women who sold imported fruits, mainly oranges and lemons, were often specifically forbidden to sell fruit grown close to home.

Vegetables were strictly home grown, with most of the women who sold them growing their own, either in their backyard gardens or in small plots right outside the city walls. The growing season was long enough to allow vegetables of some sort to be on sale throughout most of the year; as the autumn and winter root vegetables like rutabagas, turnips, large radishes, and beets were finally sold out, the early spring ones like lettuce, small radishes, and peas made their appearance. Perhaps only February and March would find a total absence of fresh produce, although dried onions and garlic would still be available. Many of these women also made and sold sauerkraut; they were able to buy cabbage at favorable prices and specifically forbidden to let rotted sauerkraut lie around.[54] They were usually limited to certain times of the day for their activities: "The old women who sell lettuce, parsley, onions, and the like are forbidden to do business before noon, but afterward they can sell as much of their lowly products as they like."[55]

Herbs, unlike spices which came in from the East and were handled by major merchants, were also a local product. Women either grew them in small gardens or collected them from the fields and woods and then sold them to doctors, apothecaries, and private citizens. They were not allowed to mix herbs or medicines, as this was to be done only by sworn apothecaries, but they could sell most raw ingredients, including poisonous ones. Often only citizens were allowed to sell, as city councils also saw this as a way of providing support for women or men who were too old or weak to do anything else.[56]

Until the middle of the sixteenth century, there were few problems with these vendors, for they appear in city council records only in a few individual cases.[57] Beginning about 1560, however, and continuing to the end of the century, the sale of fruits and vegetables was a frequent concern of city councils for a variety of reasons, which are most easily traced in Nuremberg. In 1559, because of a bad harvest, the Nuremberg fruit sellers were offering their wares at very high prices. On August 1 the council forbade them to buy or sell any fruit for one month, hoping that people would buy directly from growers. To this promulgation was added the stipulation that if the fruit sellers were later found to be raising prices on winter fruits, such as apples and pears, the council would forbid them to sell these as well.[58] Just a year later, however, after an excellent harvest, the fruit sellers and farmers' wives were allowed and encouraged to sell their fruit at the market every day.

In the 1570s more rules were added: The fruit vendors and farmers' wives were ordered to stop selling their fruit before and after the service on Sundays and to sell it only on weekdays; each vendor could have only one stand, and if husband and wife both sold, they had to share a stand. Foreigners could sell fruit for three days and then had to sell any fruit they had left to a local fruit vendor, but citizens could sell fruit from their own gardens whenever and for as long as they liked.[59]

Women were regularly discovered breaking any rule that was set. One was ordered to shut her second stand "and dismiss the maids and servants that are operating it."[60] Several fruit vendors were also found to be selling game and poultry without knowing where it had come from or how fresh it was, a practice the council found both dangerous and leading to price increases because people were not getting things directly from the game and poultry dealers. The women were ordered to stop, with a heavy fine of ten gulden—probably more than their monthly income—set as a penalty.[61] After the ban on Sunday trading, the fruit vendors complained vociferously that they had always sold fruit on Sundays and holidays, especially to farmers and tradesmen. The council grudgingly allowed them to do so again, as they were doing business anyway despite the ban, but only after the service and as long as they cleaned up their stands in the evening.[62]

What most worried the city council were rising prices, which were going up so fast "that the poor citizen does not know how to pay anymore."[63] In 1588 all those "who make such price increases and do not sell their roots and cabbage for a tolerable price" were to be arrested and taken to the city jail.[64] "Some female persons" were found to be going early to get cream (which they made into butter) from farmers and convincing them to sell their produce as well, which the women resold at a much higher price in the city. The council forbade this, demanding that the women wait until the farmers brought their cream and vegetables into town so as to prevent the women from making too much profit.[65]

The council also called for an examination of the fruit and vegetable trade, including how many vendors there were and what amount of profit they were making. All of them were called together before the council to answer certain questions: how many storage cellars and stands they had; how much fruit and at what prices they had sold it in the summer; where and how far from the city they had bought it; how many farmers they had bought it from. The council forbade them to sell anything more until further notice, as it found they were selling produce for twice what they had paid to growers. It also wanted them to list in writing the names and locations of all their farmer sources so that people could go directly to those sources.[66] A month later all the vendors were fined, ordered again to have only one stand and one storage cellar, and forbidden to sell any fruit that had been grown within 5 miles of the city. In this last case, the council wanted the farmers themselves to sell the fruit and so to keep the fruit vendors from making any profit at all on it. The woman in charge of the vendors was removed from her post for not enforcing previous regulations, and the new ordinance was hung on a placard at the city marketplace so that no one could say he or she did not know the regulations.[67] The number of women allowed to sell fruit was limited to 18, and those allowed to sell vegetables to 12, although this did not include farmers' wives or other people selling their own produce.[68]

These arrangements seem to have solved the problems in Nuremberg, for never again did such sweeping changes or restrictions appear. Similar cases did come up in other cities, however, and were handled in much the same way, with fruit vendors usually forbidden to sell fruit grown very near the city or to buy with the clear intent of storing the produce until the price went up.[69] The 1616 Frankfurt ordinance adds an interesting twist; not only were prices rising because fruit vendors were buying up everything from farmers but also, according to the council, because there were too many vendors. Although one would assume this would normally cause prices to decline as the vendors competed with each other, the paragraph following reveals the real cause for the council's concern about the number of vendors. These were not old widows who sold to support themselves but "young female persons who could easily do some other kind of work, like being a maid, but are causing great disorder by selling fruit."[70] Again the dislike of young women working—and thus perhaps living—on their own comes through.

The attention paid to fruit and vegetable vendors during this period is part of a general interest in price control spurred on by the gradual inflation of the sixteenth century. The city councils' attempts to limit the profits of these vendors indicate their concern to check rising prices in at least one area. This is a period in which the function of a merchant was only slowly being recognized, and even today there are calls for attempts to weed out "middlemen" (or women) in a time of falling farm income yet rising consumer prices.

## RELATED PRODUCTS

In addition to meats, baked products, and produce, women made and sold a number of other kinds of food and related products. They made vinegar from wine they were storing, prepared yeast for brewing and for baking, and smoked and dried meats. They sold milk, eggs, and cheese their animals produced. They bought and sold grain and flour, making contracts with farmers, millers, and customers, and sometimes shipping long distances, either by boat or overland by cart.[71] They also shipped other kinds of food, as for example a woman in Strasbourg who asked for permission to ship 37 Centner of Munster cheese that she had bought in Speyer, which the council allowed as it felt the city was already well enough supplied with cheese. Another shipped seed from Strasbourg to Freiburg in Breisgau; one shipped salt and peas regularly from Strasbourg to Basel; and yet another, wheat, barley, and flax all over the Strasbourg area.[72]

The sale of such items was generally open to all, and men working in a craft often did this as a second occupation. In fact, once something had become common as a "side occupation" for men, women were usually to be found doing it as well. City councils restricted the sale of such items only when they suspected that too many poor or elderly people, especially widows, might come into the city to do so and eventually end up needing public support.

Candle making was strictly a female occupation, with women listed in many cities as early as the fourteenth century. They received their tallow from butchers or often through a special municipal tallow office and then made the candles in their own homes.[73] In Nuremberg, candle making was considered a "sworn craft," the equivalent in Nuremberg to a guild, beginning in 1398, and the names of the women who made candles were listed in city records continuously throughout the fifteenth century.[74] This changed when the city became Protestant and the burning of votive candles was no longer considered efficacious. Not only did this cause a drop in the demand, but the candles that were still needed were only for daily use, so the registration and listing by name of the city's candlemakers was no longer regarded as important. Candle making became a "free art," still with a set of regulations, but open to anyone.

Before the Reformation, and after it in cities which remained Catholic, a number of candlemakers had special arrangements with certain churches. They were given a monopoly on the sale of votive candles in the church or else the right to have their stands directly in front of the church doors or chapel. As with those selling other types of merchandise, they were not to sell house to house, but only from their stand, and only at the price set by the city.[75]

Candles were sold by sight and length, not weighed each time, but candlemakers were to make sure the right amount of wax was in each candle.[76] Yellow wax, which was cheaper, could not be dyed green in order to make the candles more expensive; only green wax, which was of higher quality, could be dyed to make another color or a richer shade of green. New wax was not to be mixed with candle drippings to produce candles to be sold as new ones, nor were the candlemaker's maids or servants to do the work for her. Along with the candles themselves, the candlemakers also sold holders and pots to put them in, although these they did not make. Despite protests from the potmakers and ironworkers, they were allowed to continue selling these, although they were forbidden to sell anything not in some way related to candles.[77]

One of the most inventive, although also most troublesome, women to emerge from the records was a candlemaker among other things in her long and varied career. Anna Weylandin, nicknamed "Lumpen-weiblin," first appeared before the Strasbourg city council in 1573 asking for special permission to sell herring which had come in from north Germany. This was granted despite the objections of the fishers' guild, but she was soon charged with refusing to sell this herring to people unless they also bought dried and salted cod from her. The following year she was charged with buying herring outside the city instead of at the public fish market, then selling it cheaper than the established price to undersell the other fishmongers and telling her customers not to say anything.[78] She also got into the candle business the same year and was immediately charged with selling candles for less than the official price and with a number of other infractions of the candle ordinance. She answered she "would not obey any ordinance, no matter what in God's name the council made for an ordinance." At that, she was ordered to follow the ordinance and especially not to use children to sell candles illegally. Should she speak so again, the council threatened, she would be "pinched with glowing tongs, and if she works [illegally] she will be thrown in the water."[79]

Those threats apparently worked for a while, for she did not come before the council again until 1580, six years later. This time, however, the case dragged on for months. She was first charged with having candles that were too light, but when the city inspectors checked them, they were found to be all right. The council did not trust her, however, and decided "that the inspectors should watch her and send unknown people to her to buy candles, to see if we can catch her hand in the sack (so to speak)."[80] This was done, and the candles were found to be too light. Attempting to ward off all possible excuses, the council next ordered all her scales and weights to be checked secretly and candles to be bought again "so that she can be caught in the act."[81] Her scales and weights were found to be accurate, and again the candles were too light. Her husband was confronted with this, but he answered that he could not stand over every pound of candles that was made, as they often sold fifty or sixty pounds in a day, "and this wasn't saffron" (and thus very valuable ounce for ounce).[82]

Both of them were ordered to appear before the council, but she pleaded some kind of illness, and he began a long string of excuses about how the scales had not worked properly, the servants had misused them—but the council cut him off sharply, saying he and his wife were responsible and deserved severe punishment.[83] They discussed banishing them and confiscating their goods but instead decided to forbid them to buy and sell anything and fined them fifty pounds. The husband appeared before the council again, "crying and pleading for God's sake" not to have to shut the shop, but the council sent a bailiff home with him to make sure the shop was closed.[84] A further attempt to blame it all on his wife was met with the same response, although the council noted that she had merited corporal punishment as well as the fine because she had "done so much deceitfully which had done great harm to the poor." He should thank God the council had been so generous.[85] After several more supplications, the city council did allow him to sell the things he had on hand already, but his wife was to do nothing, "neither buying or selling, changing money or anything else that has to do with the business," and was not even to let herself be found in the shop. He promised "by the grace of God" never to do anything wrong again.[86]

This time the promise lasted two years, for in 1582 Lumpenweiblin was found to be selling Dutch cheese illegally—she simply switched products whenever she was forbidden to sell something. This time the council sent out a representative to order her to stop or she would be banished—she had never yet come before the council to answer any of the charges against her. This was effective, for there is no further record of her selling anything, although she did ask again in 1605, twenty-three years later, but was still forbidden to sell anything.[87] Twenty-three years of good behavior was still not enough to make the council forget all the trouble she had caused.

Lumpenweiblin, though she had perhaps gone a bit too far, had showed tremendous natural business skills, skills which could be transferred from the sale of one kind of merchandise to the sale of others. She had gone straight to producers to avoid the costs the city wholesale merchants added to any commodity; she had taken advantage of unusual opportunities; she had made sure the inspectors received products which were up to standards, had used her children to sell products which were suspicious or questionable, and had then refused to come in for questioning, sending her husband instead. In short, she was a ruthless businesswoman who used every tactic she could to increase her profits.

Similar ruthlessness was shown by the women who measured and sold firewood along the banks of the Main River at Frankfurt. Firewood was cut in the large forest on the opposite side of the river, then dragged to the river and transported across in boats or floated across. Each household received a slip from the city wood office allowing it to have its proper allocation of firewood, and then each person picking up this wood got a carrier from the woodhouse so that he or she would carry home only the proper amount. This carrier was then taken down to the riverbank where the wood was handed out by "firewood measurers." By 1610 the whole process had gotten so confusing and created such a scene of such disorder that the city issued an ordinance regulating the conduct of these women. This ordinance gives a good idea of what the women were doing, as each clause was written in response to quite specific abuses:

> A great number of complaints have come in to us recently about the women who sell firewood, that they not only try to steal customers away from others for the salary but actually force people to buy from them. Therefore we order that the wood dealers be limited to a certain number but that they not be allowed to keep someone from selling who has gotten the city council's permission to do so.
> For every gulden's worth of wood, the women are to receive only eight pence if it is measured and sold on a boat, or twelve pence if it is measured in the water.
> The wood measurers are not to collaborate with each other or force anyone against his will to use their services; even less are they to wait by the wood house and grab the carrier out of peoples' hands, as has happened so often previously, but wait patiently by the crane until someone orders wood. Nor are they to demand the order slip from anyone, but only to give wood to those who give them this slip and to no one else.
> Finally, they should measure honestly and truly, take no wood from those who they are measuring for or from the shippers without their consent, and return the carriers to the woodhouse immediately. They will be fined one gulden and forbidden to work for four weeks if they break any of these regulations, no matter what kind of excuses they try to give.[88]

The city council had a word for the ferry operators as well, many of whom were women. This same ordinance forbade them to slide their small ferries in among the big boats when the sale of firewood was going on because so doing created great confusion and allowed for the illegal or secret sale of firewood. Earlier these ferry operators had been limited to one boat each and to a penny a person per crossing, for the council had thought they were charging too much. Many of the ferries were run by older women, for this was yet another occupation seen as proper for a widow.[89]

## LIQUOR AND INNS

Although early ordinances in many cities forbade all female personnel, including the wife of the innkeeper, to serve in an inn or tavern, women were continually involved in all aspects of the liquor trade.[90] Not only was this restriction on serving totally ignored, but women brewed beer, made wine, distilled hard liquor, and operated taverns independently, and cities soon gave up on early attempts to exclude them. Consumption of alcoholic beverages was tremendous, and the business could be a lucrative one. By the middle of the fifteenth century, the number of taverns and inns in most cities was so large that city councils forbade any private citizens, male or female, to take in any noncitizen without permission, whether for payment or not. Often this was extended to include friends and relatives in an effort to provide more business for inns as well as keep track of what foreigners were in the city.

Turning first to liquor production, in many cities widows were allowed to continue brewing long after the death of their husbands.[91] A Nuremberg list of breweries from 1579 finds 7 out of 49 run by widows; seventeenth-century lists of both normal brewers and those who made wheat beer always included several women. Although most of these were widows, a few are listed without a husband's name, so they may have been the unmarried daughters of brewers. One of the women operated for more than twenty years, several of the others for ten to fifteen years. A list of brewers in Frankfurt in 1516 shows 19 men and 1 woman. She was the wife of someone who was not a brewer so had apparently not simply inherited the right to brew or at least had been able to maintain her widow's rights despite remarriage. Women could also brew independently in Strasbourg without having to be the widow of a brewer. Female brewers there paid the same taxes as their male counterparts.[92]

Women also brewed in Munich, that capital of beer production and consumption (though it did not have its current reputation in the sixteenth century). A number of female brewers brought cases to the city court demanding that overdue debts owed them be repaid. Apparently the brewers were also in the money-lending business to a small degree, for these were not only the debts of innkeepers who had taken beer on credit but also of people to whom they had made small loans.[93]

Female brewers in Munich also took care of women in childbed. In one case, a female brewer charged that a man had agreed to pay her for caring for his mistress during her delivery but had later refused to pay. He answered that he had tried to pay her but she would not accept the kind of money he offered. (She was right; the "black pennies" he offered were worth considerably less than their face value, as they had been heavily debased with copper.) She had instead taken his jacket, loaned it to others, and also worn it herself "in the wind and the rain." The court felt that since she had impounded the jacket, worth the approximate amount of his debt, she should consider the debt paid. This seems to have been a fairly standard practice.[94]

At the very end of the sixteenth century, brewers in Munich attempting to limit the rights of widows succeeded in convincing the city council in at least one case "that brewing is a learned art and given to men alone, so the request should not be granted because of her arguments about widows' rights."[95] Apparently they were not always successful, for brewers' widows appeared again in the seventeenth century, actively operating breweries.[96]

Some women brewers ran small taverns for distributing their product. In Strasbourg these were to be open only during the summer, as that was considered the proper time to drink beer, although one woman was given special permission in 1618 to keep hers open a month longer "because up until now it has been cold and uncomfortable weather to drink beer in."[97] The following year she was again given this extension on the condition that she inform the council about which brewers were operating two taverns at once, which was not allowed. To the council's embarrassment, this woman was herself guilty of this, and other brewers made the council look very foolish when they pointed it out.[98]

In addition to being commercial brewers, women also made beer for home consumption. There were no limitations or restrictions, and many households made all their own beer. Even someone as prominent as Katherine von Bora, Luther's wife, was proud of making all the beer consumed in that household often overflowing with students and guests, proud as well of its quality and reputation.

Along with making beer, women also distilled brandy.[99] Brandy was made from either wine or beer by quite a small operation easily done in a household. The earliest list of brandy makers is from Munich in 1564, when there were 15 men and 15 women, some of whom made each kind of brandy and some of whom were allowed to sell it in their houses. In 1602 there were 10 men and 3 women, and in 1689, 10 men and 6 women, several of whom are also labeled "cook."[100] Brandy was apparently more popular in Nuremberg, or else the officials were more thorough in listing everyone who made it, for the earliest extant list, from 1651, shows a total of 92 brandymakers, of whom 32 were women.[101] The city council had set a limit of 18, but there had been a rapid increase in distilleries during the Thirty Years' War, when the council was lax in cracking down on illegal operators. In Nuremberg, distillers were forbidden to sell brandy directly but had to bring it to the market immediately after it was made and sell it to the brandy-stand operators.

These brandy stands had been in operation in Nuremberg at least since 1485, when the city council specifically allowed them to be set up in the streets and on squares and gave the licenses to run them to poor and old people who could find no other work.[102] They bought their spirits in kegs and flasks at the market from the distillers but were to serve it only in smaller portions. It could be drunk immediately only on workdays, and the customer had to remain standing; on Sundays and holidays the brandy had to be taken home.

Similar restrictions were placed on brandy-stand operators in Munich. Their ordinance, first promulgated in 1526, also noted that brandy should only be sold in an open glass, not a closed beaker or pitcher, and only one penny's worth to each customer per day. If a "well-known and honorable person" needed more "for medicinal or other suitable purposes," he was to be allowed it, but no one else.[103] Brandy-stand operators were frequently fined when it was discovered they had allowed someone to sit while drinking.[104]

During the Thirty Years' War, Strasbourg saw a sharp increase in the number of brandy stands in the city, as well as the number of women who wanted to operate them. One widow asked to be given the stand of another who had remarried; that remarriage should be given as grounds for losing a stand is a clear indication that stands were seen as a means of supporting poor widows. On the request of several other widows or women whose husbands were away fighting, the city council investigated whether any of the forty stands which it allowed were vacant.[105] It found there were more than forty already operating but gave the women permission anyway "in consideration of the present hard times, which all will recognize . . . not only to support themselves better and live through this, but we hope also to bring in more taxes from those who are drinking."[106] To accomplish this second purpose, the council doubled the fees required from all who operated stands, figuring the women would raise their prices accordingly.

A few women also sold mead, hard cider, and beer by the glass, under restrictions similar to those placed on brandy-stand operators. They also operated slightly larger establishments which sold wine by the glass or by the pitcher.[107] The 1433 ordinance regulating these small taverns (*Weinschenk*) in Munich was directed to both men and women, and a count of them from the same year found 86 operated by men and 6 by women. By 1489 the tally had increased to 114 men and 7 women, and the new names added every year after that include quite a few women, some of them widows.[108]

As with all food, city councils were concerned with the purity of the wine sold. Tavern owners were regularly forbidden to sell wine or beer that had gone sour and prohibited from selling wine mixed with mustard, bacon, woad ash, brandy, or clary (a type of sage), all of which were claimed to have medicinal purposes. They were even more frequently charged with not paying the required tax on wine. In such cases, married female tavern operators who ran the place in their own names were fined, imprisoned, or even banished while no punishment was given to their husbands.[109] In some cases, these fines could be extremely heavy. In 1576 in Nuremberg forty-five tavern-keepers were charged with fraud in regard to their payment of the tax; their fines were set at up to 1,000 gulden. Their number includes two women, one fined 200 and the other 100 gulden.[110]

Permission to run a tavern was granted somewhat arbitrarily, although reasons of tradition and competition were given to explain why some applicants received it and others not. Usually the first requirement for all tavern-keepers, male or female, was that they be citizens; those who later married noncitizens occasionally lost their licenses. Women used a variety of means to convince city councils that they should be given a license: their deceased husbands had had one; they had already run a tavern a number of years; they were poor with small children to support. In some cases, they were successful, and in some, not.[111] A few arguments show more imagination; a baker in Strasbourg who was now seventy and could no longer work asked to be allowed to open a tavern "because my wife had operated a tavern for twenty-five years in Kehl [a town nearby], is known in all of upper Alsace and thus has good opportunities to buy good wine."[112] His request was denied, despite his repeated stress on his wife's skills.[113] A widow asked to open a tavern near where workers were constructing new fortifications "because the men will certainly need a tavern." The council debated "whether such a place should be run by a woman" perhaps because it would not be a normal neighborhood tavern, perhaps because the workers may have been conscripted labor and thus seen as too difficult for a woman to handle. She withdrew her request, for she left town to marry elsewhere.[114]

Occasionally a woman went to unusual lengths to get a license. One in Strasbourg had been repeatedly denied for two years but did get permission to give out wine in pitchers or bottles to be drunk at home.[115] She was discovered serving by the drink anyway, but she explained her reasons for doing so, as reported to the council: "She says that the people are now sitting in her house, and if she told them to go away it would be insulting and shameful. If they tell her to get something, she will. Two of them have been wounded and been healed by a doctor, and now the three of them are drinking in celebration of this—how could she tell them to leave?" Weary of arguing, the council finally gave her the license.[116]

Another Strasbourg woman asked to take over the license that had belonged to her mother but had lapsed because of failure to pay the required wine tax. She buttressed her argument with the fact that her husband had been forced to take work in Basel and they had been "so cruelly separated." The license would enable "we two young married persons to come together again and live in the blessed married state";

in this case as well, the council accepted her argument and granted the license.[117]

Once the license for a tavern had been given, the city council often limited other licenses in the area to assure the tavern-keeper of business. This did not stop other people from running taverns illegally, and the records are full of women, as well as men, ordered to close their unlicensed taverns.[118] The number increased whenever the number of potential customers increased, such as wartime when there were soldiers or refugees in a city. (War offered women a few opportunities, as well as many hardships). If a warning did not suffice, an official could go into a house or tavern and break all the wine jugs and even do this repeatedly until the tavern was closed. The tavern operators could be put in the stocks, jailed, forced to carry a stone around the public market, or even banished.[119]

Licensed tavern operators were frequently admonished for allowing unruly or disreputable elements into their taverns: "Frau Neuprot, the distributor of sweet wine [*Sussweinschenken*], who, in spite of a warning from the council, will not stop the disorder and nightly commotion at her place, is ordered to close her tavern completely and do no further business."[120] The Strasbourg council commented about another woman: "All kinds of rowdiness, fighting, and wantonness [*üppigkeit*] goes on at her place—besides, she stays open until midnight, beyond the curfew, and is open every day of the year."[121] Licensed operators were also accused of feeding and housing people in the tavern without a license to do so. Despite pleas that this happened without their knowledge or against their will—the men had simply passed out and could not be moved, or had secretly crawled into the attic—operators were usually allowed to feed only night watchmen who had come off their rounds and could get food nowhere else in town.[122]

Often the city council recognized that women accused of such things would simply deny what had happened or that they knew it was going on. In one case, the Strasbourg council specifically asked that only those neighbors be questioned who could be relied on not to warn the woman concerned. Apparently this failed, as she pretended to be ignorant and half-witted, and the council finally gave up on the charge.[123]

Feeding and housing people on a regular basis was the responsibility of the innkeepers, among whom were a number of women. They were responsible for feeding and caring for the horses of their guests as well and could be charged with neglect by an unhappy guest.[124] Innkeepers were not to take in peddlers or allow any merchant to sell anything from the inn; they were to send him instead to the man in charge of the market. City councils were very concerned

that innkeepers not take in suspicious persons of any type, which included "poor daughters who perform sinful work," "masterless servants," "disorderly people," and even "foreign widows with questionable reputations." [125] If an innkeeper took in a woman who seemed
honorable but who later was "suspected of immodesty because of her
unseemly company or other dishonorable or wanton conduct," she
was to be reported, or the innkeeper would be fined ten pounds, with
half the fine going to the person who reported her. In this case, the
council also noted, "Concerning this unknown woman who is wan-
dering around in such a disorderly manner: the first time she is to be
publicly thrown out of the city and the second time, either just driven
out of the city with a broom or have her nose cut off as well." [126]

Such restrictions made innkeepers think twice about taking in any
woman. A noblewoman asked the Strasbourg city council for permission to stay with friends in the city for a few days on business, although the council generally required all foreign visitors to stay in an
inn. It granted her request, with the justification "because it is difficult
for her as a woman to find any accommodations, as her husband is
not with her." [127] Even a married woman traveling alone was suspect
enough for the Strasbourg innkeepers.

A widow could usually continue operating an inn after her husband
died, as long as the taxes were paid and the house had a good reputation. Women could receive a license to operate an inn on their own as
well, although it was more difficult than receiving one to open a tavern; women thus often numbered among the illegal innkeepers found
during cities' periodic crackdowns. Once women were established as
innkeepers, they often became involved in a variety of other activities
besides simple innkeeping: housing troops during a war; storing confiscated grain or wine; housing people who had come into the city to
take medicinal baths; or money lending, either unknowingly, when
people left town without paying their bills, or knowingly, to pick up
a little extra income on the side. [128] When people refused to pay, the
woman was forced to act as a collection agent as well, in one instance
riding from Munich to Nuremberg for a 150-gulden debt. [129]

Besides these larger inns, smaller establishments existed in several
large cities to feed and house common and poor people, who were
often turned away from the large inns when they were overcrowded
or who could not pay the normal price. These were called "Garküche"
in Nuremberg, simply "sleeping houses" in Strasbourg, and offered
overnight accommodations and perhaps a simple cold meal. In 1532 in
Nuremberg 13 women, 4 men, and 32 couples were listed as running
such an inn, although their number declined slightly from then on. [130]

In many ways, the license to run a sleeping house was seen as yet
another means of supporting poor widows unable to do anything

else. Requests to the city council to be allowed to open one include the usual pleas of poverty, although the women could never say they were too disabled, for the work required some physical strength.[131] Instead they stressed their honorable lifestyle, good location, and large houses. The first was particularly important, and the woman's reputation was checked before such a license was granted.[132] In one case, her father's allowing "obviously drunk" people in after curfew was reason enough to deny a woman permission.[133] In another, a widow strengthened her request with the note that she had helped many sick people back to health and thus had beds available in her house; the council denied her permission to run a sleeping house but readily allowed her to go on taking in the sick.[134]

In the middle of the seventeenth century, the Strasbourg council decided some of the women who ran these sleeping houses were not acting with "proper modesty and decorum." They were taking in soldiers, students, and "all sorts of unmarried men," which led to "all kinds of wantonness, forbidden dancing, excessive drinking, eating, and carousing. Even more trouble and disorder may creep in as a result, through which their children and servants may be shamed and disgraced, and this city and its citizens get a bad reputation in other cities." The women were forbidden, under threat of a punishing fifty-pound fine, to take in soldiers or students. Exceptions were permitted only for those few "honorable and poor widows who have no other means of supporting themselves and their children." These widows would have to apply for special permission, and their reputations were to be thoroughly investigated before they would be allowed to take in boarders.[135]

## MARKET WOMEN

Along with the people who sold food and liquor, the marketplace of any early modern city was filled with women and men selling used merchandise of all types along with other small items. They received their merchandise from citizens who needed money, thus serving as pawnbrokers, and also when a person died and the household was being broken up. They are called a variety of things—*Keuflinnen, Gremperin, Kremerin, Täntlerin, Hockerin*—none of which translates very well into English. They were not simply peddlers or hawkers, nor were they true shopkeepers, for they sold from a small booth or stand, often no more than a bench to display their wares, not from a permanent store. Some cities divided them by exactly what kind of merchandise they sold or by what shape their booth or stand had, but these divisions are not really significant, as most regulations applied to all people who sold. For want of a better term, I call them all simply "market women."

This type of sales has been considered by a number of historians to be the most significant occupation open to women during the period. Heinrich Eckhert, in his study of the Krämers guild in southwestern Germany, finds more women in this than in any other occupation, and Helmut Wachendorf finds that there were women active at every level, from hawkers to passive investors in trading companies. Erich Maschke notes that retail sales saw even fiercer competition than long-distance trading, perhaps because there were so many women involved, and despite attempts to control it strictly. Inger Dübeck puts this in a negative light, noting that the conduct of Danish market women was "not all too flattering," particularly their attempts to fix prices and establish monopolies.[136] (These were common practices among male merchants as well, however, and do not really warrant special censure.) Luise Hess says it best: "We have here one of the most important occupations that the Middle Ages knew within its trade and industry. How gifted, farsighted, and intelligent must the medieval market woman have been, that she, a weak, legally hindered, and dependent woman was trusted with the goods and property of everyone."[137]

The importance of these women was recognized by early modern city councils as well as contemporary historians. They were often listed by name, so the city knew exactly who was to be selling. The earliest of these lists is from Frankfurt in 1359; on it, 30 male and 12 female names appear. The percentage of women increased throughout the fourteenth and fifteenth centuries, though the total number of salespeople decreased. A similar list from Nuremberg in 1396 includes 14 names, with the number there increasing to 111 by 1542 but dropping again to 48 by 1562; about one-half of those listed were widows.[138]

An early list from 1400 in Strasbourg divided the Gremper into three groups: those who had permanent stands at the market; those who sold at various places around the city, mostly near the gates; and those who could sell only from baskets or boxes without any permanent structure. The first group included 6 men and 8 women; the second, 17 women; and the third, at least 10 women, though the last pages of the list have been destroyed. They are identified in a variety of ways, either by their own first and last names; as someone's wife, daughter, or sister; or with a first name and then some identifying characteristic, as "Else from Eppisch" or "tall Agnes."[139] The city council simply used the names that these women were known by in their neighborhood.

The earliest list in Munich is from the sixteenth century and divides the Täntlerinnen into two groups, those who provided 100–gulden security, which included 1 man and 7 women, and those who provided 20–gulden security, which included 5 men and 40 women. These numbers remained roughly the same throughout the century. The Munich, Memmingen, and Frankfurt tax lists indicate that some of these women were the heads of their own households.[140] Similar numbers are to be found in other cities. The total number usually depended on how the city chose to list people, that is, whether all of those selling were listed or only those with permanent stands, but it always included a large percentage of women.[141]

These lists also include an ordinance, the earliest short and simple, and later ones much longer and more complicated as new problems arose. All ordinances are addressed to "male and female salespeople" or something similar, and oftentimes the order is reversed, "to female and male," as there were more women than men engaged in sales.[142] The 1362 ordinance for Strasbourg forbids market women to fix prices or make agreements with each other, to take more than a certain percentage as a commission for selling things, or to sell anything new. That from 1396 in Nuremberg stipulates that each woman had to pay a rental tax of one gulden annually on her stand and have two male citizens swear to her good character. A small tax like this was apparently common in most cities, as there are frequent requests from women that the rent on the stand be lowered because of difficulty paying it.[143] The first Munich ordinance from 1430 states simply that all salespeople are to be citizens, have their own household, and be married or a widow(er).[144]

During the last part of the fifteenth century, a number of cities expanded their ordinances. That from 1485 in Frankfurt forbade women who sold used clothing to sell harnesses or leather goods and required that "every third penny" they made be turned over to the city, an extremely high level of taxation.[145] Market women in Strasbourg were to collect the required taxes and tolls on all merchandise they sold and then turn these over to the city toll officer. This ordinance also gives an idea of the wide variety of merchandise these women handled: "flax; spindles; sacks with apples, cherries, or pears; short pieces of cloth; wooden dishes; glasses; ashes [for soapmaking]; doves; spoons; forks; and baskets."[146] They were forbidden to sell before eleven in the morning, or seven on market days, and specifically told not to "bring harm to anyone's honor," in other words, to call anyone names or accuse a person of anything.[147]

The Munich ordinance from 1488 and that from Nuremberg in 1504 both required that the market women—and men—prove they owned a certain amount of property as a guarantee. Those who owned at least 200 gulden in Nuremberg and 100 in Munich were allowed to sell silver dishes and jewelry, with no limit on the amount of merchandise they could sell. Those who provided only 20 gulden security could not sell things of great value and in Nuremberg could only sell up to 80 gulden worth of goods in any one day. All of them were forbidden to buy things for resale but required simply to take them on commission. All market women were to be especially suspicious of servants who brought them things to sell; they were to ask the servants where and from whom they had gotten them and why they wanted to sell them. Anything a market woman suspected was stolen was to be taken to the official in charge of the market before making any agreement to sell it.[148]

Augsburg ordinances from 1556 and 1567 and those from Frankfurt in 1594 and 1616 also specifically warned against taking any stolen goods and required 200 gulden security for all saleswomen, although this clearly did not include those who sold just a few things from small benches.[149] All these ordinances continued to require two citizens as witnesses to the woman's character and co-guarantors on her security. There is no record in any of these cities of witnesses actually required to pay back a woman's debts, however.[150]

There were also a number of restrictions on selling: the time of day was limited, usually to after ten or eleven in the morning; the number of days in the week was limited to two or three; the locations for selling were specified; and the length of time any piece of merchandise could be held was limited to a week or two. Councils tried to limit the total number of market women as well, although the attempts were never very effective.[151]

Despite all these restrictions, the number of women who wanted to get a market woman's stand or license always exceeded the number the city councils thought proper. Women thus had to appeal personally to the council and include special factors intended to swing the decision in their favor. The requests show what kind of women were favored. First of all, the woman had to be a citizen or the wife of one. She had to have the required amount of property and two persons who would swear in her behalf; it is surprising that in many cities these could be women or men, as long as they could prove they, too, had the required amount of property. Women often asked persons of high standing in the community, such as a doctor or schoolmaster, to do this for them or used their relatives if they were master craftsmen or of similar status. If the woman already knew a stand was vacant because the previous holder had died or was too old or ill to operate, she usually included the information in her request. Thus stands often passed from friend to friend, mother to daughter, or aunt to niece. Word of a vacant stand passed along the neighborhood grapevine, and then requests flooded in.[152]

Most applicants believed themselves more likely to get a stand if the council felt sorry for them, so they usually included how many children they had to support and how poor they were. Women who were widows always mentioned this fact, and a woman whose husband was still living had to explain why he could not support the family: he was too ill; business was bad in his particular craft; or he had deserted them. Many of these women were very poor, for they were receiving public support at the time of their request.[153] A woman's word alone was not always believed, however, leading the city council to investigate her claim.[154] In 1639 a cabinetmaker's wife in Strasbourg applied for a stand, saying that her husband could no longer support the family. On talking with her neighbors, the council found "that he could certainly support them if he would only work industriously, but he spends his time playing dice and drinking. He often throws his wife and children out of the house, but she is a bad housekeeper and would rather go out walking than do any work. She could make lace, and she could use the eldest of her two daughters to help her." Her request was denied.[155]

Most of the women who were able to get a stand were thus widows or the wives of craftsmen who were not very well off. A mid-sixteenth-century list from Munich confirms this. It includes 3 men with no other occupation; 8 widows, all of whose husbands had been day laborers or craftsmen; and 34 other women, 16 the wives of day laborers or men who "did nothing." Of the husbands who did have occupations listed, most were unskilled or semiskilled: woodcutters, basketmakers, shoerepairmen, hunters, and the like. Only two women were married to men in a major craft—one baker and one carpenter—and the latter woman is further identified as "Anna with the one foot," which might explain her case.[156]

Once a woman had received her stand—become "sworn" or "licensed"—she soon joined with other sworn market women to complain about those who were selling without licenses. In 1481 the Keuflinnen in Nuremberg complained, but the city council allowed some other women to sell at the market "as they have traditionally been allowed to."[157] Apparently this led to a great proliferation in women selling, for fifteen years later there was a crackdown, and everyone but the sworn Keuflinnen was forbidden to do business.[158] Gradually the rule was relaxed again, and "some old citizens' wives" were allowed to sell; this time the Keuflinnen complained of the "immorality and blasphemy" among these women and that the goods were being sold without anyone's knowing where they had come from. The council agreed, as it found "very many young, strong maids, half-grown daughters of citizens and foreigners, and so many self-sufficient women" were also at the market. A few women were still allowed to sell without being licensed, but only those who could prove their poverty to the council and could not do housework or find other employment. Even then, they were allowed to sell only if they had a special sign from the council, redated every year. If they received money through inheritance or some other way, this permission was taken from them.[159] Similar scenarios appear in every city, with the sworn saleswomen complaining, the city council first not acting on their complaints, then later deciding the situation had gotten out of hand and ordering everyone not licensed to cease selling.[160]

Anyone could sell his or her own merchandise, or have a servant sell it, as long as he or she reported first to the official in charge of the market and exhibited for him what he or she was selling. Occasionally women were also allowed to sell things they had made, like lace or other needlework, as long as they sold no other merchandise and were needy enough to warrant special consideration. City councils usually restricted the sale of such items only when they feared too many poor people might come into the city to do so and eventually end up needing public support.[161]

With the development of the printing industry and the resultant inexpensive books and pamphlets, a few women became involved in the book trade, although admittedly on a very small scale. The majority sold used books or small popular pamphlets along with other types of merchandise.[162] Some of them did become involved in the long-distance book trade, such as Margarethe Ugelheimer of Nuremberg, who continued her husband's book and art business from Venice after he died.[163] There were a few women printers, all widows or daughters of printers, although some of them carried on the shop after the master's death for many years.[164] Unfortunately there is too little information on most of these women to make generalizations about female printers and what they were printing. None of them ran afoul of the law, however, which implies that they were generally not handling controversial religious or political material.

The book dealers and peddlers did occasionally get into trouble for selling forbidden items. The material was usually confiscated, and for the first offense the woman was simply warned not to allow such things to be found in her shop again; for a second offense, or if the material was particularly controversial, the woman could also be imprisoned.[165] Female illustrators could also be punished for improper illustrations or working on a book that was itself censored.

Along with the sale of illicit books and pamphlets, illegal selling of all types went on regularly, despite attempts by city councils to forbid it. "Thieves' markets" sprang up from time to time, were closed down, opened up again in another place in town, and were closed down again. The market for used merchandise was always a good one.[166] Besides trying to weed out those who were selling without permission, the council had a difficult time trying to keep the licensed market women themselves following regulations.[167] They were admonished over and over to do business as their ordinances prescribed and were often accused of overcharging. Night sales were forbidden, as were sales in the early morning in the winter, in the belief that they were often carried out dishonestly under cover of darkness.[168]

There was a great concern about house-to-house selling (*hausieren*) throughout the period. Permission to do so was granted to only a few people and often taken from them again if the council thought they were abusing it.[169] Even carrying merchandise home for a customer was forbidden, as illicit goods could easily be slipped in. The concern over this type of sales is understandable; stands at the marketplace were in full view, and as each space was allotted, it was difficult to set up a stand with no one noticing. House-to-house sales, on the other hand, could be carried out by any sort of suspicious person, selling merchandise got from who knows where. Hygienic, symptuary, and censorship laws could be broken with forbidden merchandise.[170] Unfortunately for the councils, illegal house-to-house selling was difficult to control because of its very fluidity. Despite repeated complaints by the licensed market women that it was cutting into their business and repeated attempts to crack down, it met an obvious need and continued to flourish.

During times of emergency the councils placed other restrictions on how and what the market women could sell. For both health and protectionist reasons, they were ordered to report to the official in charge of the market when they were selling the goods of a foreigner rather than a citizen. During outbreaks of the plague, they were flatly forbidden to sell clothing or bed linen from sick people, or at least required to wash it before selling, which was not a normal practice when selling used merchandise. If there was plague in a nearby area but not in the city itself, they were ordered not to buy or sell any clothing or linen that had come in from the outside. Only things approved by the market bailiff as not coming from a "suspicious or unhealthy" place or an infected person could be sold. Innkeepers and tavern operators were also ordered to watch people who came into the city to make sure they did not sell anything.[171]

Not only did the market woman have to prove that her merchandise was not infected, she also had to prove that she had received it from its rightful owner and from people willing to sell. Booty soldiers brought in during times of war was strictly prohibited, with a woman to lose her stand were she discovered with such items. Occasionally the heirs of an estate would claim ownership and halt sales, forcing the goods to be returned to them. The market women themselves were not without rights, however; people who wanted their merchandise back had to prove they had been coerced into giving it up.[172]

In sales of clothing and other small items, small offenses often brought sharp punishment. Women were sentenced to the stocks, jailed, forced to carry stone collars around the marketplace, removed from their stands, or even banished for what seem to be minor infractions of their ordinances.[173] At one point in Nuremberg they were forbidden to sit while selling, as the council suspected they could hide prohibited products under their long skirts when seated. Some of this severity is understandable, as the market women often had the opportunity to deal in stolen merchandise and occasionally did. Any woman suspected of receiving stolen goods was called in for questioning, even if nothing incriminating had been found at her stand. All of them were informed whenever a robbery had occurred, and all were to bring any silver or gold items anyone brought them to the market bailiff for inspection before reselling them.[174]

Councils also tried to limit the straight pawnbroking activities of these women. Officially they were not to pay anyone for their goods until they had sold them, but they frequently loaned someone money with the goods serving as security, either holding the goods for a limited time until the loan could be repaid or else selling them immediately. The divisions between moneylender, pawnbroker, and used-clothing dealer were very fluid, and cities often simply gave up on their attempts to prohibit these women from petty moneylending. They even ordered borrowers to repay the women as agreed, despite the fact that such moneylending was officially prohibited.[175] It is interesting that some of these women produced written records to prove what they had lent out, including debts that were as much as five years old, so some at least had fairly good record-keeping systems.

The market women often came into conflict with other groups which claimed they were selling merchandise not allowed them. Cities relaxed their restrictions on selling once or twice during the year, during special fairs or festivals, and the women sold metalwork, spices, weapons, furs, new clothing, and glass along with their usual wares. They often kept selling these extras once the fair was over, until the group who normally sold them—tinsmiths, spice dealers, armamentmakers, furriers, tailors, or whoever—complained. The city council then examined the case, usually ordering the women to stop selling but occasionally allowing them to continue if they were very poor, sold only a few items, or sold something not made in the city, like a certain kind of toy or oil. If the women were found selling something which required reworking or preparation or could be falsified easily, like metals or spices, cities were particularly firm in their prohibitions. Even if the women offered to have a master from the appropriate craft check what they were selling for quality or purity, they were usually forbidden to sell things outside their normal range.[176]

Their most frequent disputes were with tailors, who charged them with selling new clothing but who were in turn charged by the saleswomen with selling used clothing, which was also not allowed. City councils ordered investigations of the women's booths and the tailors' shops to see if the charges were true and wearily ordered both sides to make peace with one another if no offending items were found.[177]

In these conflicts the women used a wide variety of arguments and tactics to win their cases. They used rivalries and jealousies between guilds, often selling something that two different guilds thought they had the sole right to and then turning the two guilds against each other when the case came up. They used conflicts between the city council and the guilds, turning to the council for protection from overzealous guild masters. They used geographic conflicts within the city, selling from a place selling was not allowed while knowing that the residents in that area would not complain or would even defend them because they wanted a market in that part of the city as well. As a last resort, the women used pleas of their own helplessness and incompetence, arguing that they could do nothing else and that their business was so small they could not possibly be hurting anyone by it.

Their businesses may have been small, but these women were far from helpless or reticent. Not only did they quickly bring to court anyone they considered to be intruding on their territory, but they were also very frequently involved in slander and defamation cases. They called other women and men names—asshole, whore, and thief were the most common—and then refused to apologize until the case had gone all the way to the city's highest court.[178] Even then, the woman's husband often came in first, pleading that she was "only an irrational woman, who lets talk flow so freely and unguardedly out of her mouth without thinking about it"; not until a fine was set did the woman herself come in, and then simply to ask that the fine be reduced.[179] In one case in Strasbourg, only after three weeks in prison on bread and water did the woman apologize and agree to mutter the formulaic "I know nothing but good and honor about this person."[180]

Along with all their activities at the marketplaces, honorable and licit or dishonorable and illegal, the market women were also responsible for taking inventories. An inventory of property and household goods was usually taken on all deaths, whether the person was married or single, male or female, young or old. It did not matter if there was no dispute between heirs or if there were no heirs at all. Nor did the size of the estate matter; inventories are recorded for servants who lived in one room and who owned nothing more than old clothing.[181]

Not only citizens, but also anyone passing through the city, might have an inventory taken. In 1547, for example, a French ambassador's cook was taken ill and left behind in Nuremberg when the party returned to France. Although he spoke no German, so no one could find out his name, on his death in an inn, a woman was sent in to appraise his belongings. She found a saddle, horse and trappings, some cases, and clothes, all of which she later sold to pay the innkeeper, a tailor for burial clothes, the gravediggers, and herself. Inventories of other travellers who died in various inns and those who died in city hospitals are also recorded.[182]

Inventories were also taken when anyone married a second time, to list what he or she brought into the marriage. This was done to prevent children from the first marriage from trying to lay claim to the inheritance of those from the second marriage, and vice versa. In several cases, inventories were also ordered when people were suspected of financial irresponsibility, of illegally using up their children's rightful inheritance after the death of a spouse.[183]

The items are listed right down to the penny, for example, "two tablecloths valued at forty pfennige, three old pillows at fourteen pfennige, four dishcloths at three pfennige"; "in cash there is nothing more on hand than five pfenninge."[184] Inventories were to be taken immediately after death but were often not entered into the records until the children came of age or married and the goods were to be divided. The actual list of items either remained with the family involved until it was officially entered into the records or was kept by the appraiser herself as a rough draft until she wrote up the final copy. If an inventory was not taken immediately, the surviving spouse had to account for all that had been spent or accumulated since the death, no matter how small. A widow had spent nearly all the estate to pay off debts yet still felt obliged to comment in her inventory "the little bit more that was left at my husband's demise has been used up in the five weeks since for food and drink."[185]

The surviving spouse, heirs, or their guardians enlisted the services of an appraiser to carry out this inventory and appraisal. Particularly with larger houses, she went room to room, noting all the contents and an estimation of the value of each piece. Metal objects, such as dishes, silverware, candleholders, and utensils, were divided by type of metal, weighed, and then valued according to the weight, for example, so many pounds of pewter, so many of brass, so many of silver. Wooden utensils, cloth, and linens were often appraised together, but otherwise each item was listed individually. Inventories of large estates often cover twenty to thirty folio pages, while some take less than a paragraph or have debts much larger than the value of the goods left behind.[186]

For very large estates, which included holdings in houses, workshops, fields, and woods, a male appraiser was often called in to judge the value of the immovable property, along with a female appraiser responsible for the household goods. If a workshop was being sold, a master of the appropriate craft could also be called in, to give advice on the value of tools and technical items with which the woman was unfamiliar.

The expertise these women needed was quite amazing. They not only had to know the value of every conceivable household item or article of clothing, of any age, quality, or source, but of jewelry, art objects, armor and weaponry, and raw materials as well. They also appraised books, either judging their total value or else singling out the most valuable ones and appraising them separately. This latter was especially necessary when the person who had died was a printer or bookbinder with a large stock left at his death.[187]

These appraisers were clearly literate, as payments to them were often listed "for apraising and recording" and they were sometimes hired to make extra copies of wills or appraisals if someone from the family wanted them. During the early seventeenth century some of them began a double-entry system if the estate was to be sold, listing not only an appraised price but also the price for which the items were actually sold.[188] The sale price was, it is interesting to note, always higher than the appraised price, which may have been due either to the practice of appraising low or a good market for used merchandise.

Payments for appraisal varied widely depending on the size of the estate and the length of time the job took. Appraisers were specifically ordered to appraise small estates whenever they were asked to and not wait for larger ones, for which they would be paid more. Cities limited the amount the appraisers could charge for each day they worked, although they were also expected to be given food and drink as part of their salary.[189] Of course, if they then sold all or part of the estate at the public market, they received their normal commission in addition to what they were paid for the appraisal.

The testimony of an appraiser was often included in the sale of a house or shop with all its contents, which could take place after a death when there were no heirs, or when someone was forced to sell because of debt. When smaller debts were paid off in merchandise rather than cash, an appraiser was also called in to make sure neither party was being cheated. In such cases, she had to swear that she had favored neither party nor had even been in contact with them before the agreement was made.[190]

Judging by the records in Nuremberg, where there is the best information about appraisal, there was a decline in the importance of female appraisers after about 1565. Fewer and fewer inventories mention them, and they disappeared completely from the lists of sworn city officials. This may in part be the result of the sources, as most of the inventories that survive from after that date involve ownership of land and a house or other buildings, for which the appraisal was done by a man. This cannot be the full explanation, however, for some small estates with no house or property were also handled by male appraisers after 1565. Previously all appraisal of movables had been handled by women, even if a man had appraised the house and land.

1564 is an important date in the legal history of Nuremberg, for a reformation of the city's law code was published in that year. A clue to the shift away from female appraisers may be found in its provisions dealing with inventories, which set up a tighter system.[191] Inventories were to be taken within one month after a death and were not to take more than two months, so that they were to be finished three months after any death. The living spouse was not bound to pay the creditors any more than was in the inventory, a sort of bankruptcy clause; also the creditors could not claim any debts before the inventory was completed. If someone willfully hid something, he or she was required to pay all debts and could not declare bankruptcy. If the heirs did not want the inheritance, they were not bound to take an inventory and thus not bound to pay off debts. All inventories had to be signed by two council members and brought before the council.

These last two clauses could definitely have had an effect on the activities of the female appraisers. Once heirs were given the option not to take an inventory if they foresaw nothing or very little left after debts had been paid off, they would not be likely to bother for very small estates, which make up so many of the earlier inventories. It would then be up to the creditors to claim some of what was left and the courts to decide how to divide it. Either they did not take systematic inventories to accomplish this, or they are no longer extant. If an inventory was not taken, it would have been the creditors' problem to find someone to sell off the estate and liquidate the capital, another reason for an heir simply not bothering to take an inventory.

The fact that an inventory now had to be signed by two council members also points to a general trend which adversely affected female appraisers. After the 1560s the presence of the guardians (*Vormunder*) became much more noticeable in inventories and wills in every city, especially if it was the husband who had died. These guardians were appointed by the city council when either parent died. It is often hard to determine without careful reading if the widow was even still alive, as the inventories were all now brought by the guardians, whereas earlier they invariably began, "I, Frau So and So, on the death of my husband. . . ." Even if the husband was the survivor, his children's guardians, often relatives of their mother, had to agree in writing to all clauses in the inventory.

Inventories began to include stipulations about the raising of children, giving the guardians rights to intervene even if the father was the surviving parent. The following is a good example:

> Hans Maier must raise his little daughter and provide her with the necessary food and clothing until she has reached her twelfth year and reaches maturity. If, however, Hans Maier does not support his child as she deserves and grievances arise on her account, the guardians shall have the power to take away the child (when she has not been reasonably cared for) from the father and send her elsewhere where she can be cared for according to her needs. This is with the stipulation that the father still provides the money for board, room, and upbringing, as he himself has offered and agreed to do.[192]

Even if the estate was very small, widows and widowers were required to provide a "suitable dowry" for daughters of marriageable age. In a few cases when the surviving spouse had left town and abandoned the children—in one the widow is described as a "wanton spendthrift"—the guardians alone had the inventory drawn up and made no attempt to find the errant parent.[193]

Gradually the practice evolved, perhaps spurred by frequent quarrels between the heirs, of having two men take the inventory, rather than a female appraiser, one appointed by each side, that is, the children's guardians and the living spouse. These male appraisers came to be considered actual city officials and are listed each year alongside fire inspectors, grain weighers, night watchmen, and the like in Nuremberg's register of officials. This probably meant they received a salary from the city, not solely from their customers, which would have made them less open to bribery, but there are no records of the exact amounts.

The movement away from female appraisers is not complete, however, for even after 1565 they were used for some inventories, including some which were very large.[194] Rather, there was a gradual trend toward more legalistic inventories taken by sworn men who could appear in court to defend them if there was a controversy; their word was more likely to be taken at face value by the council members demanded by the city's new law code than that of a female appraiser. She was occasionally suspected of taking bribes to supplement her income and not reporting all property to the benefit of the surviving spouse. This ties in with the rising importance of guardians, who were rarely mentioned in earlier inventories and were always male citizens.

As in other areas, increasing regulation, control, and structure in appraising and the taking of inventories led to a decrease in women's activity. With more elaborate legal language necessary in the inventories and with the clause allowing the heirs not to take an inventory if they foresaw no estate after debts, the demand for female appraisers dropped dramatically. These women certainly did not withdraw from the economic life of the city, however, but returned to the marketplace and concentrated all their attention on selling.

# Der Schellenmacher.

Ich aber bin ein Schellenmachr/
Zu Preng vnd Narrnweiß ein vrsachr/
Mach Zimbel Schellen/groß vnd klein/
Zum Schlittenzeug / sauber vnd rein/
Auch wol gestimbt auff die Stech Bahn/
Darzu Schelln für den Prittschenmann/
Auch Schellen an die Narren Kappn/
Darmits zu Faßnacht vmbher sappn.

*A Bellmaker's Wife Assisting in Production. Woodcut by J. Am-
mann from* Beschreibung aller Stände *(Frankfurt, 1568).*

# CHAPTER FIVE
# Guilds, Crafts, and Market Production

The most difficult area of the economy to explore in terms of women's work is production. One would at first assume the opposite, as many more sources exist about production—more ordinances, court cases, disputes—than about sales or services. Because of this wealth of material, more studies have been made of production in general, or of one particular craft, than of other areas of the economy. Most of these, however, both original sources and secondary studies, are totally silent about women. One could easily assume, as some authors have, that women were simply not involved in production at all.

Digging a little deeper and doing some reading between the lines of the ordinances gives a different picture. Looking inside any workshop, at the people actually working there as well as the man in charge, one finds a huge number of women. In guild shops, the master's wife, daughters, and maids often worked alongside his journeymen and apprentices, and his widow ran the shop after his death. In production organized by merchant capitalists, all members of a household might work making thread or cloth, or women might work alone while their fathers or husbands were involved in another occupation.

During the medieval period, production in all cities can be divided into two basic types, that which was free and theoretically open to any resident and that which was highly organized and regulated. Because of the nature of the first type, free and open, there is little specific information about it, but it is certain that women were involved because of their occupational labels on tax rolls.[1] Most of these "free arts" required little training, and their products were cheap and simple: wooden bowls and spoons, brushes, brooms, combs, and the like. The men and women who made them often did so as a secondary occupation, after their work as day laborers was over or during winter when there was less work available. Occasionally the people who made one of these products attempted to organize and exclude others, but the city councils usually prohibited this, as they wanted some simple occupations open to all.

There is much more information about the second type, the organized crafts. Beginning as early as the twelfth century in many cities, certain crafts began to form themselves into guilds, which set quality standards for their particular product and regulated the size of workshops, the training period, and the conduct of their members. In most cities individual guilds achieved a monopoly in the production and sales of one particular product. If one wanted to become a shoemaker, for instance, one spent about seven years as an apprentice, then at least that long as a journeyman, working in the shop of a master shoemaker, after which one could theoretically make one's masterpiece. If the masterpiece was approved by the other master shoemakers and if they thought the market for shoes large enough in their town to allow for another shoemaker, one could then become a master. In some cities each craft formed a totally separate guild, with more than one hundred different guilds in the town, while in other cities guilds combined together to form larger units.

As these guilds grew in economic power, they began to demand a share of the political power in the city and thus came into conflict with the city councils, which were usually made up of the city's major merchants, bankers, and property holders. This conflict went on for centuries in most cities, and in some, the guilds triumphed, taking over control of the city's political as well as economic life. In others, the council triumphed, reducing the guilds to dependent bodies and retaining the final say in the decisions. In still others a compromise was reached whereby the guilds were allowed some members on the city council and the council, some power over the guilds. The different results of this conflict in each city have been dealt with extensively in general histories of the crafts and in city histories and are very important to take into consideration when studying economic and political developments.

Surprisingly, in terms of women's work, however, this made no difference at all. The attitude of the crafts toward women varied from city to city and from craft to craft but did not depend on the general political power of the crafts in the cities. Nor was their ability to exclude women (which was a major aim of many crafts during the sixteenth and seventeenth centuries) solely dependent on their power and independence but on a variety of other factors as well. The specific organization of the crafts in each city—whether they were combined into a small number of large guilds or whether each craft was a totally separate body—also made no significant difference. One can generalize about women's work in the crafts more safely than about the crafts themselves.

The earliest craft ordinances, from the fourteenth and early fifteenth century, often mention both male and female masters, although it is difficult to tell if these women had been trained independently in all cases or were actually masters' widows. In some guilds the women had been trained on their own, as the ordinances regulating apprentices talk about both boys and girls. If a woman was in charge of a workshop, she had to pay whatever fees and taxes were normally required, in some cities even provide a horse and rider for the city's defense. She was not expected to bear arms herself, but then, neither were older masters. She was expected to help repair city walls and defensive works or send members of her household to do so. In general, these female masters had to carry out all the normal duties of a citizen themselves or pay someone to carry them out for them.[2]

Most of the crafts which mention female masters and apprentices are those which require nimble hands, not great strength—weaving, needlemaking, yarn spinning, hatmaking, and tailoring—but none of these early ordinances in any craft forbid women's work per se. Even in the heaviest industries, like ironmaking and roofing, masters' widows ran the shop for as much as fifteen or twenty years after the death of their husbands. Of course most of the workshops were run by men, but those run by widows and other women often made up as much as 10–15 percent in some crafts.[3]

Beginning in the mid-fifteenth century, many crafts expanded their ordinances, explicitly discussing certain things which had not been mentioned before and reediting them to conform to current practices. In many of these ordinances the words "female master" and "girl apprentice" were simply dropped, with no discussion of why this was done, which probably indicates that the ordinances were describing the actual situation and not introducing something new. The only woman explicitly mentioned in many of these ordinances was the master's widow, and her right to run the shop was usually limited. Previously she had apparently been allowed to carry on as long as she wanted, for there were no restrictions on her work in the earlier ordinances. As E. William Monter notes for Geneva: "Geneva's guild regulations thus handicapped female artisans more effectively than her social customs handicapped businesswomen."[4]

I begin my more thorough examination of women's work in production at just this point, at the time of the first restrictions. As most production continued to be carried out by guilds or organized crafts throughout the early modern period, the bulk of the chapter focuses on women's work in this type of workshop. The women involved must really be divided into four different groups, for their functions within the workshop and their ability to work varied with their status. The first group consists of masters' wives and daughters; the second, of masters' widows; the third, of maids and other female employees in the shop; and the fourth, of women working independently at a craft. These women were differentiated not by their level of training, as males working in the crafts were, but by their relationship or lack of relationship to a master craftsman. When merchant capitalists began to hire workers and households, a woman's relationship to male workers was no longer important; women's work in the new capitalist industries is thus the subject of the last section, that on women working independently.

## MASTERS' WIVES AND DAUGHTERS

The most important woman in any workshop was the master's wife. As Alice Clark notes, "The assistance of a wife was often so important in her husband's business that she engaged servants to free her from household drudgery, her own productive capacity being greater than the cost of a servant's wages."[5] Recognizing this, most crafts required that master craftsmen be married. A journeyman could make his masterpiece whether he was married or not, but he had to be married and a citizen before he could practice as a master and own a shop. His choice of a wife had to be made very carefully, however, for like the male members of a sworn craft or guild, all wives had to be of legitimate birth and have an "honorable" lifestyle. The letters proving this became more and more complicated. Not only did the letter have to contain when and where a woman's parents had been married but also who the clergyman was and who had been in attendance, so that suspicious crafts could check on the authenticity. Later such letters often had to contain a sworn statement by two male citizens that the woman had been born legitimately and that she had always maintained an "honorable" lifestyle.[6] A woman was also responsible for the behavior of her parents. Even if her father had been a craftsman, if he had acted dishonorably in any way, she was suspect and would often not be married. Women often tried to argue that they had been small children and could not have prevented their parents' misconduct, but then the crafts simply resorted to a "bad blood" argument.[7]

Crafts were concerned not only with the family background but also with the conduct and morality of master and wife. A couple whose first child was born too early in their marriage was often expelled, and appeals went all the way to the emperor, though the cities and both Protestant and Catholic churches accepted such children as fully legitimate.[8] Occasionally this concern was carried to what seem to be bizarre extremes. The shoemaker's guild in Bremen, for example, appears to have had the right physically to examine the wife of a shoemaker before the couple's first copulation to see if she was a virgin or not. In the words of the ordinance, which are, admittedly, confusing, the two youngest guild officials "sit the bride on the bed, and the sworn guild officials, with the hand they have sworn their oath with, touch or grab, as a sign of her undisturbed virginity." Following this, the young couple had to provide the two officials with a meal![9] Some authors have interpreted this to mean that the officials actually touched her sexual organs, which, given the fact that contemporary doctors did not go that far when making diagnoses, seems highly unlikely. Whatever it was the officials actually touched or grabbed, however, the crafts' close involvement and interest in the most intimate personal details of the lives of its members comes out clearly.

The crafts were much more strict than city councils or even the churches in regulating their members' conduct. A man who had committed adultery was usually immediately expelled; if his wife was guilty and he decided to go on living with her, he was also thrown out. Such cases appeared often before city courts, which had to decide between keeping households and marriages together and keeping the guilds happy; they usually decided in favor of the household and ordered the crafts to take such masters back. Even when they grudgingly agreed to do so, the craft usually at least forbade the guilty woman to accompany her husband to any public functions and often tried to deny her widows' rights or deny her children entrance rights to the guild.[10]

Although there were stringent regulations about the general conduct of a master's wife, there was generally no restriction on the work she could do in the shop. City councils did not feel they could intrude here, nor did other masters bring complaints that a wife was working too much. In general, wives seem to have been responsible for selling the merchandise their husbands made and often for collecting debts and keeping the books as well. Many of the debts owed to craftsmen listed in inventories are actually noted as owed to their wives, for example, "to the cooper's wife for six barrels."[11] Wives, as well as husbands, were held responsible for the payment of fees and taxes and for the quality of the product. In some cases, if the wife was put in the stocks or imprisoned for any infraction, the shop was not to operate until she was released.[12]

Often a wife's dedication to the business exceeded that of her husband. In 1505 Agnes Frey Dürer stayed in Nuremberg during an outbreak of the plague while Dürer himself fled to Venice, because she thought life in Venice too expensive and she had to sell his works in the city and at the Frankfurt Fair.[13] After Dürer's death she also refused to give away any works he had apparently promised to various people and demanded that they pay her for them. Nuremberg leaders and humanists, especially Lazarus Spengler, never forgave her for this and described her in their letters and writings in most ungracious terms.

Masters' wives were also very eager to have their sons accepted into the craft. They often brought appeals to the city council arguing that their sons were being illegally excluded, and one mother went so far as to forge the document proving her son was legitimate.[14] A mother's dedication could be too smothering, however, as in one case involving the Strasbourg barbers. A barber's widow asked to be allowed to continue the shop with her son as an assistant, but permission was denied by both the barbers and the city council because the son "had never properly learned the trade of barbering because he has never stayed with one master but has been locked to his mother by her misraising of him."[15]

Besides handling incoming payments, the wife was also responsible for purchases and the distribution of salaries and food to journeymen. As Natalie Davis notes, this latter function often brought her into conflict with the journeymen, who were prone to suspect she was watering the wine or in other ways shortchanging them.[16] All of these functions meant she could be dealing with large amounts of money and probably kept an account of expenditures for various items and services.[17]

If city councils decided the wives were becoming unruly in their sales methods and conduct, they restricted or even forbade their activity until they settled down. In Nuremberg, for example, the furriers' wives were often admonished about "the numerous quarrels, disputes, and brawls" at the furriers' trading house.[18] Any woman who shouted, swore, denounced another's products, or refused to allow another to sell was to be excluded and fined.[19]

In special cases, city councils gave women permission to operate shops in the prolonged absence or during illness of their husbands. Special permission was especially likely in times of war but could also be granted if the man were imprisoned or banished. Often the crafts objected because they thought it damaged the reputation of their craft

to have the wife of a criminal continue to operate. The councils usually overrode these objections, as they realized the woman might
be forced to seek public support if she could not keep running the
shop.[20]

In general, then, master's wives were free to do what they could or
wanted to in running the shop. Two cases from the seventeenth century did restrict their work somewhat and are worth looking into in
some detail, as the reasons for these restrictions were given quite
clearly. In 1605 in Memmingen the wife and daughter of a glazier were
forbidden to do any work outside their own home; the wife complied
with the order; the daughter did not. Her father then wrote to a mayor
of Freiburg in Breisgau asking his opinion on the matter and received
the answer "that no one should be forbidden to use his children to
help him in his craft either inside or outside his house." The father
included this opinion in his letter to the city council, asking that his
daughter be allowed to continue working with him until she got married "because it is normal for the unmarried daughters of other master
craftsmen as well, such as furriers, tailors, and cabinetmakers, to
work outside as well as inside their homes." He agreed with the prohibition on his wife's work, for she had broken some of the articles of
the glaziers' ordinance by running from house to house offering her
services, but he did not agree to a general prohibition of the work of
wives.[21]

The other glaziers answered that they had already forbidden foreign
journeymen to work in Memmingen and certainly were not going to
allow "some female persons" to work, as it might harm opportunities
for masters' sons. They noted his wife had not been forbidden to work
because she had broken the ordinance, "because none of the articles
apply to women, so she can't be punished for breaking them"; she had
been forbidden because all women were forbidden to do outside work.
The daughter in question was also now old enough to marry, according to the other glaziers, so she should do so and support herself in
that way, not by taking work away from masters' sons. The Freiburg
mayor, they concluded, had really meant only sons when he had referred to "children." These arguments were effective with the city
council, which flatly prohibited all glaziers to use their wives or
daughters to help them with outside work. Apparently the council's
sense of propriety was offended at seeing women working on ladders,
for this restriction was not extended to work in the shop nor to a
woman helping her husband or father outside the house in another
occupation.[22]

The second case is decidedly more complicated. In 1694 the journeyman cordmakers in Frankfurt had reported that other cities in the

empire did not allow daughters to work, so the city council prohibited this in Frankfurt as well. Two years later, the master cordmakers charged that this report was false, that the journeymen had lied. They strengthened their claim with letters from the Ulm and Nuremberg councils, saying that they could not understand why Frankfurt had prohibited wives and daughters from working, as all other crafts allowed this and as even the Bible stated clearly that woman was to be the helpmate of man. The masters also noted that times were hard and that especially the poorer masters would have to be given public support if they could not use their wives and daughters to help them. This was a convincing argument with the Frankfurt council, and women were allowed to work again. The case ends on a rather unhappy note for these women, however, with the council's calling for further investigation of where the journeymen had gotten their information. The council commented that the prohibition of masters' daughters or even wives working did not seem so outrageous. If this was the case elsewhere in some crafts, they did not want Frankfurt to be the exception.[23]

This case is a good example of two things seen in many of the added restrictions on women's work in the crafts during the seventeenth century. The attack was led by journeymen, who were willing to lie in their attempts to get women excluded, and the city council was always concerned to do what other cities were doing and not deviate from the general pattern in any way.[24] Although in this case the council's concern worked to the women's advantage, in most cases it did not, for once one city had placed some kind of a limitation on women's work, others were quick to follow.

Both cases involve masters' daughters, who made a more complicated problem for crafts than masters' wives. In general, as the above cases show, an unmarried daughter was allowed to work in her father's shop and was not restricted as to what she could do there.[25] If she married outside the craft, she was usually prohibited from working any longer, although not always. If she continued paying the normal guild fees and the guild itself did not object, a daughter often continued working after her marriage, especially in crafts that did not require many tools, such as bagmaking or tailoring. Even if the guild objected, she was occasionally given special permission to work if she was poor or had to support an elderly parent who could no longer work. Then she was strictly forbidden to use anyone to assist her, with provision that the permission would be retracted if it were discovered her husband or maid was helping her.[26]

As the glaziers in Memmingen stated in the case above, guilds would rather that their masters' daughters married than that they worked on their own. To attract prospective husbands, they usually lowered the entrance fee a journeyman had to pay or shortened the length of time required before he could make a masterpiece, provided he marry a master's daughter. In some cities, even if a daughter had first been married to someone outside the craft, her second husband could also enter her father's guild more easily or cheaply than normal. A master's son marrying a master's daughter from the same craft paid a still smaller entrance fee, in some cases even being taken in free of charge. Thus, guilds objected when part of their membership wanted to split off for one reason or another, as when the painters in Lübeck wanted to leave the glassmakers' guild. The glassmakers would not allow it, specifically because then their sons and daughters would have fewer marriage partners to choose from from within the same guild.[27]

Generally a journeyman who married a daughter—or widow—of a master was not counted in the at-times-very-limited number of new masters allowed into a craft each year, for he was not establishing a new workshop but simply taking over an existing one. As the vitality of certain crafts declined in an area, no new masters were let in at all, making marriage to a daughter or widow the only way a journeyman could establish his own shop.[28] This membership restricting happened throughout Europe during the sixteenth century, although city councils tried to fight it, believing it not for the "common good." They usually tried to force guilds to allow people in without marrying in, although they were not always very successful.

## Masters' Widows

With the death of the master craftsman, the status of the women working in his shop changed immediately. His wife was most directly affected, for the most common restrictions were those on masters' widows. The earliest guild ordinances made no mention at all of widows, who seem to have had unrestricted rights to carry on a husband's shop after his death, or at least as long as they remained unmarried.[29] Beginning in the mid-fifteenth century, however, the time a widow was allowed to continue operating the shop was limited, first usually to one or two years, later to as little as two months. In other cases, she was limited to only finishing work already begun or only allowed to work at all if there was a son who could possibly inherit the shop. If she remarried fairly soon, she might even be forbidden to sell what her first husband had made if the second was not in the same guild.[30]

Generally by the mid-sixteenth century, widows in most crafts could no longer take on apprentices or retain more than one or two journeymen. They could not hire any new journeymen or additional pieceworkers or, in some cases, buy any new raw materials. By the seventeenth century some guilds flatly forbade widows to use any journeymen at all, in an attempt to keep their shops as small as possible.[31] Sometimes restrictions on widows' work came in under the guise of technological improvement. For example, a new dyeing process was introduced in sixteenth-century Lübeck; in 1546 the city council there allowed the old dyers to continue working but not their widows. Only men who had been trained in the new techniques were to be allowed to dye cloth after the old dyers had all died out.[32]

It is no surprise that widows as a rule ran smaller workshops and had a smaller income, even when allowed to continue to work independently. Claus-Peter Clasen, in his recent study of the Augsburg weavers around 1600, finds that 15 percent of the master weavers were women but that they employed only 5 percent of the journeymen and assistants.[33] Widows in the iron industry in Nuremberg usually paid much lower taxes than masters did, which means they had a lower income.[34] Over two-thirds of the widows paid the smallest amount of taxes, a statistic repeated in other cities as well, at a time when 20–25 percent of the households in most cities were headed by women, most of them widows.[35]

Widows were quickly denied the right to continue working if there was any suspicion of immoral or dishonorable conduct on their part. They were most often accused of having sexual relations with one of the journeymen, for which one or both could be banished.[36] This measure was justified as a protection for widows from the duplicity of their journeymen, who used this means to force them into marriage so that they could take over the shop in their own right. Why the unfortunate widow as well as the conniving journeyman was to be banished is never explained.

None of these restrictions was absolute, however, and city council records are full of requests by widows that they be freed from the normal restrictions for one reason or another. Each request was considered separately, and it is difficult to discern a pattern in which were accepted and which not. The widows' requests, however, do show what lines of argument they thought might be effective. First of all, the widow usually stressed her age and infirmity, pointing out that she had no other possible means of support and that she would not be working very long anyway "because death will soon be a visitor." If she could not use old age as grounds for special treatment, then she usually mentioned the number of children she had or noted that her aged parents were dependent on her for support.[37]

Also, the widow always downplayed the amount of goods she would be making, pointing out that such a small amount could not possibly harm the guild concerned. The guild's opposition to her arose, out of "misunderstanding and envy," not from a true assessment of the situation.[38] Could she help it if her products were better than those made by other masters, and so customers came to her? She often noted as well that others were already selling what she wanted to sell, hinting that this was really a "free art" and not properly under the control of any guild. Another ploy frequently used was asserting that the guild could not supply enough of the items concerned to keep up with the demand for them in the city; this argument was most often used in times of war by a widow who wanted to make and sell military equipment.[39]

When asking to be allowed to retain a larger number of apprentices or journeymen than usual, she stressed that the apprentices were almost through with their training and were "beloved by the whole family" and that the journeyman was ready to make his masterpiece and take over the shop by marrying her. Only her "sorrow and modesty" prevented her from marrying a journeyman right away, as her first husband had only "so recently gone to his grave."[40] At the end, the widow threw herself on the mercy of the council "as the protector and shield of poor widows and orphans," begging for Christian charity and pleading that no one else would understand her problems.[41] This tactic was often successful, leading the council to justify its decision by noting that "we believe it is always better that one supports oneself than comes to the council for public charity."[42]

There are no limits to the rhetoric widows used to gain a special dispensation, as shown in the following letter from a wool-weaver's widow in Frankfurt, asking that her apprentice be allowed to remain with her though there was no master in the shop:

> How heavy and hard the hand of God, himself burdened with the cross, has come down on me, and in what a pitiful situation I find myself after the all-too-sudden death of my late husband, with my young and helpless child still nursing at my breast. My situation is known widely everywhere, and certainly well-known by you, the honorable and generous council.
> Although most Christian hearts, recognizing my misfortune, would let me go on in my occupation and livelihood and earn my meager piece of bread, the heads of the wool-weavers guild came to me, in my own house, right after my late husband's death, at the time of my greatest sorrow, and contrary to all Christian love, ordered me, with harsh and importune words, to slow down in my work. Then they ordered my apprentice, who had been raised by us at great cost and

was only beginning to be of use in the craft, to leave my workshop and go to one of theirs, under the pretense that there was no master in the shop so he could not complete his training. This was very beneficial to them, but very harmful to me.

The last council, owing to its mercy and generosity, allowed my two journeymen and this apprentice to work unhindered in my shop as they had before until a final decision had been reached. Paying no attention to this wise decision, one of the other weavers, Jacob N., began to yell at my journeymen whenever he met them, saying that my workshop was not honorable and all journeymen who worked there were (begging your pardon) bloody rogues and thieves. On the next Saturday, he came into my workshop and pushed them out, acting in blind jealousy and nastiness, and said he would write to all places where this craft is carried out that the men who work in my shop are not to be tolerated anywhere.

And now I bring you, wise, honorable, and merciful council, my humble request, as a lonely widow now even more oppressed by this shame, slander, and insult, that the honor of my journeymen be restored to them, so that I and the poor infant mouths I have to feed may be supported. And also that the apprentice be allowed to stay with me, as it is the practice everywhere else in the entire Holy Roman Empire that widows who run a workshop with journeymen are allowed to retain an apprentice until he has finished his training. I ask also that all the master wool-weavers be informed of the decision so that they will not act against your wise decision and thereby appear to be ignoring you or reducing your power, and that this workshop, which is so widely renowned, be allowed to operate freely again to the benefit of the entire city. I would be eternally thankful for a decision in my behalf and would fervently offer what modest prayers I could straight from my heart for the rest of my life for your future health and well-being.[43]

One can easily understand why widows were allowed to carry on a business: as they themselves point out, the tools, equipment, and organization were already there; contracts had been made; the household still needed to be supported; the widow was usually skilled enough to carry on the work; and cities prized order and continuity in households, which of course were the tax units. Why, then, would widow's work be restricted at all? The justifications for this are stated most clearly in a case involving the Frankfurt stonemasons.

In 1624 a stonemason's widow asked to be allowed to continue working, as she had a large amount of stone left which her husband had purchased just before his death and which no one was willing to buy. Several stonemasons answered her with the comment that it was now the practice in Frankfurt and elsewhere that widows were allowed to work only four weeks after their husband's death. They followed this with a long string of reasons as to why she should not be given special consideration. First, other widows would want the same rights, as had happened once before. Second, her husband had been the most successful stonemason in town, and the others felt he had taken business away from them and were bitter about it. If his widow continued the shop, there would be many disputes between her and the other masters. Besides, her husband had been vigorously opposed to letting any widow work longer than normally allowed, so why should they go against his wishes in the case of his own wife? Third, she could not oversee the shop properly, so stone might be destroyed and work not done properly, "which would bring shame to her and to the whole guild." Fourth, she could not control the journeymen, who might marry and have children, but if they were accused of bad work, leave their wives and children, who would then need public support. Fifth, because she could not control the journeymen, they would want to work in her shop and not for other masters. The city council in Frankfurt wrote first to Strasbourg, asking about the practice there, and on finding that the stonemasons' widows there were also limited to four weeks work, refused to allow the widow her request, despite her pleas for Christian charity.[44]

In the stonemasons' answer, one can see a number of things emerging: petty jealousy and envy of the most successful mason, suspicion between masters and journeymen, feigned or real concern about the guild's quality standards, and flagrant attempts to win over the city council with the specter of more public welfare charges. These kinds of reasons undoubtedly figure in other decisions to limit widows' rights in many crafts, but the action is often taken with no clearly expressed justification, simply with the statement that it was done "because of a number of especially important reasons, all too long to mention here, but which are known to all."[45]

In arguing their case before the city council, the guild concerned usually tried to counter each argument the widow had made as to why she should be given special dispensation. Usually they began by pointing out that "her poverty is not so severe" and her children were old enough to find work.[46] Or, they noted, "She could probably find a good husband if she only wanted to, and then her poverty would be much reduced."[47] They then took the somewhat curious tack that she was too successful and was driving other masters out of business. Because she was successful at winning customers, she was no longer a "needy widow," and the council should not feel pity for her.[48] At times this argument was accepted, and at times the council pointed out that if her products were better or more popular than those of other masters, why should she not be allowed to continue?[49]

As a last resort, the guild stressed that she was using unfair business practices, running after customers and using "feminine charms" to lure them into buying from her. They even hinted that her husband might not have died of natural causes, particularly in cases in which she asked that her journeyman be allowed to continue working in the shop. Would it not be better, the guilds commented, if she supported herself instead by "taking care of expectant mothers or some other appropriately female occupation?"[50]

Better still, in the eyes of the guild, was remarriage. Craft ordinances made it very beneficial to a journeyman to marry the widow of a master of his craft. His entrance fees were reduced or eliminated; the length of time he was required to work as a journeyman before becoming a master was greatly lessened; and of course he got a fully equipped shop and house, complete with apprentices and other journeymen.[51]

When a journeyman married a widow, he was usually given six months to make his masterpiece, during which time, the woman retained the masters' rights (*Meisterrecht*). If he did not make it, or failed the inspection, he and his wife were required to work only as pieceworkers in someone else's shop for a six-month period. After this time, he could try again, but his wife was not allowed to retain her master's rights nor reacquire them until the second husband had successfully completed a masterpiece. It is interesting that the widow herself was never required to make a masterpiece, even if she ran a workshop for as long as ten or fifteen years after the death of her husband.

The guilds encouraged rapid remarriage by their increasing limitations of widow's rights, and in some crafts in some cities, they actually required widows to marry again, unless one was too old.[52] In that case, one of the guild's journeymen was put in charge of the shop by the other guild masters, either with the idea that she was no longer capable of running the shop on her own or because they did not want her to get the notion that she could run it herself. By encouraging remarriage, the guilds came up against the city councils, who believed widows were remarrying faster than was proper. In Nuremberg in 1563, for example, the council passed an ordinance requiring any widow to wait at least three months after the death of her first husband before marrying again, or until she was no longer pregnant with his child to avoid inheritance problems.[53] Marriage ordinances in most Protestant areas required a nine- to twelve-month waiting period.

The city councils may not really have had much to worry about, however. The one statistical study of how businesses were passed down during the period, made of the joiners and corsetmakers in Vienna during the Thirty Years' War, finds that roughly 10 pecent were handed down to sons, between 12 percent and 18 percent to journeymen who married a widow or daughter, and more than 70 percent simply purchased by strangers.[54] Although this may not have been the case everywhere, it does at least point out that these guilds were not as successful at keeping businesses in the same family or caring for masters' widows and daughters as they hoped to be.

By the seventeenth century some guilds were successful in their campaigns against overly successful widows. City councils began to receive requests not only from widows asking to maintain shops but also from those asking that they be allowed to give up the shop. The small amount of business they could do with no apprentices or journeymen was not enough to pay their guild dues. A few guilds allowed a widow to pass on her rights in the guild to her children if she gave up her shop or if she remarried out of the guild. These guilds stressed that this was a sign of their "generosity," as this widow would thus be free of paying annual guild dues. The fact that she could also not produce anything was not mentioned.

Most guilds did not allow a widow to do this, which meant that by giving up the shop, she was also giving up her children's rights to remain in the guild. As all guilds by this time had very high entrance fees, it also meant that her children would generally be reduced to doing piecework, working as servants, or working in one of the "free" crafts, with very little opportunity of entering a guild again. The guilds' desire to limit the rights of widows and in this way control the number and size of workshops operating had won out over their desire to care for masters' children.[55]

## JOURNEYMEN

Thus far I have been talking about women who were in some way related to the master craftsman. Before going on to maids and other women who were not related, I need to explain a bit about the journeymen in the shop, for they became the most vocal opponents of all work by women.

Though masters were required to marry, until the sixteenth century most crafts forbade journeymen and apprentices to marry. If they did, they were not able to become masters and could be dismissed by their current master at any time. Masters who hired journeymen or ap-

prentices that they knew were married could also be fined or punished in some other way. Clauses against the hiring of foreign journeymen in many craft ordinances always identified them as married;
they were not to be hired because their wives and children often did
not come with them, and the guilds feared they would take their earn-
ings out of the city and become a financial drain. Occasionally groups
of married journeymen asked for special permission to stay in a city if
their skills were needed, but they could be ordered to leave once the
need had passed.[56] There were, however, a few crafts in which journeymen could marry. Carpenters, bricklayers, stonemasons, and
other construction trades had always allowed journeymen to marry
and have their own households because their work did not take place
in the master's house.

As opportunities declined in the sixteenth century, the only way for
a journeyman to become a master himself was to marry the widow or
daughter of a master; journeymen in all trades then began to demand
that they be allowed to marry. The prohibitions against marriage had
made sense when most journeymen could hope to move up, when
being a journeyman was simply a stage, but now that many would remain journeymen all their lives, the restriction was unrealistic. Journeymen in many trades joined together into separate journeymen's
guilds with special dress, parades, and festivities which did not include the master craftsmen. One of the first demands of these journeymen's guilds was the right to marry.[57] In most cases, they were successful in this demand, so that by the seventeenth century married
journeymen were accepted in most guilds.

The journeymen's guilds then began to make other demands and to
set rules and restrictions for their own members which were even
more stringent than those of the craft ordinances. All contact with
prostitutes or other "dishonorable" people, like the city executioner,
Jews, or bath operators, was forbidden, even standing next to them in
a public place. A journeyman who had promised to marry a woman
secretly without the knowledge of his or her parents and relatives was
to be excluded, and no honorable journeyman was to work next to
him. Journeymen often refused to work with another who had married a woman in some way "dishonorable," until guild masters or city
councils stepped in and ordered them to do so. As one can easily
imagine, the atmosphere in a workshop where this had happened was
not terribly pleasant.[58]

Though the journeymen's guilds justified their moves as attempts to
maintain standards of morality and behavior among their members,
their unexpressed aim was to exclude as many people as possible
from working in the shop so that there would be less competition for

work places. Another way they did this was to further tighten up legitimacy requirements so that one had to prove the legitimacy and good conduct not only of one's parents but also of one's aunts and uncles. Any possible grounds for excluding someone meant one less competitor for a position; if a whole family could be excluded through the actions of one member, so much the better.[59]

Journeymen next turned against a group that was much easier to identify than those who had questionable relatives or associates: the women working in the shop. They first demanded that all maids be forbidden to work, then that the master's own wife and daughters be excluded or that the tasks they did be limited to finishing and packing or other unskilled jobs. Rather than request that their own wives be allowed to work with them, they demanded instead that all women be excluded from the shop.[60] This included the master's widow, for journeymen's guilds often forbade their members to continue working for widows longer than a few weeks.

These demands went beyond, and in some cases even worked against, the journeymen's own economic interest. They lost work places when widows' rights were limited, and their wives could not work at a trade for a decent wage but were limited to domestic service, laundering, selling at the market, or other low-paying occupations. We can only understand these moves by recognizing that women working in the shop not only represented an economic threat but also had a symbolic or ideological meaning for the journeymen.

The women of the household—the master's wife, daughters, and maids—were a symbol of the patriarchal system that everyone in the household, including journeymen and apprentices, worked under.[61] Attempts to limit the power of the patriarchy—the power of the master—often struck first at the most vulnerable part of the patriarchy, the master's female dependents. As journeymen's work became proletarianized—that is, as their chances of ever becoming masters dimmed and they could expect to remain wage laborers in a master's shop their whole lifetimes—journeymen attempted to save a shred of their old position and honor by sharply differentiating their work from that of women. What they did in the shop, whether it required much training or not, was to be a male province.

## MAIDS

The group most directly affected by the journeymen's actions were maids working in a master's shop. Beginning in the mid-sixteenth century the work they could do was limited, and the number of maids the master could use to do anything at all was limited as well. For example, maids in Nuremberg leather shops were forbidden to attach buckles to belts or to hammer studs into them or to gild or paint them later. Knifemakers' maids could make sheaths and scabbards and attach handles to knives but not make or sharpen the blades themselves. In both these crafts no maid could be hired specifically for work in the shop but had to do some housework as well. Even in occupations which today seem traditionally female, such as knitting stockings, maids were restricted to carding and spinning the wool and were not to be taught to knit; this was the province of the master, journeymen, and apprentices.[62]

In 1597 the journeymen cordmakers in Frankfurt complained to the city council that though cordmaking had recently been made a guild, the masters were still hiring nothing but young women and girls, although this was not tolerated by most guilds. The masters huffily replied that their teaching of girls as well as boys was a sign of their openness and generosity; if they were to be strict like other guilds, many of the journeymen themselves would suffer, for they would have to produce a proof of legitimate birth and a letter of apprenticeship. Besides, the journeymen had refused to make small cords, so that the masters had to use women and children for this. They, the masters, and not the journeymen, should be the ones complaining. Nevertheless, ten years later the journeymen's arguments were successful, and the masters were permitted to employ only their own daughters and no other relatives or nonrelated maids. Even the number of daughters they could use was limited to two, and they were only allowed to work at "finishing small tasks."[63]

Under pressure from the journeymen, the ringmakers in Nuremberg passed an elaborate ordinance regulating women's work:

> From now on, no maid is to be used for any kind of work in this craft, nor are they to offer any assistance, with a fine of four pounds for each infraction. And since it has come up that some journeymen marry before they have become masters and then use their wives in the craft and let them work, out of which many disputes have arisen, the following has been decided and shall be promulgated: Since it is now forbidden to use any maids for this craft, so it shall also be forbidden for the women to work whose husbands have not yet become masters. And the masters' daughters who have been supported by their fathers and plan to marry, but their husbands are not masters yet (and thus they cannot marry) so they are still supported by their fathers and have not had a wedding yet, can still help their fathers. However, if a master's daughter is employed by another master as a maid she is not allowed to help work at the craft but is forbidden to as a maid.[64]

In this case, the journeymen had succeeded in preventing from working not only maids but also the wives of other journeymen and master's daughters who were not working in their father's shop.

By the late seventeenth century, most of the metal crafts had totally forbidden the use of maids. Not only were the masters to be fined if caught employing maids, but all journeymen were required to report any maid working in their shop.[65] They were not allowed to work beside a maid and were liable to pay the same fine as that required of the master, should they do so. Given the fairly low rate of pay for journeymen, this was a stringent fine.

Not only the journeymen, but also other guilds, made objections to masters employing women. In 1615 the Munich strapmakers complained that the beltmakers were employing their wives and maids to do stitching with an awl, which was forbidden to everyone but the strapmakers. The city council ordered the beltmakers not to use female hands for tasks they themselves were not allowed to do.[66] During the mid-seventeenth century the Strasbourg wool-weavers had come to such hard times that they were spinning wool for the linen-weavers, for their production of linsey-woolsey. They forced through a regulation which allowed the linen-weavers only one spinning maid instead of the large number they had had previously; all the rest of the wool thread they needed they had to buy from the wool-weavers.[67]

Occasionally these disputes ranged beyond city boundaries. The Frankfurt hatmakers refused, as long as the Fulda hatmakers continued to use "all sorts of servants, maids, women, and embroideresses," to take on journeymen who had been trained in Fulda. The abbot of Fulda answered that it had long been the custom to employ women as assistants, but now, "since the hatmakers here have been insulted and despised because of this, their children, journeymen, and apprentices hindered, and the quality of their product denigrated," he agreed to forbid women to work any longer. The Frankfurt hatmakers grudgingly agreed to accept Fulda journeymen from then on, as long as the abbot promised to punish any hatmakers who continued to use women in any capacity.[68]

The same sort of pressure was put on the Nuremberg glovemakers by those in Strasbourg. In the 1530s the journeymen glovemakers in Nuremberg objected to having to work next to a maid, but the masters and the city council allowed women to work. Shortly after, the bag- and glovemakers in Strasbourg complained about the cheap price of Nuremberg gloves and convinced the city council there to write to Nuremberg. This complaint worked, and the women were forbidden to work.[69]

This same combination of complaints—by local journeymen and a foreign city council—occurred in a later case involving Strasbourg and Nuremberg, only this time the positions were reversed. In 1563 five journeymen beltmakers left Strasbourg, complaining that "adopted daughters" of the masters were performing work that should actually be limited to journeymen. The women were often other relatives or simply maids of the masters, being called "daughters" to seem to be in compliance with the law.[70] The five went to Nuremberg, and then two beltmakers from Nuremberg were forbidden to sell their products in the Strasbourg market by the guild of beltmakers there. The Nuremberg beltmakers responded by closing their market to all Strasbourg beltmakers. The Strasbourg city council ordered the beltmakers' guild to disallow daughters to work unless they were the actual daughter of the master and sent to Nuremberg for opinions on the issue. The Nuremberg city council agreed, as its own ordinances also forbade the unrestricted use of maids or other female helpers. Eventually both markets were opened again, and the unhappy journeymen returned to Strasbourg.

Actually, as Ernst Mummenhoff points out, a much larger issue than simply the activity of maids was involved. The journeymen wanted the ultimate rights to the *Schenkwesen*, the decision as to who would be hired in a workshop, which had traditionally belonged to the masters. Princely and ducal cities often attempted to draw journeymen away from the free imperial cities by granting them the Schenkwesen. The Reichstag—imperial Parliament—had taken this away from the journeymen in 1530 and 1548, but the ruling was not obeyed by many cities, and later the right was officially given back to the journeymen. With the rise in the number of journeymen seeking employment during the late sixteenth century, the fact that their fellow journeymen had the Schenkwesen was very significant and certainly not beneficial to female employment in the crafts.

### INDEPENDENT WORK BY WOMEN

Thus a mixture of reasons were involved in all the moves to exclude women: interguild rivalries, journeymen's fears, worries about competition from guilds in other cities, conflicts between masters and journeymen or between masters and the city council or journeymen and the city council. All of these and others come to play again in respect to opportunities for women to work independently. For this category of production work, I focus on several specific crafts, for they offered the most employment for women. These include light metalwork and cloth-and-clothing production, which was by far the largest employer of women. Of course, as I have said, there were women who worked in nearly every craft in some city at some time, but almost all of these were widows, wives, daughters, or maids. The few who were not were clearly exceptions, although it is interesting to discover that there were women who ran foundries, shod horses, shipped sheet metal, and made armor.[71]

In every city there were always a few women operating independently making needles, rings, measures, thimbles, and other small articles out of iron and tin. In some cities these were "free arts," and so the women were not challenged in what they did. Only if they tried to make keys and locks or something which required a similar amount of training and was thus regulated by a guild did they come into conflict with male artisans. Even in cities where all these small metal items were supposed to be made by certain guilds, needle- and pinmaking was seen as an appropriate female task, and women were usually allowed to work on their own at it. It required few tools and nimble hands, the right kind of job for women who for some reason "can not spin or sew," the usual female occupations. If a woman tried to use her husband to help her, however, she was sharply rebuked, for then this was *Handwercksstimpeln* (dabbling in a craft one had no authority to work in).[72]

Husband and wife often worked together making thimbles and could be hired by another master to work in his shop as pieceworkers. The regulations governing couples hired in this way in Nuremberg are rather interesting:

> If the wife works without the approval of her husband and her work is found to be faulty or lacking, she will not be allowed to work at the craft, with a fine of four pounds, but her husband can still hold a workplace.
> However, if the two are working with the agreement and knowledge of each other, and faults and problems are found in the man's work, then the man will not be allowed to operate a shop nor to work at a craft (i.e., in another's shop) but will have to pay for this as he deserves. And the woman can then absolutely not work.
> These two people, wife and husband, can not be considered as one person, but two pieceworkers. And the wife as well as the husband can work with a master in his house.[73]

Thus the husband was not responsible if his wife broke a regulation or if her work was not up to standard, but she also suffered if his was faulty in some way. This fits in very well with the general lines of responsibility followed in most legal cases. Husbands were not required to pay back debts their wives had incurred without their knowledge;

the unfortunate and unwise creditor had simply lost his money.[74] Wives, on the other hand, were often included in a husband's banishment even if they had no part in the crime.

Goldsmithing was another occupation in which there were a surprising number of women. Most were goldsmiths' wives or widows, but they were usually also full members of the guild themselves, taking the oath and paying fees, which was very unusual. Perhaps the valuable nature of the raw material used led the guilds to demand that women as well as men swear to handle everything truly and honestly. The ordinances for goldsmiths' widows are longer and more elaborate than those for widows in other crafts and specifically ordered widows to keep a sharp watch on their journeymen so that no unworked gold or finished products should disappear.[75] Long after the widows in most crafts were limited to a few months' work after their husbands' deaths, goldsmiths' widows could work for many years, and they appear on lists of masters as late as the eighteenth century.

In cities with a very large gold industry, such as Nuremberg, women also worked at more specialized tasks within the gold industry, especially spinning gold threads to be used in fancy embroidery. Each goldsmith or goldbeater (men who hammered gold into very thin sheets to be used for goldleaf or inlay) was allowed two maids to whom he could teach gold spinning. Unlike other crafts, these maids could work full time in the shop and did not have to be responsible for some of the housework as well. Those who were unmarried were to live with the master, just like apprentices or journeymen. Their salaries were based on how much they could spin, and the masters were to pay them no more or no less than the established wage rate.[76]

Along with maids who lived and worked in a master's house, there were also independent gold spinners who worked either in the master's house or in their own homes. The goldbeaters frequently attempted to have the independent gold spinners forbidden from doing any work, but the city council refused their requests. As long as a woman had learned her trade from a goldbeater or another goldspinner, and as long as she did all the spinning herself, she was allowed to continue.[77]

In 1597 gold spinning itself was made a sworn craft, with a set apprenticeship system. Each spinner was to be an apprentice for no less than four years and be duly registered when she was taken on. She was then to spend at least one more year with another master, a kind of journeyman period. If she was unmarried, she was to live in a master's house and not on her own. Once she had married, however, she could still spin on her own but could use no maids to help her nor take on any apprentices. Even her own daughters were to receive their training from a master goldbeater or goldsmith.[78]

Thus, though it was restricted, gold spinning continued to be an opportunity for a woman to practice a craft other than that of her husband, independently and in her own household, as long as she was married or widowed. Those who worked outside a goldsmith's shop were paid by the piece, but there are, unfortunately, no records of how many women worked or how much they were paid. The Nuremberg city council's defense of the gold spinners' right to work despite the repeated complaints of the goldbeaters is most unusual in that in every other sworn craft, the opposition of the masters was enough to prevent any general permission of women's work.

Several factors were probably responsible for the unusual position of gold spinning in Nuremberg: it had become a sworn craft very late and had traditionally employed many women; it demanded a high degree of skill and some financial capital for an original investment, but few tools and only a small work space, so it could be done in a home; it took a great deal of time to produce a small amount of spun gold, and the demand seems to have remained high.

Another factor may have also contributed to this, and it does explain the council's sharp differentiation between single and married gold spinners. In 1600 gold spinners, lacemakers, and grapeshot makers were prohibited from having any more than eight workers, male or female, in any one shop because they had "taken on, without discrimination, a superfluous number of frivolous knaves and young wenches, who do not want to serve any master and only work when they want to. At the same moment they do not only commit wanton acts but almost every week some girls come into the hospital for syphilitics because of being often in contact with these people and infected in bad dwelling places. They freeze in the winter and are otherwise destroyed and denigrated by the stink and evil company."[79] The council obviously thought married women spinning gold were a lesser threat than the "wanton young wenches" who would otherwise be hired to work. For seventeenth-century city councils, single women living and working on their own was to be avoided at all costs.

Unlike other crafts, the production of cloth and clothing throughout most of Western history has been a women's occupation. Until the late Middle Ages, all stages of production, from carding raw wool or cooking flax to making the final finishing touches on garments, were carried out in the home, usually by female members of the family or by servants. As late as 1500 Jacob Wimpheling, in *Germania* (dedicated to the city of Strasbourg), praised Margaret, the daughter of Duke

Louis of Bavaria and wife of Phillip, the elector Palatinate, his contemporary, with the comment: "She was active during her whole life with feminine occupations, consisting mainly of spinning and weaving of wool and silk, sewing and all sorts of embroidery, which she did together with her entire female retinue."[80] She was certainly not an exception, as letter exchanges between noblewomen throughout Germany often include references to spinning and requests for yarn, with clear indication that the ladies were doing it themselves.[81]

Beginning in the thirteenth century, however, particularly in urban areas and in monasteries, male artisans began to take over some stages of production from women, gradually forming guilds of weavers, drapers, and cloth cutters. These guilds often fought with each other over who had the ultimate right to control all stages of cloth production. In some cities, the drapers won; in others, the cloth cutters; and in still others, the weavers themselves, so that the organization of production varied from city to city. As with the battle between the guilds and the city council, however, who ended up with ultimate control made little difference to women who worked in cloth production. Although some guilds allowed female members at the beginning, women were gradually excluded from most weavers', drapers', tailors', and cloth cutters' guilds in most cities. Only the initial stages, such as carding and spinning, or the production of cheaper cloth, especially that specifically made for women's clothing, such as veils, were left to unorganized women workers.

First a brief look at the medieval period. As weavers and other craftsmen were gradually forming guilds, in the late thirteenth and fourteenth centuries in Germany, women were involved in a huge variety of occupations. In Frankfurt fourteenth-century tax records list 24 somewhat different occupations for women in cloth and clothing. The Munich tax records for the fifteenth century include weavers, bagmakers, nappers, bag and glove embroiderers, and spinsters, all of whom are clearly working on their own and not simply as widows carrying on their husbands' shops. In Trier Annette Winter finds women in many of the same crafts. The only all-female guilds in Germany, except for gold spinners, were those of yarnmakers and silkweavers in Cologne.[82]

The situation was much the same in other German cities. A 1434 partial list of weavers in Strasbourg includes 68 men and 38 women, some labeled as widow or daughter but some as "single woman" (*Jungfer*) or with nothing but her name. About half of these women made a larger payment than normal, and the list bears the notation "if they want to make cloth, they will do like the others," so apparently they were paying for the privilege of being in the guild without making cloth.[83] Some of these female weavers were quite successful, for their income and property made them responsible for supporting an armored knight and horse for the city's defense. Women are also mentioned in a number of other cloth-related trades, such as glovemaking, veilmaking, and wimpel making in Strasbourg.[84]

In Brandenburg weavers' wives could buy into the guild for the same price men had to pay and could then set up a second weaving bench in the shop, at which they themselves worked. Women appear to have been independent members of weavers' guilds in Bremen, Cologne, Dortmund, Danzig, Speyer, Memmingen, Ulm, Lüneburg, and Munich, and perhaps in other cities as well, although the records are not as clear. In most of these cities veil weaving was strictly a female occupation throughout the fourteenth and fifteenth centuries, with the women sometimes members of the weavers' guild, sometimes forming their own organization, and sometimes not members of any guild at all.[85]

In addition to women who wove as members of weavers' guilds, a number of women also wove primarily for their own household use. If they had a few cloths extra, they were usually free to sell them at the market, although they were often limited as to the number they could sell.[86] Gradually these women began to weave more and more for the market; this would later lead to conflicts with the weavers' guilds.

The number of weavers of all types in a city like Augsburg or Frankfurt or Ulm—between 250 and 500—necessitated a huge number of additional workers, most of whom do not appear in any records. Each weaver, with the help of one or two journeymen, often produced as many as 60–100 bolts of cloth annually. Fifteenth- and sixteenth-century techniques of production necessitate at least 20 carders and spinners per weaver if he or she was making this much.[87] These were pieceworkers, paid by the weaver, and were generally women who carded and spun in their own homes or in the weavers' house but who are almost never identified by occupation in tax lists because they paid no independent taxes on their work, being considered members of a male-headed household. Once the cloth was woven, it was often sent back to female nappers, who straightened it and took out knots or any small particles which had worked themselves into the weave. From there it went to either male or female cloth washers before being sent to a dyer or bleacher.[88]

About thirty cities in Germany had independent female tailors, some of them assuredly masters' widows, but others women who had joined the tailors' guild on their own.[89] Female tailors in Frankfurt could pass on their guild rights not only to their children but also to their husbands; if a woman married after joining the guild, her husband had only to pay the normal entrance fee to become a master also, even if he had not been trained as a tailor or been a member of the guild before.[90] Tailors also often had female wageworkers who did much of the actual sewing for them.[91] In addition to tailors, seamstresses were to be found in every city.

In Ulm several women took part in the *Barchantschau*, the examination and approval of linen cloth, admittedly as folders and other sorts of manual laborers, but they were sworn to secrecy and ordered to do their job quickly and efficiently, just as every other official at the Schau was, and were paid the same as male assistants.[92] In Memmingen two women and one man carried out the official examination of the flax before it was made into linen.[93]

It is evident, then, that women were independently involved in a huge number of textile-related occupations well into the sixteenth century. The large majority of them were wageworkers involved in thread preparation, in finishing cloth, or as assistants to weavers; but some were weavers or tailors themselves, either carrying on a shop as widows or having somehow gained the right to run one themselves.

As early as the fourteenth century, however, restrictions began to appear and these intensified and sharpened in later centuries. Many involved masters' widows, daughters, and maids, and the general pattern is the same as in other crafts. Some restrictions are direct controls on independent work by women, regulating or limiting what they could weave, sew, knit, dye, embroider, or spin, when any of these activities were perceived as threatening by the guilds.

In Strasbourg the dispute over women weaving ranged over centuries, beginning in 1330. In that year the weavers demanded that all women weaving anything be required to buy into the weavers' guild, which many of the women could not afford to do.[94] The city council intervened and said that only those women who wove wool, serge, or other more expensive cloth would be required to join; those who wove linen cloth of all types could continue without paying the weavers' guild anything. As Gustav Schmoller points out, this really had little to do with the women's weaving but was actually one episode in the power struggle between the council and the weavers.[95]

A century later the weavers demanded that female veil-weavers also pay guild dues; four veil-weavers appeared before the council to argue that they had never paid anything before and should not have to now. Again a compromise was reached, with each veil-weaver paying a small fee, the amount depending on how many weaving benches and assistants she had. In 1484 the council elaborated further on this, continued to require veil-weavers to pay only a small fee, but began requiring the female narrow-cloth (*Halbtuch*) weavers to pay twice this amount and forbade them to have more than one weaving bench. This meant they could only weave themselves and have no assistants or apprentices. Women who wanted to weave regular cloth or use apprentices had to buy into the guild at the normal rate, pay all annual fees, and carry out all other guild duties except for serving as the nightwatch at the cloth house.[96]

This was immediately opposed by the weavers, who were no longer satisfied with simply requiring all women who wove to be members of the guild. They now wanted women strictly limited to veil weaving, not allowed even to make narrow cloth "because the majority of the male weavers have to earn their living making narrow cloth."[97] They also wanted all veil-weaving apprentices registered and their teachers clearly told not to teach them to weave anything else "because they themselves don't know how to do this properly." In addition, they wanted all rural weavers strictly prohibited from selling their cloth in Strasbourg and all peddlers and old-clothing dealers forbidden to sell any new cloth. Clearly the weavers were worried about competition from a number of groups, but the council apparently would not agree to their demands. As long as women paid the normal guild fees, they were to be allowed to weave whatever they wanted.

The Basel weavers voiced similar complaints in the mid-fifteenth century. Women who were supposed to weave only veils and headcloths were also weaving narrow cloth without paying the guild any fees. The city council there reacted the same way as the council in Strasbourg had; rather than require the women to quit weaving, it required them instead to buy into the guild. More than one-quarter of the linen weavers in Basel in 1469 were women, probably the highest proportion in all of Germany.[98] In both these cities the city council never let the weavers exclude women simply because of their sex.

These two cities were somewhat exceptional, however. Strasbourg in particular was much more liberal in many craft ordinances than most cities. Illegitimate sons were not excluded from guild membership until the late sixteenth century, nor did journeymen have to produce any proof of good conduct or family background. As Schmoller points out, "The exclusion of whole classes of society from the crafts, that frequently happened elsewhere as early as the beginning of the sixteenth century, appeared to be totally unknown in Strasbourg." He goes on to say, however, "We never experience the exclusion or limitation of the rights of women during our whole period [to 1800]. But, nevertheless, we do not see women mentioned very much later, though up until about 1500 they are frequently mentioned along with the men."[99]

The picture in other cities is much bleaker than this. Women were limited to making narrow cloth and veils in 1360 in Speyer and in 1375 in Hamburg; in 1458 even the number who could do that in Hamburg was limited to 30.[100] In 1403 women were excluded totally from weaving in Göttingen, in 1470 in Leipzig, and in 1450 in Richlitz in Saxony; in the last case, some women continued until the guild appealed to the duke of Saxony and got a ducal order demanding that they stop.[101] In 1509 women were forbidden to weave linen in Heilbronn, though the husband of one weaver ardently defended their right to do so: "My wife, who weaves linen, learned how to do so in her youth and supported her father and mother in their sickness and old age with this . . . and now she is helping me support our small children. That a woman should be forbidden to do so is unheard of in Heilbronn."[102]

A new twist was added in Augsburg in the conflict between male weavers and female veil-weavers. Up to 1560 veil weaving had been a free art; at this point the weavers and some of the veil-weavers demanded that anyone who made veils buy into the weavers' guild at the full price, justifying this with the claim that the art of weaving veils had changed and become more complicated so that only those learned in the craft should weave. The city council asked for a compromise, and in 1561 the veil-weavers were given an ordinance requiring all to buy into the guild except for those "few women" who had been weaving for many years already, and they could now have only two looms. These women also had to register immediately with the council, buy all their yarn in the city, and be married or widowed with their own households.[103] This last clause brought immediate objections from a number of single veil-weavers who had learned veil weaving "because it is a fine and honorable female trade" and who were supporting elderly parents; only in a few cases, however, did the city council make exceptions and allow single women to work.[104]

This concern about single women working on their own comes out in several other cases in Augsburg. In 1577 the weavers complained that they could not find enough maids to spin for them, as all the women coming into the city were working independently and living with other families or renting a small room somewhere. Five years later the council forbade all noncitizen women to live and work independently, but to no avail. In 1597 the weavers were even more incensed, as women were saying openly that they were not so dumb as to work as spin maids for the weavers when they could earn three times as much spinning on their own. This was an intolerable situation, according to the weavers, as these women had complete freedom as to when they worked and when not and to walk around with young journeymen all during the week; they were a bad example for girls coming in from the countryside, and even for local girls, who would thus be inclined to live on their own rather than become maids. The city council enacted a series of harsh ordinances banishing all women who made demands of their employers and forbidding all unmarried women, citizens or not, to have their own households.[105] As with the gold spinners in Nuremberg, single women working were viewed with much more suspicion and hostility than simply women working.

By the end of the sixteenth century in some areas, there was clear hostility to all women working as weavers, whether single or married, guild members or not. The 1598 weaving ordinance for a number of small towns in the duchy of Württemburg recommended that no girls be taken on as apprentices, and if one was, she was to pay a higher entrance fee than a boy. If she became a master weaver, she could only weave narrow cloth and could not use a maid or apprentice to do any weaving for her; if she married outside the craft, she could only weave veils. The Stuttgart ordinance from the same year is even more specifically antifemale, as it directly forbids the taking on of new female apprentices, establishing a huge fine for infractions, and a similarly large one for any present female weaver who took on any apprentice, boy or girl.[106] It does allow women to continue boiling flax, one of the most unpleasant tasks in cloth preparation, but only under the direct supervision of a master.[107]

According to a 1604 complaint by the Munich linen-weavers, if women were allowed to continue weaving, the result would be "great disorder among the crafts, faulty products, masters' widows and orphans left without support, poor masters who could no longer pay their taxes, customers cheated by being sold slipshod merchandise, and suspicious persons coming into the city."[108] Quite a list. The weavers in Frankfurt, Memmingen, and Nuremberg agreed, and in most cases, the guilds were able to restrict women weavers. City councils did make individual exceptions, but these were only in cases of great need and only allowed the woman to weave things which were simple and not very expensive or for one particular customer.[109] A late-sixteenth-century list of weavers in Frankfurt gives a total of 173, of which 13 were widows and only 6 single or married women. A list from Munich in 1613 shows even fewer women: only 3 widows out of a total of 159 weavers.[110]

There were still a few women weaving in Augsburg despite all the hostility to them, as Clasen's study indicates. Of the 2,165 people who actually had a loom and a weaver's bench, 115 were women; of these 115 women, 47 had no journeyman or servant. Therefore they either wove themselves or let the loom stand unused, which was very unlikely. Clasen simply does not know what to think on the matter, for there were no provisions in guild ordinances for female apprentices, and some of these women were not widows.[111] This really is not very surprising, for with only one loom each, they were not major weavers; the tax records indicate they were very poor anyway. Their presence was most likely simply tolerated because it was easier and cheaper to let them weave a bit than provide them with poor relief.

Even in Strasbourg, the weaver's guild began to bring more complaints against women around 1600. Women who had long made and sold small linen dish towels reported that the weavers were now ordering them to stop; other women who wove veils reported that they had been told to stop after they remarried, even though there was nothing in the ordinance which prohibited veil-weavers from marrying.[112] In all these cases, the city council supported the women; only one woman was totally forbidden to weave, but she had broken every rule in the book: She had bought yarn privately instead of at the public market, had not worked her sign into her cloth or brought the cloth for inspection, had kept her shop open longer hours than allowed, had hired a foreign journeyman when there were native ones out of work, and then worst of all, had had him sleep in her bedroom for two weeks, although both she and he said "nothing happened." Not only all that, but she refused to pay any legal costs for all the times she had appeared in court, and the council finally threw her in jail as well as forbidding her to work.[113] The fact that she was a woman was never even mentioned in her trial, however.

While weavers' guilds in many cities were attempting to exclude female weavers on one ground or another, tailors' guilds were often attempting to limit the kinds of work female seamstresses were allowed to do. Seamstresses had long performed a wide variety of tasks: clothing repair and alteration, the actual construction of simple women's and children's underclothing, finishing and detail work on garments made by members of the tailors guild. Some specialized in making fine ladies' slips and chemises and were then specifically called "silk-seamstresses." The number of women who made their living this way was probably very large, for seamstresses are the largest occupational group among women who received citizenship rights independently in Nuremberg, and they appear frequently on tax lists in many cities.

Seamstressing and sewing were regarded as proper female occupations and skills which could prove useful for any girl, no matter what her later situation. Small endowments were often set up to provide girls with training in seamstressing, and city orphanages had a seamstress as part of their staff, responsible not only for sewing but also for teaching.[114] In most cities seamstressing was a free art, open to any woman.[115] Only in Memmingen did seamstresses have an ordinance which required them to be citizens, have learned for one year as an apprentice and another year as an assistant, and pay a small fee annually to the tailors' guild.[116] Whether this may actually be considered a guild is questionable, as the seamstresses did not have any independent officials nor independent power to regulate themselves.

As long as the women were handling old or used clothing, there seem to have been no limitations on their work. Judging by how often things termed "plain," "simple," "old," or even "ragged" are listed in various wills and testaments, clothing repair and alteration was a good source of employment. When new clothes were concerned, however, the tailors frequently brought complaints that the seamstresses were doing work that was not allowed. Usually this resulted in the seamstresses being restricted to making things out of old cloth; or only out of cheaper, coarser kinds of cloth; or only when specifically requested to by someone who came to them.[117] In some cities seamstresses were told simply "to make nothing which is properly the work of the tailors,"[118] but this vagueness led to confusion, and cities became more specific in their restrictions, as the following decision by the Nuremberg city council points out:

> It has been decided by the honorable council that from now on no seamstress or anyone else outside the tailors' guild is to make a breast cloth, jerkin, doublet, or the like unless it is made out of simple fustian or wool cloth. They shall also not trim these jerkins or doublets with velvet or silk cloth, nor make or sell any complete doublet or jerkin from silk, camel's hair, satin, velvet, or any other kind of silk cloth. Whoever does anything contrary will have to pay a fine of five pounds for every instance.
>
> However, if anyone comes to a seamstress with the cloth they have purchased themselves, whatever the material is, she will then be able to make this up into a garment for the appropriate payment. However, she can make nothing else than a doublet or jerkin out of it [i.e., no coats or capes, which only tailors were allowed to make].[119]

As in so many crafts, cities wanted to be sure that their seamstresses were allowed to do exactly what those in other cities were. Thus the Kempten city council first wrote to Memmingen asking for a clarification of its seamstresses' ordinance before Kempten would decide in a dispute between its own tailors and seamstresses. On learning that in other cities only men were allowed to work with silk, the Munich council prohibited girls from learning this trade and allowed them to learn only "common seamstressing."[120]

Since they were limited to the production of lower priced garments of simple material, seamstresses were rarely able to do more than support themselves. They usually paid the lowest amount of taxes, if they paid any at all, and were often forced to accept public charity at the end of their lives. Even then, however, cities required them to do "some sewing or other similar work" in the hospital where they were living in return for their food and shelter.[121]

Restrictions similar to those on seamstresses were placed on female bleachers and dyers. They were permitted to handle small articles, often those which had already been used and were being remade, but could not bleach, dye, or treat whole pieces of new cloth; this was reserved to the actual guild of bleachers and dyers. A veil-weaver was allowed to bleach what she had made herself but not anything woven by someone else.[122] As their work used a great deal of water and often had an unpleasant smell, the bleachers and dyers had their own area of work in each city, either outside the city walls along a stream or set off from other crafts inside the city. The women usually worked out in the open but occasionally used the workshops of male bleachers and dyers during their off-hours.[123]

As many crafts expanded and elaborated on their regulations during the sixteenth century, they took over the production of certain items which had previously been considered "free arts," often to the detriment of the women who had been making them. The process can be seen most clearly in hatmaking, which until the middle of the sixteenth century had been relatively open to female workers.[124] Women often made small hats and other head coverings out of scraps in their own homes, learning the trade from their parents or friends and supporting themselves or supplementing their husbands' income in this way.

Beginning in the mid-fifteenth century, even this was opposed by the guild of small hat makers (*Baretmachern*) who wanted all women forbidden to do such work unless they were married to a hatmaker. The women immediately objected, pointing out that making these things was "proper work for women," and a compromise was usually reached that allowed the women to make veils or hat decorations, to repair hats, or occasionally to make a hat for an "honorable woman or girl" who specifically requested one. They were not to use maids to help them, to advertise their products, or even make them out in public so that people would know they made hats and order from them. In some cities hatmakers were also forbidden to take on female apprentices but could only use their own wives and daughters to help them.[125] Thus women were effectively excluded from the millinery trade, or at any rate from making hats which were entirely their own creations.

The same sort of thing happened in knitting. Though there is some dispute about its exact origins, knitting first appeared in Europe in Spain at the beginning of the sixteenth century and then spread quickly up through France, Germany, and England. Like all new techniques it was a "free art" at first, open to anyone who wanted to learn. Gradually the weavers' or cloth dealers' guild in many cities began to demand that knitters join them, paying the normal guild fees, although usually only male knitters were required to pay the full amount. As opportunities for weavers declined in many cities, the men turned more and more to knitting as their chief source of income. They then demanded that women either pay full guild fees or else be forbidden to knit.

Women continued to be allowed to knit woolen gloves, as long as they bought their wool through the city wool office and did all the knitting themselves. Stocking knitting, however, gradually became a male occupation. Usually some women were allowed to continue knitting if they were poor and had supported themselves in this way for a long time but were then restricted to selling only those stockings they had made themselves. Master stocking-knitters were not to teach any women or girls to knit, except their own wives and daughters, but could use unrelated maids to card and spin the yarn for them. The male knitters were never totally successful in excluding women, as city councils continued to allow both women and rural people to sell what they had knit themselves, maintaining it did no serious harm to anyone. They were forbidden, however, to use knitting frames, which greatly speeded up the process; frames were reserved for men who were members of the guild.[126]

The process whereby a free art became a craft, hence closed to women, is traceable in the case of a stocking knitter in Memmingen. In 1632 Brigitta Müller reported that her brother had told her to stop making and selling stockings, as she had not had a proper apprenticeship; she answered that knitting was a free art, open to all, and so he had no grounds to order her to stop. She had learned from their father just as he had and was supporting her family by it, as her husband could not get any work at the time. The council agreed to let her continue, suggesting that she set up her stand far away from her brother to avoid conflicts, but made no comment on whether stocking knitting was a free art or a closed guild.[127]

Thirty years later she appeared before the council with the same complaint, only this time it was a group of younger men who had ordered her to stop. In the meantime, knitting had been made a closed guild, but she had been allowed to continue "as is the case with any craft in any city when it becomes a sworn guild." Now she was a widow and supporting her children without public help, though she had lost nearly everything in the Thirty Years' War, "which these young masters who are complaining about me would know nothing about." She was only using a maid to help her, "and we must work very hard, though it is wrong to have to work this hard at my age." The masters answered that her comments were "empty women's prattle . . . nothing but hot air. . . . This poor widow (as she calls herself)" was making more stockings than most masters, teaching her daughter the trade, and probably had other, less honorable, means of support as well. Just because she had been allowed to work in 1632 when knitting was not a guild was no reason she should be allowed to now, when it was.[128]

As she rightly points out, they did not speak to her main point, that all those who were already practicing a trade were allowed to continue when it was made a guild, and she returns to this as her main argument with the council. Again she was successful, perhaps because the council agreed that she had "one foot in the grave and must earn what I need with trials and difficulties," but it allowed her to sell her goods only from her house and not from the public market, where she would have to confront the other knitters.[129] Thus in knitting as well as in weaving, tailoring, hatmaking, and dying, women were gradually excluded as guild regulations were expanded and free arts came under the control of a guild.

What, then, were women still doing? Most of all, they were spinning. When households were liquidated for debt and everything was sold down to the last spoon, the widow was still allowed to keep her spinning wheel.[130] In even the most desperate cases, women were expected to keep spinning; a woman charged with stealing had merited a harsh punishment, according to the Memmingen city council, but because she had been forced to steal by her now-deceased mother and was very sickly, she was to be chained in the paupers' room in the city hospital "in a way that she can still spin."[131] The Strasbourg city council was offered the prospect of a young woman "with no hands and only one foot, but who can still do all sorts of handwork, like spinning"; the man who had found her wanted to show her to the public, and the city council agreed, allowing him to charge a penny an onlooker.[132]

As I have noted, early modern weaving techniques necessitated a large number of spinners to keep each weaver supplied with thread, often as many as twenty per weaver. Because of this, each weaver got his or her thread from a variety of sources: some of it was spun by maids who lived in the weaver's household; some of it by pieceworkers who worked, but did not live, in the weaver's house; some of it by pieceworkers spinning in their own homes, using wool the weaver provided; and some purchased at the market from urban or rural spinners who bought their own wool. As merchant capitalists began to invest in cloth production, they often bought the wool and hired both spinners and weavers.

Whenever the weavers or investors provided wool for spinners working in their own homes, they were careful to make sure the spinners returned it all to them and did not try to short-change them. The wool was to be weighed before it went out to them and then again when it came back and also to be examined to make sure it was not wet or dirty. The spinners were forbidden to mix the wool of different masters or to take longer than four weeks to spin any wool.[133] In Frankfurt if a weaver disputed any weight, two male or female witnesses were to testify, and the wool in question was confiscated until it had been examined and the case heard.[134]

As might be expected, there were frequent court cases involving spinners, weavers, and merchants. Weavers and merchants accused spinners of falsifying weights, substituting lower quality for higher quality wool, damaging the wool by sloppy carding, or even dying and weaving themselves and not selling their thread to weavers. Spinners accused both weavers and merchant investors of making secret arrangements with other spinners to pay them less than the standard wage, of buying thread from the spinners in their houses and not at the public market so no one could see how little they were paying, of confiscating thread illegally, or of buying all their thread from rural spinners to the detriment of spinners living in the city.[135] Many of these same accusations were leveled at the merchant investors by weavers' guilds as they felt their hold on cloth production slipping.

Urban linen-spinners felt particularly threatened, for linen spinning was a growing rural occupation throughout the period.[136] Not only rural women, but also rural men, spent much of their time preparing and spinning linen and later spinning cotton when that industry grew in south Germany. Sebastian Franck noticed this when he visited the areas around Augsburg and Ulm, and he commented: "Not only women and maids, but also men and boys, spin. One sees contradictions: they work and gossip like women yet are still vigorous, active, strong, and quarrelsome people, the kind any area would want to have."[137]

Most cloth produced in south Germany was wool, linen, cotton, or blends of these, but in 1601 the duke of Württemburg attempted to start silk production in Stuttgart. He hired all kinds of people, from gardeners to weavers, male and female, to care for the mulberry trees, the silkworms, the cocoons and to handle every stage of production. The following year every town and jurisdiction in Württemburg was asked to send two boys or girls, chosen from among those receiving public support, to Stuttgart to learn silk spinning. The duke was to provide housing and support for these young people, but very few towns sent any. The industry itself was never very successful, as the German climate is somewhat harsh for silkworms, and the duke's attempts finally collapsed in the Thirty Years' War.[138] Thus silk spinning never became an important occupation for women in Germany the way it was in north Italian cities such as Florence and Lucca, in London, or in French cities such as Paris or Lyon.[139]

This short-lived experiment does point out that spinning of all ty̧ es was seen as an alternative to poor relief. Orphans and other poor children, boys as well as girls, were taught spinning, and authorities saw spinning as a way of reducing the amounts required for public welfare. Unfortunately these same authorities did not see that raising the wages paid spinners might have made them completely self-sufficient. As Alice Clark says of the seventeenth century in England, "Spinning became the chief resource of the married women who were losing their hold on other industries, but its return in money value was too low to render them independent of other means of support."[140]

Donald Woodward, another commentator on the English scene, notes that wages for spinning were so low that though this was an "essential part of many household economies," it was "rarely of sufficient importance to be considered a by-employment."[141] Though the wages were low, the frequency of spinning wheels in Woodward's household inventories makes his dismissal of the importance of spinning somewhat puzzling, however. Between one-third and one-half of the households he surveyed had spinning wheels, which to most observers would indicate that spinning was the most important by-employment available to rural English families, or certainly not one to be dismissed out of hand.

Spinners in Germany as well as England were extremely underpaid and could not support a family on their wages—or in some cases, even support themselves. As Klaus-Joachim Lorenzen-Schmidt notes for Schleswig, "seamstresses and spinners are predominantly labeled 'poor' in the city tax records," which Bücher notes for Frankfurt and Schmoller for Strasbourg as well.[142] Their wages did go up during the sixteenth century, but not fast enough to make up for the general rise in prices. Women identified as spinners frequently appealed to city councils for support, noting, "What little I make at spinning will not provide enough for even my bread."[143]

Thus by the mid-seventeenth century, women were limited to the lowest paid and the least pleasant tasks in the cloth industry, to work that they *could* do part time even if they needed to work full time to support themselves, or to work that was outside the guild structure and which men did as well as a side occupation. Whether they worked for guild masters or merchant investors, their labor was essentially proletarianized, and their economic security was minimal. They generally worked in isolation in their own homes, so unlike male weavers and also unlike market women, who worked together or in competition with one another, they developed little work identity and so did not organize as a group.

*Women Preparing Flax.* Woodcut by *Petrus de Crescentiis, in* Von den Feld und Ackerbau *(Frankfurt, 1583).*

# Conclusions

As the preceding chapters have made clear, women in the early modern period were working in a wide variety of occupations in every sector of the economy. Their work was affected by economic and technological change, religious and political developments, and intellectual movements. Because women's work was so varied, it is difficult to draw sweeping conclusions, but some general trends are discernable. To analyze these, it is useful to divide women's work into three general categories: occupations in which there was little change over the period, occupations in which both men's and women's work changed as the result of more general changes, and occupations in which women were restricted or excluded specifically because they were women.

Domestic service was affected very little by the changes of the period and continued to be the only employment option open for a number of women. It constituted a training and waiting period for many women before they married, but for others it was a permanent occupation. Servants were poorly paid and had little authority, so there were no economic or political reasons to oppose women working as servants. In fact, as the authorities' fear of disorder and masterless persons increased during the sixteenth century, domestic service appeared to them to be the perfect employment for unmarried women. The more prosperous households which could hire many servants were generally headed by men, and cities also passed laws which required single women to take positions in male-headed households only. Larger household staffs grew more fashionable in the seventeenth century, and maids were also employed at spinning and other production-related tasks in the households of merchant investors. For women who did not or could not marry, domestic service provided the best means of making sure they had masters.[1]

Women also continued to be employed in large numbers in other service occupations, particularly those society viewed as extensions of a woman's work in the home. Through the centuries women had been responsible for treating illnesses in their own families and among their servants, slaves, and serfs and for comforting the sick and dying. When these activities were transferred to hospitals and infirmaries, women, especially those in certain religious orders, continued to be involved. During the sixteenth century the majority of both Protestant and Catholic cities secularized and rationalized their public welfare and hospital systems, taking over church institutions and combining small hospitals and endowed funds into larger, more comprehensive ones. In total number and type of jobs involved, however, this process seems to have had little effect on women's employment. Lay women simply replaced the sisters, or the same women kept on working as city, rather than church, employees. A great many of the lower-level employees in the city hospitals, pesthouses, and orphanages—cooks, maids, wet nurses, and maintenance staff—were women, and most of the administration and day-to-day decision making, including medical diagnoses, were carried out by women as well.

Although most welfare distribution was handled by men, women were often responsible for distributing funds and charities which went to women alone. Dowries for poor girls and support for expectant mothers were handled by female administrators in some cities. This, too, may be seen as a continuation of a long-standing practice. Before the cities took control, these endowments had often been started by women, maintained by contributions from wealthy widows, and administered privately by other women.

Such service occupations generally remained open to women without challenges from men because the jobs required no initial capital or specialized training; wages were low, often little more than room and board; and the work was often unpleasant and physically taxing. Even though some of these positions, particularly those in hospitals, involved a great amount of responsibility, they still had low status because of low pay and lack of formal training. Many service occupations had the advantage for women of being quite flexible, allowing them to move in and out of jobs as their own family responsibilities changed; but this same impermanence also meant that these women did not organize to protect their rights, as their first loyalty was to their families.

Midwifery was the one exception among service jobs. Midwives did go through a period of training, which lengthened over the centuries of the study, and could become, if not wealthy, at least financially secure. They had an accepted public role as witnesses and medical investigators and a strong sense of work identity. Though male accoucheurs and "man-midwives" were beginning to appear in France and England during this period, in the south German cities birth remained a female affair.

Conclusions

The changes in midwifery during the period were eventually to lead to a decline in the midwives' salary, independence, and status and are part of broader cultural changes. As city authorities became more concerned about public order and morality, they used midwives to help control illegitimacy and fornication, and thus they came to demand higher moral standards of the midwives themselves. As the status of university-trained physicians rose in comparison with that of barber-surgeons and midwives, both trained through apprenticeship, cities began to put midwives under the control of male physicians. As city governments attempted to regulate all aspects of life, the ordinances regarding midwives became much longer and more complex.

These same trends can be seen in other occupations during the period, and they led in many of them to restrictions on work performed by both men and women. Cities passed stricter market regulations in their attempts to control monopolies, ensure the purity and quality of food products, prevent the selling of stolen goods, enforce political and religious censorship, keep foot and wagon traffic moving freely, protect local production, and ensure the payment of taxes and fees. These regulations were not sex specific, however, and women continued to dominate trade at the city marketplaces. In fact, throughout the period the sexual balance in sales and trade changed very little. Men continued to be the long-distance merchants and investors, and women, the local distributors. Both men and women were fishmongers, game and poultry dealers, and innkeepers, either as married couples or independently. In addition, wives were often responsible for the sale and distribution of their husbands' products, such as bread, meat, and clothing. Such occupations often required the labor of at least two persons and were rarely profitable enough to be viewed as any sort of economic threat.

Many of the ordinances and regulations governing various occupations were originally passed to make sure those practicing an occupation had been properly trained. Although they were not specifically directed against women, in practice women were more affected because they could not go through formal training programs. Women were, of course, not allowed to receive university training, which meant they could not become physicians and lawyers. A university education was increasingly required of upper-class officials, which meant that a wife could not officially assist her husband in his duties. Gradually the requirement seems to have trickled down to lower-level officials, so that positions like gatekeeper and toll collector were no longer held by couples, but by men alone. The wife may have still opened the gates or collected the tolls, but she was not considered an official and was no longer required to swear an oath of office.

Members of other occupations, such as apothecaries, barber-surgeons, and notaries, attempted to identify themselves as somehow "professional" and thus drew increasingly distinct lines between fellow professionals who were formally trained and people who simply practiced on their own. The apothecaries generally succeeded in their attempts to make theirs a respectable, learned trade. In accomplishing this, they established a sharp distinction between themselves and the women who sold medicinal herbs, even though both groups' raw materials were in many cases the same. The herb sellers were specifically forbidden to mix any herbs and gradually prohibited from selling anything which might be dangerous.

The barber-surgeons, on the other hand, never succeeded in completely defining for themselves an exclusive sphere of operations. Women who were successful at curing minor afflictions—eye infections, skin diseases, boils, and the like—were allowed to continue doing so without officials going on record that such work was normally the province of barber-surgeons alone. Some of these decisions stemmed from the sentiment that it was improper for a male barber-surgeon to treat a woman with an infection, particularly one located on the breasts or genital area, but the midwives and other women who handled illnesses dealt with children and men as well. The resultant lack of differentiation between the medical work done by women and by barber-surgeons was certainly a factor in the continued low status of the latter group.

Part of the decline of the activity of female appraisers may be traced to the growing professionalization of lawyers and male appraisers. More formal legal language became a requirement for wills and inventories, which made it difficult for women with little formal education either to draw up a will on their own or to write out a proper inventory. In one case in Nuremberg the council specifically stated that the language used by a widow in a supplication concerning her husband's will was "too raw and haughty" and told her to seek an advisor—a notary or a lawyer—to help her smooth it out.[2] The male appraisers often succeeded in becoming actual city officials, which ended the chances for women in the field. Tied to this formalization of legal procedures was an increase in the importance of the guardians in all cases of inheritance. Although women were not required to have a guardian during this period, the practice became more and more common if disputes with the children's guardians were anticipated after a husband died. By the eighteenth century guardianship for women was made law, and even unmarried women were relegated to the legal status of minors.

Women were also excluded from certain crafts under the guise of technological improvement. The Munich brewers argued that "brewing is a learned art and given to men alone"; the Lübeck dyers maintained that widows should not continue to operate shops because they had not been taught the new method of dyeing.[3] In the professions and crafts as well, then, a line was gradually drawn between the skilled and unskilled spheres of labor. Women could not enter occupations in which formal education or apprenticeship was needed and thus, along with unskilled male workers, could not rise above low-paying and low-status jobs within these sectors of the economy. Because untrained men were also excluded, however, these restrictions were not perceived as directed specifically against women. In fact, authorities often appeared more willing to make exceptions for women and let them work at an occupation normally closed to those without formal training. This attitude was the equal result of both their sympathy for widows and poor women left without a means of support and their desire to keep such women from needing public welfare. As long as the woman concerned did little more than support herself or her children, there was a tendency among authorities to overlook infractions and to order any guilds or professional bodies concerned to overlook them as well. After all, this was "only a poor widow" whose work could not be much competition and so should not be regarded as seriously as a man's.[4]

The increasing concern with public morality noted in reference to midwives also affected women's employment in other areas. Municipal brothels were closed; public baths, either closed or regarded with great suspicion. In case after case, moral considerations entered into city council decisions, both in individual cases and in the formulation of general ordinances. Women making supplications were not only investigated as to their claims of poverty and helplessness but also as to their lifestyle and general worthiness. Women were chosen for certain positions—as teachers, hospital administrators, and orphanage directors—because of their moral standards as well as their skill and training. This was also true for men in similar positions, but because the training required for women was often ill-defined or not mentioned at all, moral considerations became paramount.[5]

Moral considerations were also often the reason given by city councils for their increasing concern with women who worked and lived on their own. Here something deeper and more fundamental was at work, however, than simply the oft-noted concern of city fathers with the private lives of their cities' residents. Such women were "masterless," that is, outside the control of a male head of household. They were, as the weavers in Augsburg complained, free to work when they chose, free to walk around when they chose, and ever more vocal in defending their rights.[6] This independence became increasingly disturbing to guild masters, city councils, and journeymen and led to a variety of laws aimed at forcing women into male-headed households. The sheer number of women involved, however, made this an unattainable ideal.

This hostility to and suspicion of unmarried women was not something completely new in early modern Europe (the late medieval religious groups such as the Beguines and the Sisters of the Common Life had also experienced such hostility), but this was the first time that actual laws against secular unmarried women were enacted by city governments. Both Protestant and Catholic authorities increasingly viewed marriage as the "natural" vocation for women—for all women in Protestant areas and for most women in Catholic areas. Women who did not marry were somehow "unnatural" and therefore suspect, a fact many historians of witchcraft have noted.[7]

This widely accepted ideal of marriage had a negative effect on women's work. Though city councils recognized that some women would have to work, they always viewed this work as a temporary or stopgap measure until the women could attain or return to their "natural," married state. Thus they were never willing to make blanket statements allowing women per se to practice any highly skilled occupation and were suspicious when women made more than subsistence wages. "Women's work" came increasingly to be defined as that which required little training or initial capital, could be done in spare moments and was done by men only as a side occupation, carried low status, and was informally organized and badly paid. To be allowed to work, women themselves often stressed these factors when appealing to city councils. By down-playing their own abilities and effectiveness, some women won the right to work but in doing so, contributed to the beliefs that women's work was somehow different than men's and that women, even if doing the same work as men, deserved less pay. They should be paid less, according to city authorities, both because the quality and quantity of their work was lower and because women did not "need" as much as men, who were assumed to have families to support. The authorities recognized that women who worked did so out of necessity and not out of choice and often had families to support, whereas some men did not; but this recognition did not lead to equal pay.

All of these trends—professionalization, increasing regulation, concern with public morality, suspicion of unmarried women, devaluation of women's work—led in some cases to outright prohibition of women's work. Not only were women excluded because they were untrained or dishonorable but specifically and solely because they were women. This exclusion of women solely because of gender is also related to larger developments, particularly to political conflicts within the cities and to a growth of self-consciousness among the journeymen.

Women's work was a handy arena for the battles between guilds and city councils, or between factions within those councils, over control of the economic life of the city. When guilds prohibited "women and other untrained persons" or simply women from carrying out certain activities, the councils often responded by defending an individual woman's right to work. They did this both because the woman represented no threat to the generally wealthy, upper-class council members and because this was a way to demonstrate, for the benefit of the guilds, who had the ultimate authority in the city. Thus women's work had a symbolic importance far beyond its real economic impact; only by understanding this can one understand why such a fuss was made over an old woman making pretzels or a widow brewing beer. Women's work became the chosen arena because it was one sector of the economy in which the workers had no voice, no political power, and few formal rights; governing bodies could freely fight with each other without interference from the workers themselves.[8]

Both economic and symbolic factors led the journeymen to demand the exclusion of women from guild shops. With the general economic decline of the sixteenth century, the opportunities for journeymen to become masters decreased; they began to think of themselves as a separate group, not just masters-in-training—"*Gesellen*" (comrades) rather than "*Knechte*" (vassals). They became increasingly resentful of the power of the masters and began to form separate journeymen's guilds. These guilds demanded the right to determine who would work in a shop and seized it by refusing to work alongside those who did not have their approval. At first they excluded those who were illegitimate or regarded as somehow "dishonorable," but gradually came to exclude pieceworkers and women as well. Journeymen first demanded that the master's maids be excluded from all production-related tasks, then that his wife and daughters be barred as well. They thus assured themselves of more workplaces and also achieved a symbolic victory over the master. He may have determined their hours and wages, but the journeymen kept his female dependents out of the shop. In addition, they made sure they would never have to take orders from a woman.

As journeymen succeeded in their demands that the master's wife, daughters, and maids be excluded from the shop, they also succeeded in their demands that they be allowed to marry. Having campaigned so fervently against women's work, however, they never requested that their wives be allowed to work with them, though this could have been financially advantageous. Their sentiment against women working in the skilled trades extended to their own wives and daughters as the idea spread that working next to any woman was somehow dishonorable. Their wives and daughters were thus relegated to domestic service, sales, or employment in a "free" crafts, all of which were generally poorly paid.

Thus many different groups in early modern cities were increasingly separating women's work from men's work and simultaneously devaluing women's work. City councils did this to assure public order and decorum, while keeping some low-paying, low-status occupations open to women to prevent their requesting public assistance. By passing or agreeing with blanket prohibitions of women's work but still allowing individual women to work, councils asserted their control of the economy and at the same time reinforced the idea that women's work need not be taken seriously. Journeymen also wanted men's and women's work spatially separated and differentially rewarded, but because of their own proximity to women in pay and status, they wanted no exceptions to be made. In their supplications to guilds and city councils women themselves often found it practical to stress the distinction between their work and men's work and also the small impact their work would have.

Though in the long run women's down-playing of their own role was probably harmful, in the short run it accomplished what they wanted from it. They clearly knew what the councils wanted to hear, just as they knew where the best places for selling were, who the honest business people were, what regulations could be avoided, and what political squabbles could be used advantageously. In fact, what emerges most clearly from the records is not the dismal exclusion of women from economic life but their continued involvement in it despite all barriers and restrictions. As they were progressively excluded from the skilled crafts, they turned to sales and services or to those crafts which were informally organized.

What any woman did depended on her age, skills, marital status, energy level, and ingenuity and also on what sorts of occupations were available in her community. During the course of her lifetime, she might be involved in a wide variety of occupations, full time or part time, in her own home or in someone else's, in the fields surrounding the city or at the public market. Once she had found something which fit her needs and skills, she defended her right to work at it against guilds, city councils, and other "envious and malicious" people. She generally did this individually, not joining together with other working women, and so was not always successful, but she certainly did not submit meekly. Though women could rarely gather enough resources for significant capital investment, they could and did use modern business procedures. Many kept records, some of which involved double-entry bookkeeping; they loaned and borrowed money at interest; they made contracts which involved fairly elaborate shipping and storage instructions.

Because of the nature of most women's work, that is, frequently changing and often part time, they often did not develop the strong sense of work identity that craftsmen did. In some occupations, such as midwifery, innkeeping, and appraising, however, women did, as demonstrated by their tendency to hand down their occupations to their daughters in the same way that craftsmen did to their sons.[9] The wife of a craftsman also felt a sense of work identity based on her recognition that her role in the shop was as important as that of her husband. She would have identified herself as, for example, "the wife of the butcher," which was not simply her marital status but also her occupational title. Her neighbors recognized that she had certain skills and tasks, and her pride at being the wife of the butcher rather than, say, the wife of a day laborer came not only from her husband's stature but also from her own. For such women, family identity and work identity were linked and not antithetical.

I do not mean to sound too positive. Women were limited to an increasingly narrow range of occupations during the period, and the work they did was devalued, both economically and ideologically. As individual wages replaced family wages and journeymen forced women out of the shop, the wives of master craftsmen and merchants gradually retreated from active work in the family business; "the wife of a butcher" was less an occupational title in 1700 than in 1500. Journeymen's wives never shared responsibility for a family product the way the wives of master craftsmen did; they never appeared in court or in wills as butchers' and bakers' wives did. The wages of those who had always worked as individuals—pieceworkers, domestic servants, and day laborers—did not keep up with the rise in prices and were held down even more than men's wages because of feelings about the value of women's work.

From today's perspective one might wonder why early modern working women did not perceive what was happening, did not realize where the professionalization, increasing regulation, and the separation of men's work from women's would lead. Did they not realize that by down-playing their own skills and performance they were contributing to trends that would be extremely detrimental to them in the long run? Why did they not organize to defend their rights collectively or set up formal structures to regulate their occupations?

The answers to these questions lie, not in the realms of economic or political change or intellectual or technological developments, but in two universal characteristics of women in history. First, women make up half the population, and that means half of every class, social level, and economic level. Naturally they identify as much, often more, with the men of their class as with the women of other classes. This was particularly so in medieval Europe, where there were more restrictions and limitations by class than by sex. As Rosemary Radford Ruether comments:

> It would have been difficult to recognize women as an oppressed gender group when the primary social stratification integrated some women into roles of power. Indeed, perhaps it was not until the early modern period that the perception of women as marginalized by gender became stronger than the perception of women as divided by class. Only then could a feminist movement arise that protested the subjugation of women as a group.[10]

The increasing restrictions on women's work are an important part of that marginalization by gender, but it would have been impossible for an early modern woman to foresee the final extent of that marginalization.

Second, whether viewed positively or negatively, as biological or cultural, a woman's primary concern has traditionally been the welfare of her children and family. Work has been adapted so far as possible to family responsibilities. This adaptation was relatively easy in the medieval economy but grew increasingly difficult as occupations grew more rigid in training requirements and demanded full-time labor. This meant that a married woman with a working husband might elect to stay with her children rather than pursue one of the low-paying, low-status jobs available to her. If a woman's family depended on her income, however, she was willing to do any kind of work to support them or to use any kind of arguments to be allowed to work.

The fact that so many women's supplications in all fields—medicine, sales, the crafts, food production—stress their dependents originally struck me as simply a play for the authorities' pity. Recent studies of women's psychological and moral development prompt me to suspect that the approach may stem from something deeper. Carol Gilligan finds that women describe themselves in terms of their relationships with others, and they perceive those relationships as forming a network rather than a hierarchy. Confronted with moral problems, women tend to justify their solutions and the actions they take with a value system based on responsibility in relationships and on care rather than on rights and on rules. "The logic underlying an ethic of care is a psychological logic of relationship, which contrasts with the formal logic of fairness that informs the justice approach."[11] When they follow this approach, women are much less likely to base their decisions or actions on abstract principles or absolutes than on individual context.

Although there are evident dangers in applying twentieth-century psychological theory to earlier periods, the parallels between the women Gilligan studies and the women making supplications about their work are very striking. The early modern working women also based their appeals on their responsibility to others—to people who were actually related to them and about whom they cared. They saw themselves first as part of a network of relationships which included family, relatives, friends, neighbors, and acquaintances rather than as members of a hierarchical system such as a guild. They rarely argued that they had a "right" to do something because of precedent or regulations but often that the circumstances surrounding their case might even warrant a break with the rules and the past. The appeals that were successful often involved the supplicant throwing herself on the mercy of the authorities "as the protector and shield of poor widows and orphans," but rather than reflecting actual feelings of helplessness, the approach may as easily have been motivated by sense of responsibility to others and recognition that this kind of rhetoric might bring the results necessary to meet that responsibility. A supplicant using this tactic certainly recognized that, in the eyes of male authorities, widows as a group deserved charity and pity and that her request was thus more likely to be granted if she convinced them that she was especially needy and would otherwise need public poor relief.

Reconstructing women's thought patterns or even determining which phrases were their own and which belonged to the notaries in these supplications is very difficult and must be done with reservations. Nonetheless, it seems unlikely that these women—who hired someone to write the supplication; provided the facts of the case; and appeared personally before city councils, ducal courts, and other bodies—were in fact as weak and pathetic as they attempted to appear. Journeymen may have felt it was dishonorable to work next to a woman, but questions of honor, or even modesty and physical strength, do not appear as considerations for women seeking to support themselves and their parents, children, and husbands. Nor did questions of sisterly solidarity; women were often willing to separate themselves from other women to win permission to work.

There were a few women, though, who had a broader view of what was happening, who argued for the rights of all women. Some of these were literary women—like Louise Labé, Christine de Pisan, and the Mesdames DesRoches—who expressed their thoughts in poetry, fiction, and treatises.[12] Others figured in this study, like Katherine Carberiner, Elizabeth Heyssin, and Brigitta Muller, whose ideas are recorded only because they came into conflict with the authorities. The voices of most working women from the period have not been heard, but there may have been many others who agreed with Katherine Carberiner that "women have more trust in other women" and felt about their work as Elizabeth Heyssin did when she asserted that "such are fine things for women to do."

# Abbreviations

| | |
|---|---|
| Augsburg | Augsburg Stadtarchiv |
| BB | Bürgerbücher |
| Frankfurt | Frankfurt Stadtarchiv |
| BMB | Bürgermeisterbücher |
| Ver | Verordnungen |
| Freiburg | Freiburg im Breisgau Stadtarchiv |
| Memmingen | Memmingen Stadtarchiv |
| BB | Bürgerbücher |
| RPB | Ratsprotokollbücher |
| Munich | Munich Stadtarchiv |
| HGS | Heilig-Geist-Spital |
| RSP | Ratsitzungsprotokolle |
| Nuremberg | Nuremberg Staatsarchiv |
| AStB | Amts- und Standbücher |
| RB | Ratsbücher |
| RV | Ratsverlässe (Verlässe des Inneren Rats) |
| Nuremberg Stadt | Nuremberg Stadtarchiv |
| Inven | Inventarbücher |
| Lib Litt | Libri Litterarum (Stadtgericht der Reichsstadt Nürnberg Grundverbriefungsbücher) |
| QNG | Quellen zur Nürnbergische Geschichte |
| Strasbourg | Strasbourg, Archives Municipales |
| XV | Akten der XV |
| XXI | Akten der XXI |
| RB | Der erneuerte grosse Rathsbuch |
| Stuttgart | Stuttgart, Württembergisches Hauptstaatsarchiv |
| Stuttgart Stadt | Stuttgart Stadtarchiv |
| Findbuch | Stadt Stuttgart Historisches Archiv Findbuch |

Archival collections are fully identified in the bibliography, which also includes full details of publications of books and articles. Articles from collections of essays are cited by author in the notes, but such volumes are sometimes listed under the editor's name in the bibliography.

# Notes

## INTRODUCTION

1. Gerda Lerner has stated this most emphatically in "The Challenge of Women's History" in *The Majority Finds Its Past*, 169.
2. George Unwin, *Industrial Organization in the Sixteenth and Seventeenth Centuries*; W. Abel, *Agrarkrisen und Agrarkonjunktur*; Hermann Kellenbenz, *The Rise of the European Economy*; Myron P. Gutmann, *War and Rural Life in the Early Modern Low Countries*; Perez Zagorin, *Rebels and Rulers 1500–1660*, vol. 1, *Society, States and Early Modern Revolution: Agrarian and Urban Rebellions*; Barrett Beer, *Rebellion and Riot: Popular Disorder in England during the Reign of Edward VI*; Peter Kriedte, *Peasants, Landlords and Merchant Capitalists: Europe and the World Economy 1500–1800*.
3. See Natalie Zemon Davis, *Society and Culture in Early Modern France*; Peter Burke, *Popular Culture in Early Modern Europe*; Lawrence Stone, *The Family, Sex and Marriage in England 1500–1800*; Steven Ozment, *When Fathers Ruled: Family Life in Reformation Europe*; Linda Pollock, *Forgotten Children: Parent–Child Relations from 1500 to 1900*; Thomas Max Safley, *Let No Man Put Asunder: The Control of Marriage in the German Southwest, 1550–1600*. There are also many biographies of exceptional women and studies of men's ideas about women.
4. Alice Clark, *Working Life of Women in the Seventeenth Century*.
5. Karl Bücher, *Die Frauenfrage im Mittelalter*, 16. Bücher's argument here is not based on statistical findings, for he does not continue his survey of the Frankfurt population into the sixteenth century. Despite the fact that the fifteenth century in Frankfurt saw an increase in the percentage of taxpayers who were female—24.26 percent for the century as a whole as compared with 20.35 percent for the fourteenth century—and the fact that the last half of the fifteenth century saw a steady increase in that percentage, Bücher feels that somehow this must have ended by the sixteenth century. His own reasoning at this point is a good example of wishful thinking, of trying to explain something he clearly saw happening—a decline in the number of occupations open

to women—by ignoring his own statistical findings. It is certainly difficult to see how he could otherwise have called the early sixteenth century "peaceful times which must have brought a gradual leveling in
the significant sexual imbalance evident in the Middle Ages." Unfortunately the sources he used, the Bedebücher, have been destroyed, so
there now are no statistics on the sexual balance of the Frankfurt population after 1500.

6. Bücher, *Frauenfrage*; Friedrich Bothe, *Beiträge zur Wirtschafts- und
Sozialgeschichte der Reichsstadt Frankfurt*; idem, *Frankfurts wirtschaftliche-
soziale Entwicklung vor dem Dreissigjährigen Kriege und der Fettmilchaufstand (1612–1616)*; Gerd Wunder, "Die Bewohner der Reichsstadt Hall
im Jahre 1545"; idem, *Die Stuttgarter Steuerliste von 1545*; Barbara
Kroemer, "Die Einführung der Reformation in Memmingen."

7. Helmut Wachendorf, *Die wirtschaftliche Stellung der Frau in den deutschen
Städten des späteren Mittelalters*, 147–148.

8. Rudolph Wissell, *Das alten Handwerks Recht und Gewohnheit*, 445.

9. Sibylle Harksen, *Die Frau im Mittelalter*, 28.

10. See Annette Winter, "Studien zur sozialen Situation der Frauen in der
Stadt Trier nach der Steuerliste von 1364," 20–25; Martha Congleton
Howell, "Women's Work in Urban Economies of Late Medieval North-
western Europe: Female Labor Status in Male Economic Institutions";
Edith Ennen, "Die Frau in der Mittelalterlichen Stadtgesellschaft Mit-
teleuropas"; Margaret Wensky, *Die Stellung der Frau in der stadtkölnische
Wirtschaft im Spätmittelalter*.

11. See especially Louise Tilly and Joan Scott, *Women, Work and the Family*.

12. Robert Reynolds, *Europe Emerges: Transition toward an Industrial World
600–1750*; Wilhelm Wilda, *Das Gildenwesen im Mittelalter*, 288–344;
Karl Bosl and Eberhard Weis, *Die Gesellschaft in Deutschland*; Fernand
Braudel, *Civilization and Capitalism in the Fifteenth–Eighteenth Centuries*, vol. 2, *The Wheels of Commerce*; Ernst Pitz, *Wirtschafts- und Sozialgeschichte Deutschlands im Mittelalter*.

13. Olwen H. Hufton, "Women and the Family Economy in Eighteenth-
Century France"; Barbara Mayer Wertheimer, *We Were There: The Story
of Working Women in America*; Tilly and Scott, *Women, Work*; Susan Estabrook Kennedy, *If All We Did Was to Weep at Home: A History of White
Working Class Women in America*; Olwen H. Hufton, "Women, Work
and Marriage in Eighteenth-Century France"; Alice Kessler-Harris,
*Out to Work: A History of Wage-Earning Women in the United States*.

14. Bücher, *Frauenfrage*; Winter, "Studien"; Gerd Wunder, "Unterschichten
der Reichsstadt Hall," in Erich Maschke and Jürgen Sydow, eds., *Städtische Unterschichten*; Wachendorf, *Stellung*, 24.

15. Bücher, *Frauenfrage*.

16. Bothe, *Beiträge*; Kroemer, "Einführung"; Bothe, *Entwicklung*; G.
Wunder, "Bewohner"; idem, *Steuerliste*.

17. Bothe, *Entwicklung*; Oscar Westermann "Die Bevölkerungsverhältnisse
Memmingens in ausgehende Mittelalter"; G. Wunder "Bewohner";

idem, *Steuerliste*; Erich Maschke, *Gesellschaftliche Unterschichten in den südwestdeutschen Städten*, 27; Edith Ennen, "Die Frau im Mittelalter," 92. Similar situations may be found in other European cities as well, e.g., Leiden, Copenhagen, Malmø, and Schleswig. Howell, "Women's Work," 85; Grethe Jacobsen, "Women's Work and Women's Role: Ideology and Reality in Danish Urban Society, 1300–1550," 15, n. 73; Klaus-Joachim Lorenzen-Schmidt, "Zur Stellung der Frauen in der frühneuzeitlichen Städtegesellschaft Schleswigs und Holsteins," 329–333. All of these tax lists must be used very carefully, however, as there is no standard procedure for identifying a woman's marital status. Some city scribes were quite thorough and listed women who paid taxes as single (*ledig*), widowed (*witfrau*), or wife (*uxor*), but others labeled some women and not others. I assume, for instance, that all those labeled "widow" were widows but not that there were no widows among those not labeled as such. Some women labeled "widow" or "single" are also labeled "servant," and so it is difficult to tell whether these women lived on their own or lived in their employer's household. Simply because they are not listed as paying any taxes does not necessarily mean they were not heads of household; for that particular collection, the "Habenichtsen" may have been charged nothing but simply listed by name. Claus-Peter Clasen attempts to deal with many of these problems in his study of the Augsburg tax lists, but questions still remain. For example, why do a few women have property taxed separately from that of their husbands? And what about married women who lived apart from their husbands? (Clasen, *Die Augsburger Steuerbücher um 1600*). Because of the nature of the documents, all the percentages given in the preceding documents must be seen as estimates. As I refer to a number of different types of money, a word about coinage is necessary. The basic monetary unit was the silver pfennig (d), which was further divided for small purchases into two heller (hl). Six pfennige made up one schilling (s), which did circulate as a coin as well. The pound (£), which was strictly a money of account, was originally figured at 30d, but during the fifteenth century the "new pound," worth four times as much as the old one (120d) came to be the more common unit. In addition to these silver coins, several others circulated freely, such as the Bohemian groschen, worth 7.5d, and the kreuzer (kr), worth 4d. The standard unit for figuring large sums of money was the golden gulden, or florin (fl), which was minted in some south German towns from the early fifteenth century. This was originally exchanged for silver at a rate of 8 old £, 12d per florin, but increased in value during the sixteenth century as silver became more plentiful relative to gold. Most comparisons I make are between amounts given either in pfenninge—such as daily wages and food prices—or in gulden—such as annual salaries or property—so the exchange rate is not often an important variable. Volumes have been written about monetary and price history during the early modern period, as it is an extremely complex and involved issue, so I have tried to keep all references to coinage to a minimum or, wherever possible, translated them into real terms.

18. Memmingen RPB: November 10, 1557; July 7, 1570; June 16, 1598; December 4, 1603; October 15, 1604; June 12, 1612; July 20, 1618. Frankfurt BMB, 1600, fols. 50b, 81b. Munich RSP, 1607, fols. 158, 130.

19. Natalie Zemon Davis, "City Women and Religious Change," in idem, *Society and Culture*, 65–96; Joan Kelly, "Early Feminist Theory and the Querelle des Femmes, 1400–1789."

20. R. H. Tawney, *Religion and the Rise of Capitalism*; Christopher Hill, "Puritans and the Poor"; Natalie Davis, "Women on Top," in idem, *Society and Culture*, 124–151; John Bellamy, *Crime and Public Order in England in the Later Middle Ages*; Gordon Schochet, *Patriarchalism in Political Thought: The Authoritarian Family and Political Speculations and Attitudes Especially in Seventeenth-Century England*; John Yost, "The Value of Married Life for the Social Order in the Early English Renaissance"; Michael Weisser, *Crime and Punishment in Early Modern Europe*; Heide Wunder, "'L'espace privé and the Domestication of Women in the Sixteenth and Seventeenth Centuries." See chapter 1 for a fuller discussion of legislation against women living independently.

21. Joan Kelly [Gadol], "Did Women Have a Renaissance?"

22. Jane Dempsey Douglass, "Women and the Continental Reformation"; Margaret King, "Thwarted Ambitions: Six Learned Women of the Italian Renaissance"; John Yost, "Changing Attitudes toward Married Life in Civic and Christian Humanism"; Margaret King, "Book Lined Cells: Women and Humanism in the Early Italian Renaissance"; Susan Karant-Nunn, "Continuity and Change: Some Effects of the Reformation on the Women of Zwickau."

23. See the debate in *New Left Review* 83, 89, 94: Wally Secombe, "The Housewife and Her Labour under Capitalism"; Jean Gardiner, "Women's Domestic Labour"; Margaret Coulson, Branka Magaš, and Hilary Cartwright, "The Housewife and Her Labour under Capitalism: A Critique"; Wally Secombe, "Domestic Labour: Reply to Critics." See also Eli Zaretsky, *Capitalism, the Family and Personal Life*; Annette Kuhn and Ann Marie Wolpe, eds., *Feminism and Materialism: Women and Modes of Production*; M. Barrett, *Women's Oppression Today: Problems in Marxist and Feminist Analysis*; E. Malos, ed., *The Politics of Housework*; Olivia Harris, "Households as Natural Units."

# CHAPTER ONE:
## POLITICAL, ECONOMIC, AND LEGAL STRUCTURES

1. Karl Bücher, *Die Bevölkerung von Frankfurt am Main in 14. und 15. Jahrhunderts*; Friedrich Bothe, *Geschichte der Stadt Frankfurt*; Hans Mauersberg, *Wirtschafts- und Sozialgeschichte zentraleuropäischer Städte in neuerer Zeit*; Gerald Lyman Soliday, *A Community in Conflict: Frankfurt Society in*

the Seventeenth and Early Eighteenth Centuries; *Frankfurt um 1600: All-tagsleben in der Stadt.*

2. Julius Rathgeber, *Strassburg im 16. Jahrhundert*; Ulrich Crämer, *Die Verfassung und Verwaltung Strassburgs von der Reformationszeit bis zum Fall der Reichsstadt (1521–1681)*; Franklin L. Ford, *Strasbourg in Transition, 1648–1789*; Miriam U. Chrisman, *Strasbourg and the Reform: A Study in the Process of Change.*

3. G. W. K. Lochner, *Die Einwohnerzahl der ehemaligen Reichsstadt Nürnberg*, 19; Caspar Ott, *Bevölkerungsstatistik in der Stadt und Landschaft Nürnberg in der ersten Hälfte des 15. Jahrhundert*; Willi Rüger, *Die Almosenordnungen der Reichsstadt Nürnberg*; Rudolph Endres, "Zur Einwohnerzahl und Bevölkerungsstruktur Nürnbergs im 15./16. Jahrhunderts"; Otto Püchner, "Das Register des Gemeinen Pfennigs (1497) der Reichsstadt Nürnberg als bevölkerungsgeschichtliche Quelle."

4. Westermann, "Bevölkerung"; Karl Bosl, ed., *Handbuch der historischen Stätten Deutschlands.*

5. Erich Keyser, *Württembergisches Städtebuch*; Max Miller, ed., *Handbuch der historischen Stätten Deutschlands.*

6. Bosl, *Handbuch*, 464–484; Fridolin Solleder, *München im Mittelalter.*

7. Memmingen BB; Nuremberg AStB, nos. 299–300, 305–306; Augsburg BB.

8. Benno Schmidt and Karl Bücher, *Frankfurter Amts- und Zunfturkunden bis zum Jahre 1612*, 512. Frankfurt BMB: 1495, fol. 26a; 1505, fol. 15b. Beata Brodmeier, *Die Frau im Handwerk*, 14–20.

9. The idea that women did not swear oaths or assume any military responsibilities and were thus a kind of second-class citizens can be found in a number of authors. Where they got this idea remains a mystery, however, as the sources are full of women swearing all kinds of oaths—as witnesses, officials, citizens—and providing all kinds of horsemen, armor, and archers and even working themselves on city walls and fortifications. They certainly took as active a part in the city's defense as any older male citizen, who would also simply have provided soldiers and not buckled on his old, rusty armor himself. Female citizens did not vote for city officials, but then, neither did a large share of the male citizenry. As with Bücher's contention that the imbalance between the sexes must have ended in the sixteenth century, this may be another example of an imaginary justification for legal and economic restrictions on women. It may also be the result of extrapolating backward from the actual situation in nineteenth-century Europe.

10. Munich RSP, 1544.

11. Quote is from ibid., 1610, fol. 180. Similar cases in Augsburg BB: 1559, 1562; Memmingen RPB, October 13, 1570; Munich RSP, 1600, fol. 92.

12. Frankfurt BMB, 1471, fol. 141; Nuremberg RB, 3, fol. 198 (1482); Nuremberg AStB, nos. 305–306.

13. Memmingen RPB, March 23, 1571.

14. Nuremberg AStB, no. 306, fols. 206–207.

15. Munich RSP: 1601, fol. 24; 1598, fol. 171.
16. Memmingen BB, 269/1.
17. Strasbourg XXI, 1631, fol. 40.
18. Strasbourg XV, 1580, fols. 5, 95.
19. Memmingen BB, 269/1; Augsburg Schätze, vol. 16, fol. 379 (1632).
20. Strasbourg XXI: 1620, fol. 53; 1623, fol. 250.
21. Memmingen BB, 269/2 (1583); Munich Ratsmandata, vol. 60B3 (1628).
22. Strasbourg Statuten, vol. 18, no. 3, fol. 74; reissued 1594, 1627, 1687. Memmingen RPB: June 21, 1602; March 13, 1616. Augsburg BB, 1580 and elsewhere. Strasbourg XXI, 1613, fol. 392.
23. Frankfurt Ver, vol. II, no. 57 (July 31, 1623).
24. Frankfurt Gerichtssachen, Ugb. 51, no. 27 (1691); Stuttgart Stadt Cannstadt, no. 1098 (1532–1549).
25. Otto Reiser, "Beweis und Beweisverfahren im Zivilprozess der freien Reichsstadt Nürnberg," 45.
26. "Kaiser Ludwigs Rechtbuch 1346," in Maximilian Freiherr von Freyberg, ed., *Sammlung historische Schriften und Urkunden*, nos. 56–59.
27. Joseph Baader, ed., *Nürnberger Polizeiordnungen aus dem 13. bis 15. Jahrhundert*, 29–30.
28. Reiser, "Beweis," 74; Nuremberg Stadt, *Der Statt Nürmberg Verneuerte Reformation*, sec. 29:4; Stuttgart Polizeiakten, A38, Bü. 5, "Fürstenthumbs Württemburg Gemeinen Landtrecht (1576)," secs. 1:36, 2:29; Freyberg, *Sammlung*, no. 104.
29. Strasbourg Statuten, vol. 24, fol. 62 (1465).
30. Ibid.
31. Ibid., vol. 18, fol. 104 (1471).
32. Johannes Geiler von Kaisersberg, *Die aeltesten Schriften*.
33. Strasbourg RB, vol. 1, no. 89 (1552): "Wie es mit dem ungeerbten aussgohn hinfuhrter gehen soll."
34. Augsburg Schätze, vol. 16, fols. 164–166 (1578), 272–273 (1615).
35. Augsburg Gedruckte Verordnungen, "Erneuerte Witwen und Waisenordnung" (1668).
36. Strasbourg XXI, 1606, fol. 42b; Strasbourg XV, 1633, fol. 26; Frankfurt BMB, 1509, fol. 136b; Munich RSP, 1522; Stuttgart Polizeiakten, A38, Bü. 1, "Witwen und Waisenordnung (1540)."
37. Munich RSP, 1522; Augsburg Schätze, vol. 16, fol. 164 (1578); *Frankfurt um 1600*, 77, quoting 1611 Frankfurt *Eherecht*; Bertha Kipfmüller, "Die Frau im Recht der freien Reichsstadt Nürnberg: Eine rechtsgeschichtliche Darlegung auf grund der verneuerte Reformation des Jahre 1564," 19.
38. Memmingen RPB, February 16, 1618. This is similar to the English principle of coverture, although in England the husband was then responsible for the debts; in German cities, as I show later, the creditor had simply lost his loan.
39. Strasbourg RB, vol. 1, no. 108.
40. Ibid., vol. 2, no. 133.
41. Sec. 73 of "Ansbach Landrecht," in Freyberg, *Sammlung*, no. 350.

42. Baader, *Polizeiordnungen*, 29–30.
43. Stuttgart Polizeiakten, A38, Bü. 5, "Furstemthumb Württemburgs Gemeinen Lantrecht" (1576); Nuremberg Stadt *Nürmberg . . . Reformation*, sec. 29:5.
44. *Der Statt Frankfurt erneuerte Reformation*, sec. 2, tit. 16:9.
45. Ibid.; Baader, *Polizeiordnungen*, 29–30.
46. Wilhelm Ebel, *Forschungen zur Geschichte des lübischen Rechts*; Quotations are from Luise Hess, *Die deutschen Frauenberufe des Mittelalters*, 52. This was also the case in London. A married woman who conducted business on her own was declared a "femme sole" and was thus responsible to pay all rents and debts. She could even be imprisoned for debts, and her husband was untouched, both in person and property (A. Abram, "Women Traders in Medieval London," 280). Market women also received special consideration in Denmark, though the exact nature of their position is not spelled out as clearly as it is in London or the German cities (Inger Dübeck, *Købekoner og Konkurence*, 184).
47. Baader, *Polizeiordnungen*, 29–30.
48. Frankfurt BMB, 1505, fol. 118b.
49. Nuremberg Stadt *Nürmberg . . . Reformation*, sec. 28:6.
50. *Frankfurt . . . Reformation*, sec. 3, tit. 7:12.
51. Ebel, *Forschungen*, 121.
52. *Frankfurt . . . Reformation*, sec. 5, tit. 5:6.
53. Ibid.
54. Strasbourg RB, vol. 1, no. 89 (1552).
55. Ibid.
56. Strasbourg XV, 1584, fols. 128–129.
57. Munich Stadtgericht, 867, 1598; Ebel, *Forschungen*, 10.
58. Munich Stadtgericht, 867, 1595.
59. The same situation existed in London during the fifteenth and sixteenth centuries. Women could make public declarations that they intended to trade as "sole merchants"—*femmes sole*—but the number of women designated as such far exceeded those who actually made such a formal declaration (Marian K. Dale, "The London Silkwomen of the Fifteenth Century," 328). Perhaps the public declaration in both German cities and in London simply served as a way of assuring creditors that one was really a market woman or femme sole, so that one could borrow more easily, but was not absolutely necessary. In both areas this again points up the gap between legal codes and actual practice.
60. Munich Stadtgericht, 867, 1592–1600; Frankfurt BMB, 1609, fols. 78a, 55b, 88b; Frankfurt Gerichtssachen, Ugb. 69, no. 5 (1638); Bothe, *Beiträge*, 129, 161.
61. H. Planitz, *Die deutsche Stadt im Mittelalter*; Erich Maschke, "Verfassung und soziale Kräfte in der deutschen Stadt des späten Mittelalters"; Karl Czok, "Die Bürgerkämpfe in Süd- und Westdeutschland im 14. Jahrhundert."
62. For studies of the all-female guilds, see E. Dixon, "Craftswomen in the

Livre des Métiers"; W. Behagel, "Die gewerbliche Stellung der Frau im mittelalterlichen Köln"; Wachendorf, *Stellung*; Hess, *Frauenberufe*; Wensky, *Stellung der Frau*.

63. D. Schuster, *Die Stellung der Frau in der Zunftverfassung*; Brodmeier, *Handwerk*.

64. Peter-Per Krebs, "Die Stellung der Handwerkswitwe in den Zünft von Spätmittelalter bis zum 18. Jahrhundert"; Wissell, *Handwerks*; Bosl and Weis, *Gesellschaft*; Unwin, *Industrial Organization*; Kellenbenz, *European Economy*. See chapter 5 for a fuller discussion of these trends in the six cities I studied.

65. Wilfried Reininghaus, "Zur Entstehung der Gesellengilden im Spätmittelalter." Ernst Mummenhoff, "Frauenarbeit und Arbeitsvermittlung: Eine Episode aus der Handwerksgeschichte des 16. Jahrhunderts"; Paul Kampffmeyer, *Vom Zunftgesellen zum freien Arbeiter*; Georg von Schanz, *Zur Geschichte der deutschen Gesellenverbände*.

## Chapter Two: Hospitals, Healing, and Health Care

1. Gerhard Pfeiffer, ed., *Nürnberg: Geschichte einer europäischen Stadt*, 43.
2. Nuremberg AStB, no. 101, "Amts- und dienstleut Pflicht," fol. 57.
3. Ibid., fol. 294.
4. Ibid., fol. 400.
5. Munich HGS, no. 9 (1485 Ordnung).
6. Ibid., no. 10 (1517 Ordnung).
7. Ibid., no. 249.
8. Memmingen RPB, July 12, 2590; Stuttgart Stadt Cannstadt, nos. 439 and 440 (1618 and 1633).
9. Memmingen Spital, no. 85 (1549 Ordnung und Aid and 1669 Ordnung).
10. Strasbourg Spitalordnungen (1540).
11. Ibid. (1547).
12. Memmingen RPB: March 14, 1578; February 6, 1622. Augsburg BB, 1598.
13. Memmingen RPB, October 27, 1613. Munich RSP: 1596, fol. 16; 1597, fol. 138. Nuremberg RB, 48, fol. 66 (1589). Nuremberg RV, 1572, fol. 7 (1589).
14. Otto Winckelmann, *Das Fürsorgewesen der Stadt Strassburg*, 2:76.
15. Jurgen Dieselhorst, "Die Bestrafung der Selbstmörder im Territorium der Reichsstadt Nürnberg," 87.
16. J. M. Lotter, *Sagen, Legenden und Geschichten der Stadt Nürnberg*, 208–214.
17. Munich HGS, no. 275, Pfrundner und Personalverzeichnis 1573–1598. Nuremberg RB: 36, fol. 255 (1578); 37, fol. 16 (1578).
18. Munich HGS, no. 9; Nuremberg RB, 13, fol. 201 (1526).
19. Strasbourg Statuten, vol. 4, "Ordnung der Beginen zum Thurn" (1548).

20. Strasbourg XV, 1581, fols. 52, 104; Nuremberg RB, 68, fol. 568 (1611).
21. Nuremberg RB, 31, fol. 197 (1561).
22. Munich HGS, no. 10 (1517).
23. Memmingen RPB: February 9, 1588; July 18, 1610. Nuremberg AStB: no. 101, fol. 160; no. 234, fol. 64, "Ordnung der Lazarett" (1561). Hess, *Frauenberufe*, 107.
24. Augsburg Collegium Medicum, fasc. 5.
25. Ibid.
26. Wilhelm Stricker, *Geschichte der Heilkunde und der verwandten Wissenschaften in der Stadt Frankfurt a. M.*, 144.
27. Memmingen RPB, August 29, 1586; Munich HGS, no. 310; Winckelmann, *Fürsorge*, 1:46; Ernst Mummenhoff, "Das Findel und Waisenhaus zu Nürnberg," 153.
28. Memmingen Spital, no. 85 (1549 Spitalordnung); Nuremberg AStB, no. 101, fol. 76.
29. Memmingen Spital, no. 85 (1549 Spitalordnung).
30. Nuremberg RB: 31, fol. 102 (1560); 57, fol. 99 (1597).
31. Rüger, *Almosenordnungen*, 71; Nuremberg RB, 4, fol. 6 (1493); Memmingen Spital, no. 85 (1549 Spitalordnung).
32. Mummenhoff, "Findel," 232; Memmingen Spital, no. 85 (1549 Spitalordnung); Strasbourg XV, 1581, fol. 99.
33. Hirschmann, "Frauen in Nürnbergs Geschichte."
34. Mummenhoff, "Findel," 222.
35. Nuremberg RB, 17, fol. 170 (1536).
36. How many middle- and upper-class women chose to send their infants out to wet nurses or to hire wet nurses in their own homes is impossible to determine for this period. There have been numerous studies of wet-nursing in the eighteenth century, when it became a concern of moralists and physicians, but none for an earlier period (see Mary Lindemann, "Love for Hire: The Regulation of the Wet-Nursing Business in 18th-Century Hamburg"). This reflects the lack of sources for the earlier period, but whether this lack is the result of the fact that wet-nursing itself was not very common or that no one was bothered by the practice and so never commented on it, is difficult to say. In the eighteenth century, wet-nursing did provide employment for a significant number of lower-class women who also worked as laundresses and spinners. These women were even charged with having (and then occasionally killing) illegitimate children so that they would be able to act as wet nurses.
37. Frankfurt BMB: 1485, fol. 84b; 1505, fol. 106b. Memmingen RPB: August 5, 1545; June 20, 1606; October 17, 1610. Strasbourg XXI: 1602, fol. 136; 1605, fol. 179.
38. Mummenhoff, "Findel," 178; Winckelmann, *Fürsorge*, 1:46, 154.
39. Munich Kammereirechnungen, 1480, 1491, 1500. Strasbourg XXI: 1602, fol. 136; 1605, fol. 179; 1616, fol. 140 (quoted). Frankfurt BMB: 1485, fol. 84b; 1505, fol. 106b. Memmingen RPB: August 5, 1545; June 20, 1606; October 17, 1610.

40. Memmingen RPB: March 30, 1565; October 9, 1588; September 17, 1606; July 24, 1611; April 27, 1612; February 9, 1620.
41. Stuttgart Stadt Cannstadt, no. 1100 (1621–1622); similar case in Munich Stadtgericht, 867, 1598.
42. Quotation is from Memmingen RPB, November 9, 1531. Similar cases in Frankfurt BMB, 1485, fol. 55a; ibid., 1590, fol. 53a; Memmingen RPB, May 10, 1529; Munich Steuerbücher, 1560–1640; and Munich RSP, 1608, fols. 250, 318, 322.
43. Karl Sudhoff, *Die ersten Massnahmen der Stadt Nürnberg gegen die Syphilis in den Jahren 1496 und 1497*, 20, quoting from Nuremberg RV, September 13, 1497.
44. Memmingen Ausgaben (1488); Frankfurt BMB, 1550, fol. 18a; Memmingen RPB; January 17 and August 13, 1593.
45. Nuremberg RB, 69, fol. 545 (1614).
46. Ibid.: 5, fols. 188 (1491), 213 (1492); 15, fol. 126 (1530).
47. Ibid., 51, fol. 305 (1592).
48. Winckelmann, *Fürsorge*, 1:108.
49. Max Bauer, *Deutscher Frauenspiegel: Bilder aus dem Frauenleben in der deutschen Vergangenheit*, 2:173.
50. G. Wunder, *Die Bürgerschaft der Reichsstadt Hall von 1395–1600*; Wachendorf, *Stellung*, 23–26; Karl Bücher, *Die Berufe der Stadt Frankfurt im Mittelalter*, 25.
51. Bücher, *Berufe*, 25, quoting Frankfurt BMB: 1436, fol. 17; 1446, fol. 47; 1491, fol. 96.
52. Bruno Kiske, "Die Frau im mittelalterlichen deutschen Wirtschaftsleben," 152; Hess, *Frauenberufe*, 101.
53. Karl Weinhold, *Die deutschen Frauen in dem Mittelalter*, 1:160.
54. Stuttgart Polizeiakten, A38, Bü. 1; Augsburg Schätze, vol. 16, fol. 282.
55. Munich RSP, 1528.
56. Nuremberg RB, 15, fols. 196, 236, 243 (1531–1532).
57. Ibid.: 17, fol. 92 (1535); 22, fol. 6 (1543).
58. Memmingen RPB, March 12 and July 23, 1554.
59. Ibid.: December 6, 1560; November 22, 1564; January 15, 1565.
60. Memmingen Zünfte, 405, no. 12.
61. Memmingen RPB, November 1, 1598.
62. Memmingen Zünfte, 405, no. 12.
63. Ibid.
64. Ibid.
65. Ibid.; Memmingen RPB, August 10, 1610.
66. Nuremberg RB: 13, fol. 242 (1527); 48, fol. 35 (1585); 56, fol. 477 (1595). Strasbourg XV, 1597, fol. 57b. Memmingen RPB: February 26, 1606; December 16, 1614; February 7, 1617. Stuttgart Oberrat Malefizakten, A209, Bü. 368 (1608).
67. Strasbourg XV, 1636, fol. 242.
68. Memmingen RPB, December 16, 1614; Nuremberg RB, 57, fols. 99, 107 (1597); Munich Kammereirechnungen, 1552–1562. Clark found a

similar situation in seventeenth-century England, especially if the women were treating poor people (*Working Life*, 239).

69. Munich Gewerbeamt, no. 1020 (Medizinalia Pfuscher).
70. It is difficult to understand how Richard L. Petrelli could assert (in "The Regulation of French Midwifery during the Ancien Regime") that "during the Middle Ages the midwife practiced her art with virtually no regulation by the clergy, town fathers, or medical profession" (276). Regulation began in the German cities in the fourteenth century and even in France, the focus of Petrelli's study, as early as 1460 in Lille. Petrelli's further basic assumptions are also highly questionable and, unfortunately, shared by many historians of midwifery: "Not only was she uneducated, and of low social class, but she was feared by those whom she served, for her art was based more on superstition than on professional skill. Because of her low social class and the stigma of her profession, most doctors avoided any interference with the midwife's practice. In turn, the bellicose midwife of the early Renaissance guarded the lying-in chamber from all medical interference, particularly male" (277). To imply that midwives were all of low social class or that sixteenth-century physicians were any more "professional" and any less "superstitious" shows a lack of awareness about both midwifery and early modern medicine.

Early modern physicians actually avoided the birthing room because they knew very little about delivery and because this was seen as a female province; the latter point has been made most provocatively by Ivan Illich in *Gender*, 123–126. Illich is several centuries off in his timing of the first male incursions into this female province, however, as he notes, "Up to about 1780, medical treatises and public ordinances viewed childbirth as woman's domain" (123). As the German sources clearly indicate, there were public ordinances about childbirth as early as the fifteenth century, several hundred years before male accoucheurs and physicians took over the actual delivery. Formal instruction and licensing of midwives began long before "childbirth ceased to be an event of and among women" (124), though Illich sees the two as contemporaneous.

71. W. Kallmorgan, *Siebenhundert Jahre Heilkunde in Frankfurt a.M.*, 66; Georg Kriegk, *Deutsches Bürgerthum im Mittelalter*, 1:14; Wachendorf, *Stellung*, 7; Friedrich Baruch, "Das Hebammenwesen in Reichsstädtische Nürnberg," 8; Nuremberg Aemterbüchlein, nos. 1–139.
72. Memmingen RPB, every year. Nuremberg RB: 6, fol. 57 (1494); 28, fol. 311 (1555); 36, fol. 238 (1578). Frankfurt BMB: 1500, fol. 98; 1590, fol. 208, Frankfurt Medizinalia, Ugb. 8a, no. 6 (1531). Munich RSP, 1603, fol. 176. Strasbourg XXI, 1623, fol. 11.
73. *Gesetze und Statutensammlung der freien Stadt Frankfurt*, 319–320.
74. Baruch, "Hebammenwesen," 15. Nuremberg RB: 15, fol. 118 (1530); 71, fol. 41 (1619). Frankfurt Medizinalia, Ugb. 8a, 1499. Frankfurt BMB: 1499, fol. 29a; 1590, fols. 175, 192. Jean-Pierre Leffte, "Aperçu

historique sur l'obstétrique de Strasbourg avant la grande révolution," 13. Freiburg Eidbücher, Rep. B 3(o), no. 4, fol. 26 (1494). Memmingen RPB: May 21, 1571; December 6, 1591; March 30, 1678. Augsburg Baumeisterbücher.

75. This makes it the first city in present-day France to have a system of midwives. Paris did not have official midwives until 1560. Nuremberg Aemterbüchlein, no. 5 (1463); Munich Kammereirechnungen; Kallmorgan, *Heilkunde*, 61; Memmingen RPB, every year; Leffte, "Historique," 18.

76. Augsburg Schätze, no. 42 (1466).

77. Nuremberg AStB, no. 101, fol. 100, "Aide der Frauen so zu den gepernde Weiber verordnet."

78. Frankfurt Medizinalia, Ugb. 8a, fols. 35–46 (1696–1697).

79. Nuremberg RB: 3, fols. 178 (1482), 265 (1483); 4, fol. 54 (1484); 11, fol. 102 (1517); 29, fol. 268 (1556). Nuremberg Aemterbüchlein, nos. 7–14 (1480–1490). Memmingen RPB: May 22, 1579; June 30, 1606.

80. Mcmmingen Hebammen, 406(2) no. 12 (1618). Memmingen RPB: November 9, 1554; October 26, 1607; November 19, 1613. Munich RSP, 1599, fol. 85.

81. Quotation is from Memmingen Hebammen, 406, no. 22 (1625). Similar cases in ibid., nos. 19 (1623) and 23 (1628).

82. Augsburg Schätze, no. 282; Freiburg Eidbücher, Rep. B 3 (o), no. 4, fol. 26 (1494); Nuremberg RB, 6, fol. 155 (1496).

83. Baruch, "Hebammenwesen," 12.

84. Memmingen Hebammen, 406, nos. 3–7 (1536).

85. Ibid., nos: 8–11.

86. Ibid., nos. 13 (1620); 15–18 (1621); 20–21 (1624); 49(7) (1685). Memmingen RPB: July 30, 1585; September 5, 1621.

87. Baruch, "Hebammenwesen," 12, quoting from the Briefbücher, Nuremberg Staatsarchiv, Rep. 6, no. 57; Nuremberg RB, 64, fol. 236 (1606).

88. Stuttgart Generalreskripta, A39, Bü. 1 (1549).

89. Frankfurt Medizinalia, Ugb. 8a, 1519 and elsewhere. Frankfurt BMB: 1469, fol. 64b; 1525, fol. 107b. Nuremberg RB, 19, fol. 245 (1539). Strasbourg XXI, 1607, fol. 41a.

90. Frankfurt BMB, 1468; Kriegk, *Deutsches Bürgerthum im Mittelalter*, 2:16.

91. There are no studies of the birth rate in sixteenth- and seventeenth-century Nuremberg, nor would one be possible. This figure comes from studies of other preindustrial European populations which are somewhat comparable. Josiah Cox Russell, *British Medieval Population*; T. H. Hollinsworth, *Historical Demography*; D. V. Glass, D. E. C. Eversley, *Population in History: Essays in Historical Demography*.

92. Memmingen Hebammen, 406, no. 24 (July 31, 1629).

93. Munich Zimilien, no. 41 (Eidbuch 1488).

94. Frankfurt Eidbuch, vol. II, no. 240 (1509); Augsburg Schätze,

no. 194a, "Hebammen Eid"; Stuttgart Stadt, Findbuch, "Medizin"; Freiburg Eidbücher, Rep. B 3(0), no. 4, fol. 26, "Der hebammen Eyd mit der Ordnung."
95. Freiburg Eidbücher, Rep. B 3(0), no. 4, fol. 26.
96. Nuremberg AStB, no. 100, fol. 101–105.
97. Freiburg Eidbücher, Rep. B 3(0), no. 4, fol. 26.
98. Nuremberg AStB, no. 100, fol. 104.
99. Memmingen Hebammen, 406, no. 1.
100. Stuttgart Polizeiakten, A38, Bü. 1 (1585).
101. Memmingen Hebammen, 406, no. 1.
102. Ibid.
103. Nuremberg AStB, no. 101.
104. Strasbourg Statuten, vol. 7, fol. 19.
105. Ibid., vol. 9, no. 80.
106. Ibid., vol. 33, no. 75.
107. Ibid., no. 60; Munich Zimilien, no. 29.
108. J. H. Aveling, *English Midwives: Their History and Prospects*, 2–3.
109. Stuttgart Generalreskripta, A39, Bü. 1 (1549).
110. Jacob Springer and Heinrich Institorius, *Malleus Maleficarum*.
111. Nuremberg Stadtbibliothek Norica Sammlung, PI, SII, *Eines Hoch Edlen und Hochweisen Raths des heiligen Reichs Stadt Nürnberg verneuerte Hebammen-Ordnung*; Frankfurt Eidbuch, vol. III (1767); Memmingen Hebammen, 406, no. 1, 1704 printed midwives' ordinance.
112. Audrey Eccles, *Obstetrics and Gynecology in Tudor and Stuart England*, 119–120.
113. Baruch, "Hebammenwesen," 18.
114. *Gesetze und Statuten*, 300; Memmingen Hebammen, 406, 1740 ordinance.
115. Nuremberg, AStB, no. 103, fol. 323, "Einer Hebammen auf dem Land verneuerte Pflicht."
116. Bauer, *Deutscher Frauenspiegel*, 184–186;
117. Hess, "Frauenberufe," 107. The first significant contribution to obstetrical literature by a woman published anywhere, however, was a treatise on midwifery published in Paris in 1609, written by Louise Bourgeois, the midwife to Maria de Medici (Aveling, *English Midwives*, 302).
118. Frankfurt Medizinalia, Ugb. 8a; Memmingen Hebammen, 406.
119. Frankfurt Medizinalia, Ugb. 8a, no. 5 (1550s); Stuttgart Polizeiakten, A38, Bü 1, (Württembergische Landesordnung 1549).
120. A facsimile reprint of the first Hagenau edition was published in 1910 at Munich as volume 2 of the series Alte Meister der Medizin und Naturkunde, with accompanying notes by Gustav Klein.
121. Memmingen Hebammen, 406, no. 1, 1668.
122. Aveling, *English Midwives*, 12.
123. Nuremberg, Germanisches Nationalmuseum, "Schuld und Rechnungsbuch Dr. Christoph Scheurl," fol. 10.

124. Frankfurt BMB, 1545, fols. 133–134.
125. Munich RSP: 1523; 1533, fol. 131; 1600, fol. 188; 1610, fol. 166. Nuremberg RB: 19, fol. 238 (1539); 50, fol. 189 (1591); 55, fol. 231 (1596); 63, fol. 517 (1605). Strasbourg XXI, 1604, fol. 196a. Frankfurt Medizinalia, Ugb. 8a, no. 12 (1636).
126. Nuremberg RB, 12, fol. 96 (1522); Munich RSP, 1545, fol. 114; Memmingen RPB, October 23, 1542.
127. Munich RSP: 1524; 1532; Memmingen RPB, February 27, 1570.
128. Nuremberg RB, 27, fol. 6 (1553).
129. Frankfurt Medizinalia, Ugb. 8a, no. 14.
130. Ibid., nos. 16, 18, 20, 24, 26, 29.
131. Stuttgart Oberrat Malefizakten, A209, Bü. 233 (1656).
132. Munich Kammereirechnungen: 1380; 1412; 1420; 1430. Nuremberg RB: 16, fol. 148 (1534); 43, fol. 53 (1584); 44, fol. 106 (1585). Memmingen RPB: October 12, 1519; March 10, 1550; October 10, 1580; May 22, 1583; December 10, 1585.
133. Frankfurt BMB, 1600, fol. 253a.
134. Nuremberg Ratschlagbücher, no. 10 (1530).
135. Frankfurt BMB, 1505, fol. 69b; Stuttgart Malefizakten, A43, Bü. 2 (1526); Nuremberg RB, 40a, fols. 290, 297, 378 (1580); Munich RSP, 1599, fol. 67; Strasbourg XXI, 1604, fol. 335a.
136. Strasbourg XXI, 1603, fols. 143a, 257a (quoted), 286b.
137. Nuremberg RV: 1034, fol. 24 (1549); 1109, fols. 1, 3, 9, 25 (1554). Stuttgart Malefizakten, A43, Bü. 2 (1526). Strasbourg XXI, 1606, fol. 8b. Reinhold Schmidt, ed., *Kaiser Karl des fünften peinliche Gerichtsordnung (Carolina Constitutio Criminalis)*.
138. Frankfurt BMB, 1520, fols. 2–3; Augsburg Schätze, no. 282.
139. Nuremberg RV, 1141, fols. 33–34.
140. Memmingen RPB, November 4, 1603. Munich Stadtgericht, 865 (1523). Nuremberg RB: 29, fol. 354 (1557); 35, fol. 125 (1578); 56, fol. 507 (1597).
141. Nuremberg RB, 33, fol. 219 (1568).
142. Nuremberg AStB, no. 226a (1549).
143. E. William Monter, "Women in Calvinist Geneva," 196.
144. Nuremberg AStB, no. 221, fol. 49 (1419). Nuremberg RB: 12, fol. 96 (1522); 69, fols. 545, 548 (1614). Nuremberg Ratschlagbücher, no. 61, fol. 62 (1580).
145. Baader, *Polizeiordnungen*, 69–70.
146. Gottfried Seebass, "Das Problem der Konditionaltaufe in der Reformation."
147. Nuremberg RB: 28, fol. 53 (1554); 37, fol. 176 (1578); 69, fol. 53 (1614). Nuremberg AStB, no. 250. Strasbourg Statuten, vol. 33, no. 60 (1687).
148. Claus-Peter Clasen, *Anabaptism: A Social History, 1525–1618*, 149.
149. Strasbourg XV, 1584, fol. 121b.
150. Natalie Zemon Davis, "Women in the Arts Mécaniques in Sixteenth-Century Lyon," 143.

CHAPTER THREE: PUBLIC, DOMESTIC, AND CARNAL SERVICE

1. Munich Zimilien, nos. 29, 41. Frankfurt Eidbuch, vol. II, no. 280. Karl Pfaff, *Geschichte der Stadt Stuttgart*, 354. Strasbourg Statuten, vol. 1, fol. 85 (1463). Memmingen RPB, December 17, 1491. Munich RSP, 1483. Frankfurt BMB: 1500, fols. 92a, 116a; 1530, fol. 65b.
2. Frankfurt BMB: 1495, fol. 44; 1535, fol. 361; 1545, fols. 13b, 145b, 156a. Munich RSP, 1607, fol. 131. Memmingen RPB, April 23, 1589. Strasbourg XXI, 1602, fol. 146b. Strasbourg XV: 1571, fol. 237b; 1573, fol. 209; 1593, fols. 24, 35, 52.
3. Strasbourg XXI, 1620, fol. 146.
4. Munich RSP: 1459, fol. 21; 1559, fol. 132; 1599, fol. 137. Memmingen RPB, April 22, 1607, Wachendorf, *Stellung*, 6.
5. Memmingen RPB: March 3, 1525; December 14, 1556. Eugene Nübling, *Ulms Baumwollweberei im Mittelalter*, 67.
6. Augsburg Schätze, no. 31 (Hochzeitsordnungen 1575 and 1599); Memmingen RPB, September 20, 1616.
7. Nuremberg AStB, no. 106, fol. 129b, "Pflicht der Frau Pflegerin über die Findel"; Nuremberg RB, 31, fol. 261 (1561).
8. Johann C. Siebenkees, *Nachrichten von Armenstiftungen in Nürnberg*, 175.
9. Memmingen RPB, February 3 and 10, 1570. Munich RSP: 1535; 1544, fol. 43.
10. Rüger, "Almosenordnung," 43. Nuremberg AStB, no. 341, "Stiftungsbuch 1341–1495," fol. 40. Nuremberg RB: 12, fols. 74 (1522), 175 (1523); 13, fol. 30 (1525); 15, fol. 31 (1529); 20, fol. 110 (1540).
11. See W. H. Bruford, *Germany in the Eighteenth Century: The Social Background of the Literary Revival*; Günther Franz, ed., *Beamtentum und Pfarrerstand 1400–1800*; Franklin Kopitzsch, *Aufklärung, Absolutismus und Bürgertum in Deutschland*; Charles McClelland, *State, Society, and University in Germany, 1700–1914*.
12. Ennen views this exclusion of women from higher education as very important in determining their status in early modern Europe, when "ein Bildungsbürgertum neben dem Gewerbebürgertum erwachsen sollte" ("Frau in der Stadtgesellschaft," 19).
13. Hess, *Frauenberufe*, 127; Kriegk, *Deutsches Bürgerthum im Mittelalter*, 77; Bücher, *Berufe*, 68.
14. Quotation is from Bauer, *Deutscher Frauenspiegel*, 1:294. Similar cases in Stuttgart Stadt Findbuch, 1563, and 1581 and in Nuremberg RB: 5, fol. 260 (1493); 17, fol. 181 (1536); 41, fol. 80 (1583).
15. Nuremberg RV: 1488, fol. 9b; 1599, fol. 1. Wachendorf, *Stellung*, 20. Memmingen RPB, December 12, 1524. Munich RSP, 1601, fol. 134.
16. Strasbourg XXI, 1604, fol. 42b.
17. Frankfurt BMB, 1610, fol. 9a.
18. Hess, *Frauenberufe*, 127.
19. Stuttgart Stadt Findbuch, 1573; Strasbourg XXI, 1604, fols. 42, 43, 98; Memmingen RPB, November 27, 1620.

20. *Frankfurt um 1600*, 83; *Die Chroniken der fränkischen Städte: Nürnberg*, 4:382.
21. Nuremberg RV, 1519–1520, 1, fol. 1.
22. Ibid., 1585–1586, 1, fol. 35.
23. Ibid.: 1479, 5, fol. 15; 12, fol. 7.
24. Memmingen RPB: September 2, 1510; May 31, 1559.
25. Memmingen Deutsche Schulwesen, 397/1, "Ordnung der Köningen in der Mädchenschule" (1587).
26. Ibid. (1643).
27. Memmingen RPB: August 21, 1529; April 24, 1570; January 21, 1622.
28. Memmingen Deutsche Schulwesen, 397/1 (1587).
29. Stuttgart Stadt Findbuch, 1563, 1581, 1584, 1685, 1686.
30. Leonard Lenk, *Augsburger Bürgertum im Späthumanismus und Frühbarock, 1580–1700*, 122.
31. Memmingen RPB, April 24, 1570.
32. Nuremberg AStB, no. 101, fols. 558–567; Strasbourg Statuten, vol. 18, fols. 30–34; Munich Gewerbeamt, no. 1569 (1580).
33. Ibid.
34. Munich Gewerbeamt, no. 1569 (1580); Strasbourg Statuten, vol. 29, fol. 186; Nuremberg AStB, no. 101, fol. 563.
35. Ibid.
36. Strasbourg XV, 1587, fol. 168b.
37. Strasbourg RB, vol. 1, no. 150; similar language in Munich Zimilien no. 29.
38. Ibid.
39. Munich Gewerbeamt, no. 1569 (1580).
40. Nuremberg AStB, no. 324, fol. 181.
41. Nuremberg RB: 5, fol. 260 (1493); 6, fol. 96 (1495); 17, fol. 181 (1536); 41, fol. 80 (1583). Munich RSP: 1586, 1593. Munich Gewerbeamt 5170 (1577, 1684).
42. Nuremberg RB, 15, fol. 111 (1530).
43. Nuremberg Aemterbüchlein, nos. 30, 33, 43, 53, 61, 67, 68, 82.
44. Nuremberg AStB, no. 101, fol. 567.
45. Nuremberg RB: 6, fol. 59 (1499); 9, fol. 48 (1508).
46. Frankfurt BMB, 1604, fol. 29.
47. Nuremberg AStB, no. 100, fols. 558–567.
48. Strasbourg Statuten, vol. 18, fol. 30.
49. Nuremberg AStB, no. 100, fol. 567.
50. Strasbourg Statuten, vol. 29, fol. 186 (1556).
51. Ibid., vol. 18, fol. 30.
52. Ibid.
53. Ibid., fol. 35.
54. Stuttgart Generalreskripta, A39, Bü. 3 (1562).
55. Stuttgart Landwirtschaft A58, Bü. 26 (1555).
56. Munich Gewerbeamt, no. 1569 (1580).
57. Ibid.
58. Frankfurt BMB, 1600, fol. 50b. Strasbourg Statuten: vol. 10 (1628); vol.

9, fol. 140 (1643); vol. 33, no. 61 (1665 and 1687). Frankfurt Ver., vol. III, no. 65 (1654).

59. Strasbourg Statuten, vol. 33, no. 61 (1665).
60. Hufton, "Women, Work and Marriage," 189.
61. Nuremberg RB, 5, fol. 255 (1493); Nuremberg AStB, no. 260, "Aller Handwerk Ordnung und Gesetz Verneuerte Anno 1535."
62. Frankfurt BMB, 1480, fol. 73b. Nuremberg RB: 5, fol. 30 (1488); 34, fol. 60 (1570); 58, fol. 283 (1600). Munich RSP: 1533; 1535; 1599, fol. 141; 1600, fol. 27.
63. Frankfurt BMB: 1505, fol. 77a; 1545, fol. 79b. Memmingen RPB, June 20, 1561. Strasbourg XXI, 1607, fol. 110.
64. Munich Stadtgericht, 867, 1595 on.
65. Nuremberg RB, 56, fols. 290 and 295 (1596). Strasbourg XXI: 1602, fol. 182; 1608, fol. 74a. Frankfurt Gerichtssachen, Ugb. 69, no. 33 (1694). Bauer, *Deutscher Frauenspiegel*, 313.
66. Munich Stadtgericht, 867, 1601.
67. Memmingen RPB, August 23, 1529.
68. Nuremberg RB, 42, fol. 215 (1583).
69. Kriegk, *Deutsches Bürgerthum im Mittelalter*, 248.
70. Friedrich Bothe, "Das Testament des Frankfurter Grosskaufmanns Jakob Heller vom Jahre 1519," 374; Anton Tucher, *Haushaltbuch (1507 bis 1517)*, 107; Abram, "Women Traders in Medieval London," 277.
71. Memmingen RPB: October 26, 1569; April 5, 1570; February 3, 1570; October 2, 1581. Munich RSP: 1599, fol. 164; 1607, fol. 196. Strasbourg RB, vol. 1, no. 67 (1557). Strasbourg XV, 1586, fols. 167–168.
72. Munich RSP: 1535; 1544, fol. 43; 1603, fols. 213; 1607, fol. 185.
73. Ibid., 1600, fol. 178.
74. Munich Ratsmandata, vol. 60A1, "Ordnung der Ehehalten" (1645); Strasbourg XV, 1579; Memmingen RPB, March 17, 1585.
75. Maschke, *Unterschichten*, 30; Ennen, "Frau in der Stadtgesellschaft," 17.
76. Noted in London by Vivien Brodsky Elliot, "Single Women in the London Marriage Market: Age, Status and Mobility, 1598–1619," 89.
77. Maschke, *Unterschichten*, 29; Westermann, "Bevölkerung"; Ott, *Bevölkerungsstatistik*; Endres, "Einwohnerzahl," 249.
78. As Theresa McBride points out, urban domestic service "was of key importance to the employment of women until the twentieth century." It not only provided an outlet for surplus rural population but "played a vital role in lower-class adaptation to modern urban society" by giving servants some basic education, the opportunity to accumulate savings, geographic mobility, and perhaps a chance at upward mobility through marriage. Service thus offered opportunities that work in more "modern" factories did not. ("The Modernization of 'Women's Work,'" 231, 245.)
79. Sally Alexander, Anna Davin, and Eve Hostettler, "Labouring Women: A Reply to Eric Hobsbawn," 177.
80. Quote is from Stuttgart Landwirtschaft, A58, "Ordnung der Tag-

lohner"; similar provisions in Munich Ratsmandata, vol. 601A, "Ordnung der Tagwerker auffm Land 1645"; Frankfurt Ver, vol. II, no. 3, "Ordnung der Weingarten u. Feldarbeit"; Hess, *Frauenberufe*, 46. This was also true for women who were permanent servants in the households of farmers, as Ann Kussmaul has discovered (*Servants in Husbandry in Early Modern England*, 37).

81. Stuttgart, Generalreskripta, A39, Bü. 1, "Taglohner Ordnung, 1550."
82. Ibid., and Munich Stadtgericht, 919, "Taglohnerordnung" (1511); Memmingen Taglohner Taxe, 265(5) (1639).
83. Michael Roberts, "Sickles and Scythes: Women's Work and Men's Work at Harvest Time," 27.
84. Ibid., and Keith D. M. Snell, "Agricultural Seasonal Unemployment, the Standard of Living and Women's Work in the South and East: 1690–1860"; Heide Wunder, "Zur Stellung der Frau im Arbeitsleben und in der Gesellschaft des 15.–18. Jahrhunderts: Eine Skizze," 244.
85. Strasbourg Statuten, vol. 10, fol. 79, "Taglohner Taxe" (1633).
86. *Frankfurt um 1600*, 40; Munich Ratsmandata, vol. 60A1; Frankfurt Ver, vol. III, no. 65 (1654); Memmingen Taglohner Taxe, 265(5) (1639).
87. Nuremberg AStB, no. 101, fol. 553, "Weschin Pflicht und Ordnung."
88. Nuremberg Aemterbüchlein, nos. 2–4, 8, 26, 52, 62, 81.
89. Nuremberg RB: 6, fols. 22 (1493), 241 (1497); 23, fol. 353 (1545); 26, fol. 275 (1552).
90. Memmingen RPB, November 10, 1557; Munich Stadtgericht 867, vol. 1 (1592).
91. Nuremberg RB, 26, fol. 275 (1552).
92. Munich RSP, 1603, fol. 176.
93. Iwan Bloch, *Die Prostitution*, 1:788.
94. Munich Gewerbeamt, no. 2794 (1608).
95. Barton C. Hacker, "Women and Military Institutions in Early Modern Europe: A Reconnaissance," 649. Hacker notes that all early modern armies had a huge number of female camp followers, often outnumbering the actual soldiers. Along with soldiers' wives and prostitutes, many of these women were sutlers trading in meat, drink, and supplies. He comments: "The most striking fact about women's activities in the army is how little they differed from the ordinary run of women's work outside it—finding, cooking, and serving food; making, washing and mending clothes; tending the sick, the infirm and the wounded; sporting with men, helping other women when they could, bearing and raising children" (652). Martha Howell also finds women listed among the sellers of victuals to city-mounted military expeditions in Leiden ("Women's Work," 241).
96. Strasbourg XV, 1607, fol. 141b; Strasbourg Statuten, vol. 33, fol. 26 (1684); Memmingen RPB, April 6, 1548; Munich RSP 1563.
97. Strasbourg Statuten, vol. 33, fol. 26 (1684).
98. Wachendorf, *Stellung*, 63; Bücher, *Berufe*; Hess, *Frauenberufe*, 135; Munich RSP, 1609, fol. 77.

99. Hess, *Frauenberufe*, 136; Augsburg Hantwercksordnungen, Badeordnung 1553.
100. Werner Danckert, *Unehrliche Leute: Die verfemten Berufe*, 78–79. On the latter point, see a number of Geiler von Kaisersberg's sermons (Geiler von Kaisersberg, *Aeltesten Schriften*).
101. Stuttgart Stadt Findbuch; Anton Schichthörle, *Die Gewerbsbefügnisse in der Königliche Haupt- und Residenzstadt München*, 12.
102. Frankfurt Zünfte, Ugb. C-52 (1421).
103. Strasbourg Statuten, vol. 2, fol. 120 (1487).
104. Ibid.
105. Munich RSP: 1529; 1532.
106. Kriegk, *Deutsches Bürgerthum*, 35.
107. Munich Ratsmandata, 60B1, fol. 93b; Strasbourg XXI, 1634, fol. 80b, 152a.
108. Strasbourg XXI, 1642, fol. 15a.
109. I. Bloch, *Prostitution*, 740–745.
110. Max Bauer, *Liebesleben in deutschen Vergangenheit*, 148.
111. Johann C. Siebenkees, *Materialien zur nürnbergische Geschichte*, 4:578; Memmingen Stadt Denkbuch; Strasbourg Statuten, vol. 2, fol. 2.
112. Kriegk, *Deutsches Bürgerthum*, 2:308; Munich Zimilien no. 41 (Eidbuch 1488).
113. Nuremberg RB: 24, fol. 128 (1548); 26, fol. 356 (1553).
114. Quotation is from Baader, *Polizeiordnungen*, 119–120. Similar clauses in Strasbourg Statuten, vol. 3, fol. 4.
115. Munich Zimilien, no. 41.
116. Kriegk, *Deutsches Bürgerthum*, 2:308.
117. Ibid., 316; Bauer, *Liebesleben*, 134.
118. Baader, *Polizeiordnungen*, 120.
119. Munich Zimilien, no. 41; Strasbourg Statuten, vol. 3, fol. 4 (1500); Frankfurt BMB, 1545, fol. 47; Baader, *Polizeiordnungen*, 119–120.
120. Strasbourg Statuten, vol. 3, fol. 5.
121. Nuremberg RB: 6, fol. 268 (1498); 11, fol. 107 (1517).
122. Nuremberg RB: 6, fol. 268 (1498); 11, fol. 506 (1520); 31, fol. 188 (1561).
123. Püchner, "Register," 909–998.
124. Frankfurt Eidbuch, vol. I, fol. 31b; Frankfurt BMB, 1495, fol. 78a.
125. Munich RSP, 1536, fols. 211, 222.
126. *Chroniken der fränkischen Stadte*, 4:328.
127. Kriegk, *Deutsches Bürgerthum*, 2:322; Wachendorf, *Stellung*, 120.
128. Memmingen RPB, December 19, 1526.
129. Nuremberg RB: 19, fol. 252 (1539); 20, fol. 255 (1541).
130. K. A. Weith-Knudsen, *Kulturgeschichte der europäischen Frauenwelt*, 173.
131. Nuremberg RB: 1b, fol. 324 (1455); 7, fol. 59 (1499).
132. Kriegk, *Deutsches Bürgerthum*, 2:306; Frankfurt BMB, 1510, fol. 19b.
133. Baader, *Polizeiordnungen*, 120. Siebenkees, *Materialien*, 4:578. Nuremberg RB: 1c, fol. 143 (1468); 14, fol. 286 (1529).

134. Nuremberg RB: 9, fol. 17 (1508); 19, fol. 342 (1542); 20, fols. 44, 87 (1544); 23, fols. 202, 205 (1546).
135. Kriegk, *Deutsches Bürgerthum*, 2:306; Bauer, *Liebesleben*, 133; Danckert, *Unehrliche Leute*, 150.
136. Strasbourg Statuten, vol. 2, fol. 70.
137. Ibid., vol. 29, fol. 34 (1469).
138. Ibid., vol. 2, fols. 78, 130, 137; vol. 29, fols. 154, 156.
139. Ibid., vol. 2, fols. 75, 78.
140. Ibid., vol. 2, fol. 130.
141. Danckert, *Unehrliche Leute*, 150.
142. Strasbourg Statuten, vol. 29, fol. 154.
143. Ibid., vol. 2, fol. 137 (1497).
144. Kriegk, *Deutsches Bürgerthum*, 2:340; Bauer, *Liebesleben*, 159.
145. Nuremberg RB, 31, fol. 316 (January 5, 1562).
146. Nuremberg Ratschlagbuch, no. 34, fols. 137–150 (January 19 and 22, 1562).
147. Karl Sudhoff, *Massnahmen*, 109.
148. Ibid.
149. Munich RSP, 1498.
150. Nuremberg Ratschlagbuch, no. 34, fols. 150–153.
151. Nuremberg RB, 31, fol. 350 (March 18, 1562).
152. Ibid., 36, fol. 15 (1577).
153. Frankfurt BMB, 1546, fol. 14b; Bauer, *Liebesleben*, 159.
154. Munich Stadtgericht, 713 (1585).
155. Strasbourg Statuten, vol. 29, fol. 154; Bauer, *Liebesleben*, 157.
156. Frankfurt BMB: 1445, fol. 28; 1451, fol. 36; 1460, fol. 30; 1468, fol. 6; 1489, fol. 39; 1590, fol. 109.
157. Kriegk, *Deutsches Bürgerthum*, 2:389.
158. Bauer, *Liebesleben*, 148.
159. Frankfurt BMB: 1570, fol. 65; 1575, fol. 174.
160. Strasbourg Statuten, vol. 33, fol. 26b (1684).
161. Frankfurt BMB: 1470, fol. 13b; 1525, fol. 30b; 1530, fol. 89b. Nuremberg AStB, 228a, quoted in Walter Grönert, "Die Entwicklung des Gaststättenrechts in der freien Reichsstadt Nürnberg seit dem 14. Jahrhundert," 103. Nuremberg RB, 2, fol. 232 (1478).
162. Frankfurt BMB: 1455, fol. 98b; 1493, fol. 36. Munich RSP, 1530. Nuremberg RB 21, fol. 180 (1543). Siebenkees, *Materialen*, 4:586. Bauer, *Liebesleben*, 148.
163. Frankfurt BMB: 1460, fol. 20b; 1525, fol. 21; 1530, fol. 21b; 1535, fol. 113b; 1545, fol. 60b; 1570, fol. 81b; 1580, fols. 82b, 95b; 1590, fol. 225a. Nuremberg RB: 7, fol. 232 (1478); 22, fol. 249 (1543); 23, fol. 65 (1545). Memmingen Ausgaben, 1479; Memmingen Zuchtordnung, 265/1 (1532); Munich RSP, 1609, fol. 35b; Strasbourg XXI, 1620, fol. 150.
164. Frankfurt BMB: 1485, fol. 37a; 1610, fol. 138b. Strasbourg XXI, 1601, fol. 14. Munich RSP, 1602, fol. 73.
165. Theodor Hampe, *Die Nürnberger Malefizbücher als Quellen der reichsstädtische Sittengeschichte von 14. bis zum 18. Jahrhundert*, 57.

166. Nuremberg RB: 20, fol. 171 (1540); 33, fol. 277 (1569).
167. Munich Stadtgericht, 865, 1503. Frankfurt BMB: 1505, fols. 66a, 68b; 1600, fol. 134a. Nuremberg RB, 35, fol. 68 (1575). Munich RSP, 1599, fols. 52, 56.
168. Frankfurt BMB, 1525, fols. 60a, 103b; Munich Stadtgericht, 865, 1500–1595; Memmingen RPB, August 5, 1618.
169. Stuttgart Malefizakten, A43, Bü. 2 (1526).
170. Quotation is from Munich RSP, 1544, fol. 109. Similar cases in ibid., fol. 115; Stuttgart Malefizakten, A43, Bü. 2 (1545); Memmingen Criminalia, 132 (6); Frankfurt BMB, 1570, fol. 150b.
171. Munich RSP: 1535, fol. 120; 1596, fol. 172. Stuttgart Oberrat Malefizakten, A209, Bü. 2, no. 649 (1579). Strasbourg XV, 1596, fol. 4. Strasbourg XXI, 1603, fol. 241a. Memmingen RPB, August 3, 1618.
172. Frankfurt BMB: 1530, fol. 3b; 1600, fols. 129a, 134a.
173. Albrecht Keller, ed., *Meister Franntz Schmidts Scharfrichters inn Nürnberg all sein Richten*, 23.

## CHAPTER FOUR: THE SALE AND TRADE OF LIFE'S NECESSITIES

1. It is very difficult to determine exactly what percentage of a family's income was spent on food. In 1695, according to Gregory King's estimates, 60.7 percent of English household expenditure was devoted to diet, with poor households spending 74.1 percent of their expenditure on diet. Carole Shammas thinks these figures might be too high, as "King wanted to alert the government to the disastrous impact of the war with France on the laboring population" so might have skewed them somewhat ("Food Expenditures and Economic Well-Being in Early Modern England," 92). Her own calculations for the early modern period, 1560–1760, find that laborers given their food as part of their pay received less than half that of those given no food, which indicates employers and authorities calculated that more than half a laborer's pay would go for food and drink. As this food allocation did not include the food and drink for the laborer's family and as the amount of food is figured for male individuals, who often received twice what women did, King's estimates do not seem unreasonable, however. Erich Maschke also finds that construction workers in German cities could choose to be paid totally in money or could eat on the site. When they chose the latter, 40–50 percent of their wages were deducted for the day's food, though this again was food only for the worker, not for his or her family (*Unterschichten*, 43).
2. This is not to say that there were no women involved as long-distance wholesale traders. Numerous accounts and letters of merchants from a number of German cities show that their wives did everything while they were away on business—took in and gave out payments; handled workers and shipments; made business decisions, investments, and loans. The daughters of such merchants were often given

tutors specifically to teach them "writing and figuring." (Erich Maschke, *Die Familie in der deutschen Stadt des späten Mittelalters*, 40; "Das Rechnungsbuch der Nürnberger Grosskaufmanns Hans Praun von 1471 bis 1478," 93; Aloys Schulte, *Geschichte des mittelalterlichen Handels und Verkehrs zwischen Westdeutschland und Italien*, 1:18, 122; Wachendorf, *Stellung*, 92; Fr. Bastian, "Das Manuale des Regensburger Kaufhauses Runtinger und die mittelalterliche Frauenfrage," 417; Georg Steinhausen, *Deutsche Privatbriefe des Mittelalters*; Hermann Werner and Erika Neuhauser, *Die Schwäbin*, 83; Memmingen RPB, June 16, 1606.) I have decided not to discuss female long-distance traders in great detail, however, as their total number was so small and their ability to act determined by relationship to a male merchant. Such women rarely continued doing these things when they were widowed, at least until they married again. The few regulations of mercantile or entrepreneurial guilds that exist do not mention widows' rights. A few women also traveled as merchants themselves, especially to the fairs in Frankfurt and other cities, but these were also isolated exceptions (see Frankfurt BMB, 1515, fol. 146b, for one such example).

Alexander, Davin, and Hostettler ("Labouring Women") point out that nineteenth- and twentieth-century labor studies have ignored women's work in the same way that early modern studies of merchant capitalism have. These labor studies have traditionally concentrated on trade unions and sustained organizations, not on informal organizations and part-time, unskilled work, which always involved more women.

3. Clark, *Working Life*, 51.

4. Kroemer, "Einführung," 20.

5. Friedrich Bock, *Der Nürnberger Hauptmarkt*; Anton Herzog, *Die Lebensmittelpolitik der Stadt Strassburg im Mittelalter*, 107–109; Nuremberg RB, 11, fol. 85 (1517).

6. This is also true in Denmark, as Jacobsen has discovered ("Women's Work and Women's Role"). It contrasts, however, with the situation in Italy. Judith Brown has found opposition to women selling coming from a variety of moralists, civic leaders, and religious figures and even from writers like Leon Battista Alberti. Because women were seen as the guardians of religious and moral values, yet weak and easily led astray, they were kept out of peddling and hawking ("A Woman's Place Was in the Home: Women's Work in Renaissance Tuscany"). The difference cannot be explained solely by religion, for Catholic cities in Germany made no mention of women selling.

7. Munich RSP, 1531; Frankfurt Zünfte, Abt. II, 52, 1623; B. Schmidt and Bücher, *Frankfurter*, 350–351.

8. Frankfurt Zünfte, Abt. II, 52, 1377; Maschke, *Familie*, 35, in reference to Cologne.

9. Munich Stadtgericht, 925.

10. Memmingen RPB, March 20, 1618. Munich RSP: 1594, fol. 105; 1596, fol. 142; 1601, fol. 41. Munich Stadtgericht 925, 1612 and 1615.
11. Strasbourg XV, 1622, fol. 118b.
12. Quotation is from Nuremberg RB, 63, fol. 342 (1605). Similar cases in ibid., 67, fol. 382 (1608); in Strasbourg XV: 1621, fols. 86, 87, 167; 1628, fols. 46, 54; and in Frankfurt Zünfte, Abt. II, 52, no. 65 (1654).
13. Frankfurt Zünfte, Abt. II, 52, no. 65 (1648).
14. Ibid., no. 582a (1654).
15. Strasbourg XV, 1645, fol. 176b; Augsburg Schätze, no. 37/I, 1645 Bürgerliste.
16. Stuttgart Stadt Findbuch.
17. Memmingen RPB, July 29, 1605.
18. Ibid.: July 14, 1553; February 4, 1572. Memmingen Zünfte, 453(1). Munich Stadtgericht, 867, 1597 and 1598. Munich RSP, 1602, fol. 82. Strasbourg XV, 1615, fols. 73, 86, 124, 135, 157, 173. Munich Steuerbücher, 1630 and 1640.
19. Strasbourg XV: 1614, fols. 154, 173, 178; 1615, fols. 73, 86.
20. Ibid., 1615, fol. 124.
21. Ibid., fol. 135.
22. Ibid., fol. 157.
23. Ibid., fol. 173.
24. Nuremberg Stadt Inven., no. 1, fol. 4b (1529).
25. Frankfurt BMB: 1535, fol. 92a; 1550, fol. 113b. Strasbourg XV: 1580, fols. 201, 205; 1610, fol. 122b; 1633, fols. 204, 211. Munich Stadtgericht, 925: 1599, 1612–1614.
26. Munich Stadtgericht, 925, 1599.
27. Frankfurt BMB, 1535, fol. 92a. Strasbourg XV: 1623, fol. 139a; 1639, fols. 39, 54, 71, 78.
28. Frankfurt BMB, 1535, fol. 18b.
29. Strasbourg XV, 1626, fol. 199.
30. Ibid., fol. 290.
31. Bücher, *Berufe*; Munich Steuerbücher, 1462, 1508, 1570; Memmingen RPB, July 29, 1530; Nuremberg RB, 20, fol. 255 (1541); Munich Stadtgericht, 867, 1592.
32. Munich Steuerbücher, 1532, 1610; Frankfurt BMB, 1535, fol. 15b; Munich Stadtgericht, 867, 1587; Memmingen RPB, September 28, 1601.
33. Marianne Ebert, "Geschichte des Nürnberger Lebkuchens vom Handwerk zur Industrie," 213.
34. Housed in the cookbook collection of the Germanisches Nationalmuseum in Nuremberg.
35. Nuremberg RB: 20, fol. 255 (1541); 52, fol. 28 (1598). Strasbourg XV: 1593, fol. 96a; 1602, fols. 88a, 136; 1633, fols. 49, 321, 324; 1640, fol. 311a; 1634, fols. 29, 34; 1645, fols. 8, 98, 121; 1645, fols. 55, 95, 97. Munich Gewerbeamt, no. 2307 (Küchlbäcker), nos. 2 (n.d.), 6 (1625), 10 (1699).

36. Strasbourg XV, 1632, fol. 29.
37. Ibid., 1634, fol. 34.
38. Nuremberg RB, 62, fol. 4 (1603).
39. Strasbourg XV, 1616, fol. 101.
40. Ibid., fol. 168.
41. Nuremberg RB, 69, fol. 239 (1610).
42. Munich Gewerbeamt, no. 2307 (Küchlbäcker), no. 5 (n.d.).
43. Ibid., no. 9 (1636), in ibid.
44. Bücher, *Berufe*; Wachendorf, *Stellung*, 101, quoting from 1454 and 1505 Cologne guild statutes; Munich Stadtgericht, 917, 1433, 1511; Memmingen Steuerbücher, 1450; Frankfurt Zünfte, Ugb. C-46: Pp (1623) and Xxx (1668).
45. Nuremberg RB, 5, fol. 214 (1491); Frankfurt Zünfte, Ugb. C-46, Bbb (1675).
46. Frankfurt BMB: 1470, fol. 76b; 1505, fol. 99b; 1545, fol. 5b. Nuremberg RB, 8, fol. 249 (1506). Strasbourg XV, 1573, fol. 9a. Munich Stadtgericht, 925, 1599 and 1644.
47. Strasbourg XV, 1595, fol. 91b.
48. Nuremberg RB, 9, fol. 204 (1511); Munich Stadtgericht, 925, 1599.
49. Nuremberg Aemterbüchlein, nos. 8, 26, 52, 62, 81.
50. Strasbourg XV, 1593, fols. 91a, 99b; Frankfurt Gerichtsbuch 1405, fol. 100a, quoted in Bücher, *Berufe*, 50.
51. Nuremberg RB: 21, fol. 100b (1542); 59, fols. 249, 282 (1600). Nuremberg AStB, no. 232, fol. 321.
52. Nuremberg RB, 33, fol. 234 (1568).
53. In Vienna, fruit vendors even had a separate guild and separate banner that they hung with fruit and carried in the city's Corpus Christi parades (Rudolph Till, "Die berufstätige Frau in mittelalterlichen Wien," 117).
54. Nuremberg RB, 15, fol. 23 (1529).
55. Nuremberg AStB, no. 232, Wandelbuch Ordnung und Gesetze, fol. 35, "Fürkauf wachsender Frucht."
56. August Jegel, "Heilkräutergebrauch im alten Nürnberg," 141; Nuremberg RB, 16, fol. 37 (1532).
57. Frankfurt BMB 1530, fol. 4b; Nuremberg RB: 19, fols. 230 (1539), 238 (1539); 20, fol. 232 (1541).
58. Nuremberg RB, 30, fol. 298 (1559).
59. Ibid., 35, fol. 89b (1575).
60. Ibid., 38, fol. 48 (1579).
61. Ibid., 39, fol. 222b (1580).
62. Ibid., 44, fol. 5 (1585).
63. Nuremberg AStB, no. 234, fol. 81, "Marktordnung" (1562).
64. Nuremberg RB, 47, fol. 272b (1588).
65. Ibid., 70, fol. 185 (1616).
66. Ibid., 47, fol. 272b (1588).
67. Ibid., fol. 301 (1588).
68. Ibid., 50, fol. 93 (1591).

69. Frankfurt BMB, 1580, fol. 12b. Strasbourg XV: 1597, fols. 3, 8; 1599, fol. 95; 1628, fol. 46b. Memmingen RPB, September 5, 1604. Munich Stadtgericht, 925, 1614 and 1615.
70. Frankfurt Ver., vol. 1, no. 107, 1616 Obsthocken Ordnung.
71. Frankfurt Bedebücher, 1346–1500, quoted in Bücher, *Berufe*. Frankfurt BMB: 1520, fol. 28b; 1530, fol. 67a. Strasbourg XV: 1572, fol. 51a; 1573, fol. 104a; 1578, fol. 104a; 1584, fols. 128b, 129b; 1587, fols. 108a, 126b, 168b; 1615, fol. 10b; 1622, fol. 56b; 1623, fol. 106b; 1626, fols. 135–136; 1636, fol. 16a.
72. Strasbourg XV: 1622, fol. 206a; 1587, fols. 108a, 168a.
73. August Jegel, *Ernährungsfürsorge des Altnürnberger Rats*, 142.
74. Nuremberg AStB, no. 101.
75. Nuremberg RB: 2, fol. 88 (1476); 4, fol. 36b (1484); 5, fol. 251 (1493); 9, fol. 252 (1511). Bücher, *Berufe*, 68. Strasbourg XV, 1632, fol. 125b.
76. Nuremberg AStB, no. 101, fols. 100, 219. Strasbourg XV: 1575, fol. 68; 1634, fol. 34a. Munich Stadtgericht, 925, 1664.
77. Nuremberg RB, 22, fol. 73b (1544).
78. Strasbourg XV, 1573, fols. 9, 47, 130b.
79. Ibid., 1574, fol. 136b.
80. Ibid., 1580, fol. 7.
81. Ibid., fol. 17.
82. Ibid., fol. 24.
83. Ibid., fol. 25.
84. Ibid., fol. 30.
85. Ibid., fol. 52.
86. Ibid., fol. 59.
87. Ibid., 1582, fol. 92b; 1605, fol. 22a.
88. Frankfurt Ver, vol. I, no. 73, "Holzordnung" (1610).
89. Ibid., and Frankfurt Ver, vol. I, no. 47 (1598).
90. Satzungsbuch der Stadt Nürnberg von 1302, fol. 86, quoted in Grönert, "Entwicklung," 14.
91. Grönert, "Entwicklung," 57.
92. Nuremberg Stadt, Archiv der Nürnberger Handwerker, Rep. E5/1, no. 10; Frankfurt Eidbuch, vol. II, no. 238; Strasbourg XV, 1581, fol. 22b.
93. Munich RSP, 1595; Munich Stadtgericht, 867: 1592, 1595, 1597.
94. Munich Stadtgericht, 867: 1593, 1596.
95. Munich RSP, 1599, fol. 164.
96. Munich Stadtgericht, 925: 1637, 1672.
97. Strasbourg XV, 1618, fol. 138.
98. Ibid., 1619, fols. 68, 78, 126, 127, 154, 260.
99. Munich RSP, 1597, fol. 12; Munich Stadtgericht, 925, 1599; Memmingen RPB, November 5, 1604.
100. Munich Gewerbeamt, no. 2866.
101. Jegel, *Ernährungsfürsorge*, 159.
102. Ibid. Clark found a similar situation in seventeenth-century England: "A tendency was shown by public opinion to regard licenses [to sell

beer and brandy] as suitable provision for invalids and widows who might otherwise require assistance from the state. They were granted to 'ancient people past their labours and invalids to keep them from starving'" (*Working Life*, 230).

103. Munich Ratsmandata, vol. 60A1, 1526 Branntweinordnung.

104. Munich Stadtgericht, 925, 1590.

105. Strasbourg XV, 1636, fols. 70, 162, 167, 216.

106. Ibid., fol. 167.

107. Memmingen RPB: February 11, 1527; November 16, 1580; March 17, 1619. Frankfurt BMB: 1530, fol. 31a; 1600, fols. 108a, 126a. Munich Stadtgericht, 925, 1590, 1612. Strasbourg XV, 1607, fol. 120a. Frankfurt Zünfte, Ugb. D-24, L (1698).

108. Munich Stadtgericht, 917, 1433 Bussordnung; Munich Gewerbeamt, nos. 1411, 1418.

109. Nuremberg RB, 8, fol. 155b (1505). Strasbourg XV: 1584, fols. 95–99, 102–108; 1587, fol. 150a; 1596, fol. 60b; 1598, fol. 197; 1623, fol. 289b; 1626, fol. 57a; 1632, fol. 143a; 1640, fols. 104, 106.

110. Nuremberg RB, 35, fol. 200b (1576).

111. Frankfurt BMB, 1520, fol. 95a. Nuremberg RB, 38, fols. 269b, (1579) 310 (1579). Strasbourg XV: 1584, fol. 133a; 1598, fol. 197; 1612, fol. 192b; 1614, fol. 109b; 1632, fols. 29a, 135a. Memmingen RPB, January 3, 1603.

112. Strasbourg XV, 1612, fol. 84a.

113. Ibid., fol. 92b.

114. Ibid., 1634, fol. 58b.

115. Ibid.: 1598, fol. 197; 1599, fol. 166b.

116. Ibid., 1601, fol. 127b.

117. Ibid., 1617, fol. 171.

118. Nuremberg RB, 43, fol. 278b (1585). Strasbourg XV: 1605, fol. 53b; 1624, fols. 178, 227; 1636, fol. 4.

119. Nuremberg RB: 23, fol. 128 (1547); 67, fol. 88 (1607). Strasbourg XV, 1634, fol. 14, 15. Strasbourg Statuten, vol. 9, no. 104 (1637).

120. Nuremberg RB, 23, fol. 80a (1545).

121. Strasbourg XV, 1634, fol. 238b.

122. Strasbourg XV, 1585, fols. 77b–79b; Munich Stadtgericht, 867, 1592; Memmingen RPB, April 12, 1622.

123. Strasbourg XV, 1612, fols. 6, 9, 15, 26, 31, 34.

124. Strasbourg Statuten, vol. 19 (1362); Frankfurt BMB, 1510, fol. 11a; Munich Stadtgericht, 925, 1590.

125. Nuremberg RB, 2, fol. 232 (1478); Strasbourg XV, 1631, fol. 140; Munich RSP, 1597, fol. 80; Frankfurt BMB, 1590, fol. 59a.

126. Strasbourg Statuten, vol. 33, fol. 26b (1684).

127. Strasbourg XV, 1580, fol. 14.

128. Munich Stadtgericht, 925, 1512; 867, 1599. Strasbourg XV: 1587, fol. 70b; 1592, fol. 7; 1611, fol. 181b; 1626, fol. 112; 1631, fol. 140.

129. Munich Stadtgericht, 867, 1602.

130. Nuremberg RB, 23, fol. 80b (1545); Grönert, "Entwicklung," 63; Strasbourg XV, 1613, fols. 212, 220.
131. Strasbourg XV: 1613, fol. 22a; 1628, fol. 349b; 1640, fols. 75, 98; 1665, fol. 115a.
132. Ibid., 1620, fol. 168a; 1625, fol. 107a.
133. Ibid., 1628, fols. 51, 57.
134. Ibid., 1636, fols. 178, 189.
135. Strasbourg Statuten, vol. 9, fol. 144 (1644).
136. Heinrich Eckhert, *Die Krämer in süddeutschen Städten bis zum Ausgang des Mittelalters*; Wachendorf, *Stellung*, 97–104; Maschke and Sydow, *Mittelschichten*, 27; Dübeck, *Købekoner og Konkurrence*, 398.
137. Hess, *Frauenberufe*, 94.
138. Bücher, *Berufe*, 126; Nuremberg Aemterbüchlein, nos. 26, 52, 62, 81.
139. Strasbourg Statuten, vol. 30, fol. 136 (1400).
140. Munich Gewerbeamt, no. 5170; Munich Steuerbücher, 1410–1565; Memmingen Steuerbücher, 1450; Bücher, *Berufe*.
141. Wachendorf, *Stellung*, 89.
142. Augsburg, Danzig, Esslingen, Landshut, Ulm, Worms, Ingolstadt in Hess, *Frauenberufe*, 94 and in Strasbourg Statuten: vol. 13, fol. 103; vol. 14, fol. 26.
143. Strasbourg Statuten, vol. 19 (1362); Nuremberg, Aemterbüchlein, no. 1; Munich RSP: 1530, 1534; Nuremberg RB, 64, fol. 30b (1605).
144. Munich Gewerbeamt, no. 5083 (1430).
145. Bücher, *Berufe* (Gesetzbuch 3, fol. 32).
146. Strasbourg Statuten, vol. 13, fol. 247 (n.d. [late fifteenth century]).
147. Ibid., vol. 14, fol. 76.
148. Munich Gewerbeamt, no. 1569; Nuremberg AStB, no. 101, fol. 279 (1504).
149. Augsburg Schätze, no. 282; Frankfurt Ver, vol. I, no. 42 (1594), no. 107 (1616).
150. Nuremberg Aemterbüchlein, nos. 1–5; Frankfurt Eidbuch, vol. II, fol. 57.
151. Strasbourg Statuten, vol. 3, fol. 59 (1516); Frankfurt BMB, 1530, fol. 34a; Nuremberg RB, 30, fol. 38 (1557); Nuremberg Aemterbüchlein, no. 81; Nuremberg AStB, no. 101, fol. 109b.
152. Frankfurt BMB, 1490, fol. 103a. Nuremberg RB, 17, fol. 35b (1535); 50, fol. 434 (1593); 69, fol. 164b (1614). Munich RSP, 1548, fol. 110; 1597, fol. 133; 1600, fol. 97; Munich Gewerbeamt, no. 5170 (1578). Memmingen RPB, November 12, 1565; October 9, 1570; September 6, 1598; June 1, 1608. Strasbourg XV, 1631, fols. 60b, 109a, 172a; 1632, fol. 93a; 1633, fols. 130–135; 1634, fols. 168, 178.
153. Nuremberg RB: 5, fol. 2 (1488); 5, fol. 80 (1489); 20, 75 (1539); 52, fol. 30b (1593). Munich RSP, 1600, fol. 53. Munich Gewerbeamt, no. 5170. Memmingen RPB, February 1, 1621. Strasbourg XV, 1632, fol. 146b; 1633, fols. 296, 317; 1634, fol. 209b; 1639, fol. 146b.
154. Strasbourg XV, 1636, fols. 176, 179.

155. Ibid., 1639, fol. 107.
156. Munich Gewerbeamt, no. 1569.
157. Nuremberg RB, 3, fol. 143 (1481).
158. Ibid., 6, fols. 223b, 236b, 237, 256 (1497).
159. Ibid., 27, fol. 1554 (1554).
160. Frankfurt BMB: 1494, fol. 21a; 1500, fol. 67b. Memmingen RPB: September 25, 1580; February 23, 1582; January 9, 1590; February 8, 1605; October 9, 1610. Strasbourg XV, 1591, fols. 35–36. Munich RSP: 1600, fols. 39, 144; 1605, fol. 99.
161. Memmingen RPB, August 26, 1510; Munich RSP, 1535; Nuremberg AStB, no. 101, fol. 189 (1554 and 1566); Nuremberg RB, 30, fol. 38 (1557).
162. Nuremberg Aemterbüchlein, nos. 50–80; Munich RSP, 1544.
163. Wachendorf, *Stellung*, 90.
164. Nuremberg Aemterbüchlein, nos. 52–71. Kunigunde Wechter carried on a print shop from 1532 to 1551. Davis has discovered several women printers in Lyon ("Arts Mécaniques"), and Miriam U. Chrisman several active in Strasbourg, particularly Margaretha Prüss, who was married to three different printers (*Lay Culture, Learned Culture: Books and Social Change in Strasbourg, 1480–1599*, 15–22). Beatrice Beech from Western Michigan University is currently working on a study of women printers and publishers and has presented several papers on the subject, the most recent of which is "Yolande Bonhomme: A Printer of Religious Books."
165. Nuremberg RB: 12, fol. 212b (1523); 26, fol. 118 (1550); 27, fol. 336 (1579). Strasbourg XXI, 1630, fol. 111.
166. Nuremberg RB, 10, fol. 9b (1514); 53, fol. 203 (1593). Nuremberg AStB, no. 101, fol. 187.
167. Jacobsen links the level of illegal selling and the level of regulation together in the case of Danish cities. She notes, "Indeed, the problem of the illegal involvement of women in trade, whether they ignored the monopoly of a guild or engaged in forestalling or regrating, seems to have grown in direct proportion to the regulations and organization of trade. It was to become a major and constant problem in the early modern period, when the relatively open structure of the medieval city had given way to a tightly organized and carefully controlled local and national economy" ("Women's Work and Women's Role," 13).
168. Nuremberg RB: 1c, fol. 21 (1462); 2, fol. 63 (1476); 7, fol. 255b (1503); 9, fol. 107b (1509); 10, fol. 179 (1515); 22, fol. 126 (1544); 35, fol. 26b (1574); 52, fol. 93 (1593). Nuremberg AStB, no. 101, fol. 190.
169. Nuremberg RB: 6, fol. 223b (1497); 49, fol. 80 (1591). Frankfurt BMB, 1510, fol. 81a. Munich RSP: 1531; 1544, fol. 57. Memmingen RPB: April 24, 1560; March 12, 1660.
170. Brown finds another objection to women selling house to house in Florence. The guild of used-clothing dealers in Florence barred women from this type of sales, claiming they "infiltrated people's

houses and persuaded the housewives to buy to the detriment of their husbands" ("Women's Place").

171. Nuremberg RB: 16, fol. 95 (1533); 22, fol. 408 (1545). Memmingen RPB, September 2, 1573; November 2, 1575; January 15, 1593; October 20, 1606. Munich Gewerbeamt, no. 1569.

172. Nuremberg RB: 8, fol. 347 (1507); 16, fol. 134 (1534); 23, fol. 331 (1546); 48, fol. 672 (1590). This last is an interesting case because the goods had been sold to the Jews in Furth. The original owners tried to claim the goods had been stolen from them by the market woman, in which case the goods concerned would normally be confiscated from the Jews with no recompense given, returned to the original owners, and the market woman admonished. (The rights of the Jews to merchandise they had bought were not considered.) In this case, the market woman argued she had been given the merchandise willingly and had paid the original owners for it (after taking a fee for her services). The authorities agreed, and the case was dropped.

173. Nuremberg RB: 2, fol. 245 (1478); 6, fol. 236b (1497); 8, fol. 380 (1507); 11, fol. 45 (1516); 16, fol. 85 (1533); 16, fols. 166 (1534), 169 (1534); 17, fol. 145b (1535). Memmingen RPB, December 10, 1589; January 15, 1590. Strasbourg XV 1591, fol. 131; 1636, fol. 176. Munich RSP, 1609, fol. 67.

174. Nuremberg RB: 3, fol. 220b (1481); 48, fol. 90b (1589); 67, fol. 181b (1608). Frankfurt BMB, 1490, fol. 16b. Memmingen Zünfte, 462(1). Memmingen RPB, December 16, 1588. Munich Stadtgericht, 867, 1602. Munich Gewerbeamt, no. 1569. Strasbourg XV, 1619, fols. 91, 95.

175. Nuremberg RB: 5, fol. 242 (1491); 14, fol. 120 (1528); 17, fol. 162 (1536). Frankfurt BMB: 1515, fol. 60b; 1570, fol. 130b; 1580, fol. 48b. Munich Gewerbeamt, no. 5083 (1576). Munich Stadtgericht, 867. Strasbourg Statuten, vol. 13, fol. 247. Baader, *Polizeiordnungen*, 30. A *Verbot* (literally, "prohibition") was a legal order, issued by a city council, forbidding a Krämerin to sell or exchange any goods until she had paid off her debts. One could be issued on the goods of any person whose creditors feared they would not be repaid.

176. Nuremberg RB: 6, fol. 215 (1497); 21, fol. 265 (1543); 22, fol. 36 (1543). Nuremberg AStB, no. 234, fol. 81, "Marktordnung" (1562). Munich Gewerbeamt, no. 5083 (1576); no. 1569 (1580). Frankfurt BMB 1600, fol. 198a. Strasbourg XV: 1600, fols. 36, 45; 1612, fols. 292–293; 1617, fol. 223; 1621, fols. 199, 205; 1636, fol. 176b; 1650, fol. 20b; 1660, fol. 4.

177. Memmingen RPB, October 10, 1530. Nuremberg RB: 28, fol. 162 (1555); 32, fol. 261b (1564).

178. Nuremberg RB 21, fol. 268 (1543); 60, fol. 490 (1602); Munich Stadtgericht, 867, 1588.

179. Strasbourg XV, 1634, fol. 35.

180. Ibid., 1588, fols. 104, 117, 121, 124, 125 (quoted).

181. Frankfurt BMB, 1470, fol. 50b; Nuremberg Stadt Inven; Munich Gewerbeamt, no. 5172 (1656).

182. Nuremberg Stadt Inven., no. 3, fols. 160 (1547), 163b (1547); Frankfurt BMB, 1500, fol. 38a.
183. Nuremberg Stadt Inven., no. 3, fol. 103b (1545); Strasbourg RB, vol. 1, no. 89, "Constitutio und Satzung: Wie es mit dem ungeerbten Aussgohn hinfuhrter gehalten soll" (1552).
184. Nuremberg Stadt Inven, no. 1, fol. 7 (1524); no. 17, fol. 5 (1547).
185. Ibid., no. 4, fol. 109 (1547).
186. Ibid.: no. 3, fol. 169b (1530); no. 2, fols. 83b–84 (1537); no. 4, fol. 41b (1544). Howell, "Women's Work," 233.
187. Nuremberg Stadt Inven: no. 16, fol. 60 (1552); no. 1, fols. 200–213 (1530).
188. Ibid., no. 1, fol. 185 (1530); Nuremberg Stadt Lib Litt, no. 28, fols. 96–97; Munich RSP, 1607, fol. 160; Jacobsen, "Women's Work and Women's Role," 10.
189. Pfaff, *Geschichte der Stadt Stuttgart*, 308. Munich Zimilien, no. 41. Strasbourg Statuten, vol. 19. Frankfurt Ver, vol. I, no. 42. Nuremberg Stadt Inven: no. 2, fol. 92 (1537); no. 2, fol. 48 (1544).
190. Nuremberg Stadt Lib Litt: no. 15, fol. 73b; no. 12, fol. 170b. Strasbourg Statuten, vol. 19. Munich Zimilien, no. 41.
191. Nuremberg Stadt, *Nürmberg . . . Reformation*, sec. 38.
192. Nuremberg Stadt Inven, no. 17, fol. 112 (1569).
193. Nuremberg Stadt Heilig-Geist-Spital Inventarbücher, no. 6648 (1597).
194. Ibid., nos. 1138–1145, 4021, 4031, 4571, 4648, 6644, 6771. The largest of these, no. 4031, is very interesting, not only for its sheer size but also for the economic activities of the wife, which it demonstrates. It was taken by the widow on the death of one Peter Rheimer, a moneylender, in 1602. Their house had twenty rooms, for the furnishings are listed room by room, and the total estate came to 24,900 fls. Of this money, 15,667 fls was lent out, however, of which the wife had lent 4,147 fls in her own name. They owned 1,313 fls worth of silver dishes and utensils, among other items, and she owned 309 fls worth of clothes, while he had 119 fls worth. Among her possessions were a number of books, including Luther's Bible (1 fl), Spangenberg's *Hauspostill* (£4), a chronicle by Sebastian Franck (£2) and the old Nuremberg *Reformation* from 1484 (£5).

## CHAPTER FIVE: GUILDS, CRAFTS, AND MARKET PRODUCTION

1. Brodmeier, *Handwerk*, 13.
2. Wachendorf, *Stellung*, 30–32.
3. Rainer Stahlschmidt, *Die Geschichte des eisenverarbeitende Gewerbes in Nürnberg von der ersten Nachrichten im 12.–13. Jahrhundert bis 1630*, 186–187.
4. Monter, "Women in Calvinist Geneva," 204.
5. Clark, *Working Life*, 294.
6. Frankfurt BMB: 1465, fol. 31b; 1520, fol. 49a; 1550, fol. 7b; 1575,

fol. 62b. Lorenzen-Schmidt, "Stellung der Frauen," 322. Wissell, *Handwerks*, 1:254. Frankfurt Zünfte: Ugb. D-11, Z, no. 7 (1540): Ugb. C-44, Q (1667).

7. Frankfurt BMB: 1560, fol. 104b; 1590, fol. 175a. Frankfurt Zünfte: Ugb. C-53, Ff, no. 4 (1587); Ugb. C-44, Q (1667); Ugb. C-33, Aaa (1688–1689). Wissell, *Handwerks*, 1:258.

8. Frankfurt Zünfte: Ugb. C-44 (1618); Abt. II, 52 (1649); Ugb. C-43 (1669).

9. Wissell, *Handwerks*, 1:262–263.

10. Frankfurt BMB, 1505, fol. 95a; Frankfurt wool-weavers (1455) and stonemasons (1521) quoted in B. Schmidt and Bücher, *Frankfurter*, 87; Strasbourg XXI, 1619, fol. 186.

11. Nuremberg Stadt Inven, no. 4, fol. 109 (1547).

12. Frankfurt BMB: 1500, fol. 115b; 1530, fol. 70a. Nuremberg RB 63, fol. 342 (1605); 67, fol. 382 (1608).

13. Emil Reicke, "Ein Blick in das Alltagsleben der Pirckheimerzeit," 87.

14. Frankfurt BMB: 1520, fol. 49a; 1540, fol. 102b; 1550, fol. 61a.

15. Strasbourg XV, 1613, fols. 293b–294a.

16. Davis, "Arts Mécaniques," 145.

17. Nuremberg Stadt QNG, no. 168, "Abschrift des Journals des Sebastian Welser (1530–1539)."

18. Nuremberg RB, 15, fol. 72a (1529).

19. Nuremberg Stadt QNG, no. 68/I, 273 (1535).

20. Nuremberg RB: 1c, fol. 100 (1465): 21, fol. 85 (1542); 38, fol. 636b (1579). Memmingen RPB, August 7, 1559. Strasbourg XXI, 1605, fol. 270. Strasbourg XV: 1617, fol. 20; 1619, fols. 69, 176; 1621, fol. 43b; 1655, fols. 43–44. Frankfurt Zünfte, Ugb. C-59, Aa, no. 6 (1676); Ugb. D-9, Cc, (1680).

21. Memmingen Zünfte, 422, Gläser (1605).

22. Ibid.

23. Frankfurt Zünfte, Abt. II, 62, fols. 240–244 (1694–1697).

24. Howell has found that organized journeymen in Leiden also objected to work by masters' wives, at least in the fulling industry ("Women's Work," 215–220).

25. The watchmakers in Geneva were an exception, for as early as 1690 master watchmakers were prohibited from teaching the essential parts of their craft to any women, even their wives and daughters (Monter, "Women in Calvinist Geneva," 203).

26. Nuremberg RB, 17, fol. 90 (1535). Nuremberg Stadt QNG, no. 68/I, 374 (1538). Strasbourg XV: 1572, fol. 72; 1628, fols. 173, 209, 217, 254; 1632, fol. 151; 1636, fols. 117, 124, 133, 144, 147, 153, 168, 175. Strasbourg XXI, 1606, fol. 195b.

27. Wissell, *Handwerks*, 2:47.

28. Nuremberg Stadt QNG: no. 68/I, 210; no. 68/II, 686; no. 68/III, 1185. G. K. Schmelzeisen, *Die Rechtstellung der Frau in der deutschen Stadtwirtschaft*, 53.

29. A Frankfurt tailors' ordinance, printed in B. Schmidt and Bücher,

*Frankfurter*, 513, even allows widows who married nontailors to continue in the craft as long as they made a special payment.

30. Munich RSP, 1461, fols. 39, 42. Nuremberg RB: 2, fols. 31 (1475), 282 (1479), 318 (1479). Frankfurt BMB, 1580, fol. 189b. Memmingen Zünfte, 451(3), Hutmachern (1613). Strasbourg XV, 1634, fols. 116, 127. Munich Stadtgericht, 925, 1664.

31. Frankfurt BMB, 1515, fol. 112b. Nuremberg RB: 11, fol. 324 (1520); 22, fol. 236 (1544). Munich RSP, 1526. Frankfurt Zünfte, Ugb. D-3 (1527). Nuremberg Stadt QNG, no. 68/II, 506; no. 68/I, 115 (1535). Strasbourg XV, 1612, fol. 201b. Frankfurt Zünfte: Ugb. D-3, L (1588 and 1596); Ugb. C-54, M (1640).

32. Gustav Schmoller, *Die Strassburger Tucher und Weberzünft: Urkunden und Darstellung*, 2:510.

33. Claus-Peter Clasen, *Die Augsburger Weber: Leistungen und Krisen des Textilgewerbes um 1600*, 23.

34. Stahlschmidt, *Geschichte*, 186–187.

35. Munich Steuerbücher.

36. Nuremberg RB: 19, fol. 187b (1538); 37, fol. 59b (1578). Munich Gewerbeamt, no. 5083, 1636 Käuflerordnung, 1655 Kurschnerordnung. Frankfurt Zünfte, Ugb. D-26, N2.

37. Strasbourg XV: 1619, fols. 74, 169; 1655, fols. 15, 30, 45, 59, 79, 82, 83 (quoted).

38. Quote is from Frankfurt Zünfte, Ugb. C-43, L (1600). Similar cases in Frankfurt BMB: 1600, fol. 271a; 1610, fol. 45a and in Strasbourg XV: 1607, fol. 147; 1618, fols. 8, 14, 20, 28, 119.

39. Strasbourg XV: 1610, fols. 146, 156, 198, 225; 1633, fols. 88, 154, 173, 177, 178, 230, 232.

40. Quotes are from Frankfurt Zünfte, Ugb. C-54, M. Similar cases in Frankfurt Zünfte, Ugb. D-2, F (1506); Ugb. C-59, Gg, no. 3, and Aa, no. 4 (1672) and in Memmingen RPB: September 15, 1556; November 8, 1560 and in Strasbourg XV: 1606, fols. 90, 92; 1609, fols. 128, 144, 149.

41. Frankfurt Zünfte, Ugb. D-24, L4 (1698).

42. Strasbourg XV: 1617, fols. 84, 144, 247 (quoted); 1665, fols. 15, 30, 40, 59, 79, 82, 83. Dübeck has discovered that in Denmark, as well, city governments did occasionally grant widow's privileges against the wishes of the guild (*Københoner og Konkurrence*, 395–404).

43. Frankfurt Zünfte, Ugb. C-32, R, no. 1 (1663).

44. Ibid., Ugb. C-38, Z.

45. Ibid.

46. Strasbourg XV, 1674, fol. 175.

47. Ibid., 1674, fol. 195.

48. Frankfurt Zünfte, Ugb. D-25, P, no. 2 (1692).

49. Ibid., Ugb. C-59, Cc (1639).

50. Ibid., Abt II, 62, no. 174 (1670).

51. Nuremberg Stadt QNG: no. 68/I, 311, 412 (1583); Strasbourg XV, 1627,

fols. 133, 162, 180, 202. Similar case noted in Denmark in Jacobsen, "Women's Work and Women's Role," 19.
52. Wissell, *Handwerks*, I:439.
53. Nuremberg RB, 32, fol. 72b (1563).
54. Heinz Zatschek, "Aus der Geschichte des Wiener Handwerks während des 30 Jährigen Krieges: Eine soziologische Studie," 39.
55. Nuremberg RB, 22, fol. 62b (1544); Munich Gewerbeamt, no. 2293; Strasbourg XV, 1608, fol. 22.
56. Wissell, *Handwerks*, 2:446. Frank Göttman, *Handwerk und Bundnispolitik: Die Handwerkerbände am Mittelrhein vom 14, bis zum 17. Jahrhundert*, 33. Nuremberg Stadt QNG: no. 68/III, 1099; no. 68/I, 230 (1535); 616 (1562); no. 68/III, 1298 (1601).
57. Strasbourg XXI, 1620 on.
58. Göttman, *Handwerk und Bundnispolitik*, 153; Wissell, *Handwerks*, 2:140, 271; Strasbourg XV, 1628, fols. 152, 164; B. Schmidt and Bücher, *Frankfurter*, 280.
59. Clark notes the same trend in seventeenth-century England. She comments, "The keystone of the journeymen's position lay in their ability to restrict their own numbers by the enforcement of a long apprenticeship and the limitation of the number of apprentices. On gaining this point the journeymen in any trade secured a monopoly which enabled them to bargain advantageously with the masters . . . when their organization was strong enough, the journeymen allowed no unapprenticed persons to be employed upon any process in their trade, however simple or mechanical, a policy which resulted in the complete exclusion of women, owing to the fact that girls were seldom, if ever, apprenticed in these trends" (*Working Life*, 298).
60. E.g., Nuremberg Stadt QNG, no. 68/III, 1108.
61. I thank H. Wunder, who, both in her article "Stellung der Frau" and in personal conversation, stressed the importance of this patriarchal structure.
62. Nuremberg RB, 10, fol. 96b (1513); 11, fol. 180b (1519). Nuremberg Stadt QNG: no. 68/I, 115 (1535), 271 and 372 (1538), 119 (1568); no. 68/II, 905. Augsburg Handwercksordnungen, 1550, Nestler and Huter.
63. B. Schmidt and Bücher, *Frankfurter*, 417–420; quotation on 420. The language of the 1607 ruling is somewhat ambiguous, as it states first that "only daughters whose parents have been in the guild before, and not simply blood-relatives," could be employed by a master and then states that "only two girls may do anything at all in the shop, whether they are daughters or not" (420). The best resolution of the ambiguity, I think, is to read the last statement as a restriction on the number of daughters and the work they could do, not a contradiction of the first statement. In other words, masters could employ only their own daughters to do craft work and, if they employed a maid to clean the shop or prepare materials, could only use one daughter. In

no case was the number of girls in the shop to exceed two, no matter what they were doing.

64. Nuremberg Stadt QNG, no. 68/II, 663.
65. Ibid.: no. 68/I, 441; no. 68/II, 674, 847, 853, 873; no. 68/III, 1093, 1107, 1189.
66. Munich Gewerbeamt, no. 1020.
67. Schmoller, *Strassburger*, 541.
68. Frankfurt Zünfte, Ugb. C-36, Cc (1649, Huter).
69. Wachendorf, *Stellung*, 63.
70. This incident is related in Mummenhoff, "Frauenarbeit."
71. Nuremberg RB: 1c, fol. 176b (1469); 2, fols. 31 (1475), 282, 318 (1479); 3, fol. 25b (1480). Frankfurt BMB, 1570, fol. 17b. Strasbourg XV: 1628, fol. 214b; 1643, fols. 58, 67, 93, 135. Stahlschmidt, *Geschichte*, 184.
72. Nuremberg Stadt QNG, no. 68/I, 195 (1569). Nuremberg RB, 35, fol. 389b (1577). Strasbourg XV: 1610, fols. 198, 225, 246, 256; 1621, fol. 43b; 1628, fols. 173, 209, 217, 254; 1632, fol. 151a. Monter, "Women in Calvinist Geneva," 200.
73. Nuremberg Stadt QNG, no. 68/III, 1107.
74. Baader, *Polizeiordnungen*, 30.
75. Munich RSP: 1461, fol. 42; 1484, fol. 19. Munich Gewerbeamt, 1020. Stuttgart Landwirtschaft, A58, Bü. 26 (1584 goldsmiths' ordinance).
76. Nuremberg Stadt QNG: no. 68/III, 1100 and 1097 (1560). Gold to be spun is first beaten and stretched out into very thin sheets; then these are put together into "books," or quires. As stated in the ordinances, all of these activities were often done by female gold spinners.
77. Ibid., 1100.
78. Ibid., 1307 (1597) and 1315 (1613).
79. Ibid., 1305 (1600).
80. Quoted in Hess, *Frauenberufe*, 11.
81. Steinhausen, *Privatbriefe*, 1:57, 82, 125.
82. Bücher, *Berufe*; Munich, Steuerbücher; Winter, "Studien," 20–25; Wensky, *Stellung der Frau*.
83. Schmoller, *Strassburger*, 32–37.
84. Jacques Hatt, *Une ville du XVe siècle: Strasbourg*, 53–55.
85. Wissell, *Handwerks*, 440; Bücher, *Frauenfrage*, 16; Wachendorf, *Stellung*, passim; G. Wunder, *Bürgerschaft der Reichsstadt Hall*; Erich Kober, *Die Anfänge des deutschen Wollgewerbes*, 85; Memmingen Zünfte, 475(2).
86. Memmingen Stadt Denkbuch.
87. B. Kreutzer, "Beiträge zur Geschichte des Wollengewerbes in Bayern," 446; Schmoller, *Strassburger*, 503, from a survey by A. Becher in Augsburg in 1673.
88. Bücher, *Berufe*, 97, 118, 138; Kober, *Anfänge*, 71; Memmingen Steuerbücher.
89. Schmoller, *Strassburger*, 446.
90. B. Schmidt and Bücher, *Frankfurter*, 506, 513.
91. Hess, *Frauenberufe*, 71.

92. Nübling, *Ulms Baumwollweberei*, 67.
93. Memmingen RPB: March 3, 1525; December 14, 1556.
94. This was often the first move any guild made in trying to restrict work by women. The linen guild in Florence also argued that female tailors should pay the same fees that male tailors did if they wanted to work, though they probably earned significantly less than most male tailors (Brown, "Women's Place," 6).
95. Schmoller, *Strassburger*, 402.
96. Ibid., 40–41.
97. Strasbourg Statuten, vol. 28, fol. 361.
98. Wachendorf, *Stellung*, 57.
99. Schmoller, *Strassburger*, 521, 523.
100. Wissell, *Handwerks*, 441; F. G. Mone, "Die Weberei und ihre Beigewerbe von 14.–16. Jhd.," 174.
101. Wissell, *Handwerks*, 452.
102. Hess, *Frauenberufe*, 70, quoting from Urkundenbuch der Stadt Heilbronn, III, 162.
103. Clasen, *Augsburger Weber*, 130.
104. Ibid., 132.
105. Ibid., 132–133.
106. Stuttgart Landwirtschaft, A58(2), Bü. 19.
107. Jacobsen finds similar restrictions in Danish cities, where women were hired as seamstresses, flax preparers, and laundresses but never as weavers or tailors ("Women's Work and Women's Role," 16).
108. Munich Gewerbeamt, no. 2730.
109. Nuremberg RB: 3, fol. 44b (1480); 3, fol. 136 (1481); 5, fol. 25b (1488); 21, fol. 79 (1542). Memmingen RPB, October 29, 1554.
110. Frankfurt Zünfte, Ugb. D-26; Munich Gewerbeamt, no. 2730.
111. He leaves it as a question, actually: "Dürften sie den Webstuhl selbst betreiben, obwohl sie doch das Weben selbst gar nicht gelernt hatten?" (Clasen, *Augsburger Weber*, 59).
112. Strasbourg XV: 1592, fol. 21a; 1593, fol. 134; 1597, fols. 39b, 47a; 1615, fols. 163, 172.
113. Ibid.: 1600, fols. 61, 81, 139, 169; 1601, fols. 68, 69; 1605, fols. 40, 49, 60, 70, 104, 112.
114. Memmingen RPB: October 20, 1589; September 28, 1610. Mummenhoff, "Findel," passim.
115. Alexander Dietz, *Frankfurter Handelsgeschichte*, 323.
116. Memmingen Zünfte, 471(1); Memmingen RPB, October 16, 1616.
117. Frankfurt BMB, 1460, fol. 28b; Memmingen RPB, February 7, 1529; Munich RSP, 1531; Munich Gewerbeamt, no. 1019; Schmelzeisen, *Rechtstellung*, 53; Hess, *Frauenberufe*, 70 (Mainz, Constance, Freiburg in Breisgau).
118. Nuremberg Stadt QNG, no. 68/II, 867.
119. Nuremberg AStB, no. 260, fol. 430.
120. Memmingen Zünfte, 471(5) (1641); Munich Gewerbeamt, no. 1019 (1469 Seidennäterordnung).

121. Quotation is from Memmingen RPB, August 30, 1577. Similar cases in Frankfurt BMB, 1489, fol. 76b; Memmingen RPB, September 1, 1520.
122. Nuremberg Stadt QNG, no. 68/I, 311; Munich RSP, 1559, fol. 133; Frankfurt BMB, 1590, fol. 201a; Strasbourg XV, 1655, fols. 33, 34.
123. Strasbourg XV, 1617, fol. 21.
124. Bücher, *Berufe*, 60; Frankfurt BMB, 1505, fol. 6b; Hess, *Frauenberufe*, 77; Nuremberg Stadt QNG, no. 68/III, 1302 (1597).
125. Nuremberg Stadt QNG: no. 68/III, 1302 (1597); 1303 (1603). Munich Gewerbeamt, no. 1020, 1603 Krämerordnung. Memmingen Zünfte, 451(3) (1613). Strasbourg XV: 1639, fols. 120, 154, 164, 171, 182; 1665, fol. 94.
126. Schmoller, *Strassburger*, 234, 304, 307–309; Memmingen Zünfte, 441(1). Joan Thirsk also finds rural knitters in England were more likely to escape aulnage (monopoly patent fees) because their work was on such a small scale as to escape the attention of the aulnage collectors (*Economic Policy and Projects: The Development of a Consumer Society in Early Modern England*, 63–65).
127. Memmingen Zünfte, 441(3).
128. Ibid.
129. Ibid.
130. Frankfurt BMB, 1495, fol. 5a.
131. Memmingen RPB, February 8, 1581.
132. Strasbourg XXI, 1616, fol. 186.
133. Schmoller, *Strassburger*, 161; Stuttgart Landwirtschaft, A58, Bü. 19; Hess, *Frauenberufe*, 60, relating cases in Heilbronn, Schweinitz, and Stuttgart.
134. E. Fromm, "Frankfurts Textilgewerbe im Mittelalter," 98, quoting Gesetze der Wollenweber von 1377.
135. Memmingen RPB: January 30, 1553; November 22, 1592. Stuttgart Landwirtschaft, A58, Bü. 19 (1598). Munich RSP, 1606, fol. 75. Frankfurt Zünfte, C-50, Ss, no. 4 (1615). Schmoller, *Strassburger*, 446. Hess, *Frauenberufe*, 61, relating cases in Lüneberg, Basel, and Markgrafschaft Baden.
136. Schmoller, *Strassburger*, 439; Nübling, *Ulms Baumwollweberei*, 171; Fromm, "Frankfurt," 69; Brodmeier, *Handwerk*, 54; H. Wunder, "Stellung der Frau," 242. Howell finds complaints about cloth producers using rural spinners and carders in contravention of regulations in Leiden as well ("Women's Work," 72).
137. Schmoller, *Strassburger*, 519.
138. Stuttgart Generalreskripta, A39, Bü. 4 (1601); Pfaff, *Geschichte der Stadt Stuttgart*, 299.
139. Brown, "Women's Place"; Abram, "Women Traders in Medieval London," 278; Dale, "Silkwomen"; Dixon, "Craftswomen," 218–220. Davis has discovered that silk winding, lacemaking, and cotton spinning were often taught to poor and orphan girls in Lyon in small centers set up by the city and run by older women. These centers thus served as a substitute for poor relief both for the girls and the women

in charge and gave the girls a trade, which the city fathers hoped would keep them from needing public support later in life as well ("Arts Mécaniques," 142).
140. Clark, *Working Life*, 9.
141. Donald Woodward, "Wage Rates and Living Standards in Pre-Industrial England," 39.
142. Lorenzen-Schmidt, "Stellung der Frauen," 339; Bücher, *Frauenfrage*, 24; Schmoller, *Strassburger*, 161.
143. Frankfurt Zünfte, Ugb. C-50, Ss, no. 4 (1615).

## Conclusions

1. Stone has commented, "The household was a most valuable institution for social control at the village level. It helped to keep in check potentially the most unruly elements, the floating mass of young unmarried males" (*Family*, 28). This study shows the household was also regarded as the perfect institution for controlling young, unmarried females as well.
2. Nuremberg RB, 26, fol. 103b (1551).
3. Munich RSP, 1599, fol. 164; Schmoller, *Strassburger*, 510.
4. Strasbourg XV, 1619, fol. 74; Thirsk finds that aulnage (monopoly patent fees) was collected from some stocking knitters and not from others, which she attributes to the location of the knitter; urban knitters were forced to pay aulnage, while rural knitters escaped it. From her examples, it appears that women were also less likely to be pressed for aulnage, though Thirsk herself does not make this conclusion. William Cecil did use the phrase "widows in outhouses and cottages" to refer to those rural knitters who escaped aulnage in the parliamentary debate on monopoly, thus downplaying their importance in his answer to the towns' objection to rural industry (*Economic Policy and Projects*, 63–65).
5. Brown finds this concern with morality to be even more important in limiting women's work in Renaissance Tuscany ("Women's Place").
6. Clasen, *Augsburger Weber*, 96.
7. H. C. Eric Midelfort, *Witchhunting in Southwestern Germany, 1562–1684*; Donald Kelley, *The Beginning of Ideology*; Ian MacLean, *The Renaissance Notion of Women*; Yost, "Changing Attitudes"; idem, "Value."
8. Margaret Strobel has recently noted similar conflict over women in contemporary Zambia. When young men go to work in the copper mines, they are no longer under the control of village elders, who then only have control over women. The young men and the mine owners want women to follow men to the mining communities so that stable communities will be established and the men will not be tempted to go to South Africa, where wages are higher. The village elders want women to stay in the villages, as does the government, which does not want to have to provide social services in the mining towns. The opinions of

the women concerned are not considered. Their location, like their work in sixteenth-century Germany, is a symbol in the fight over political power and control among male power groups ("Current Research in African Women's History").

9. This is something which bears further investigation. We have long assumed that it was natural for fathers to hand down occupations, and it would appear just as natural for a mother to hand down her skills, equipment, reputation, and customers to a daughter who seemed interested and competent. To my knowledge, this has never been explored fully, though Hufton does refer to it in her 1975 study of women in eighteenth-century France ("Family Economy"). Natalie Davis has suggested that women's identity and power revolved around their status in a neighborhood, rather than an occupation. She has discovered that certain women were often chosen as godmothers and were turned to for advice, which indicates that they were highly regarded ("God-Parentage: Conflict and Community in Sixteenth-century Lyon"). This, too, would be fascinating to investigate, though women's informal networks of influence are very difficult to trace in sources.
10. Rosemary Radford Ruether, *Sexism and God-Talk*, 63.
11. Carol Gilligan, *In a Different Voice: Psychological Theory and Women's Development*, 73.
12. Labé quoted in Julia O'Faolain and Lauro Martines, *Not in God's Image: Women in History from the Greeks to the Victorians*, 185; Christine de Pisan, *The Book of the City of Ladies*; Tilde Sankovitch, "Inventing Authority of Origin: The Difficult Enterprise."

# Bibliography

ARCHIVES

Augsburg, Stadtarchiv
    Baumeisterbücher (1570–1589)
    Bürgerbücher (1460–1630)
    Collegium Medicum
    Gedruckte Verordnungen (Anschlage und Dekreta)
    Hantwercksordnungen (1550–1589)
    Schätze: vol. 16 (Verordnungen) and nos. 31, 36, 37/I, 42, 71, 194a, 282
Frankfurt, Stadtarchiv
    Bürgermeisterbücher (1460–1610)
    Eidbücher: vols. I–III
    Gerichtssachen: Bürger wieder Fremde, Ugb. 51, 54, 57, 69, 72
    Medizinalia: Ugb. 8a (Hebammen)
    Verordnungen: vols. I–III
    Zünfte: Abt. II, 62 (Posamentierer); Abt. II, 52 (Metzger); Ugb. C-32
        (Wollenweber); Ugb. C-33 (Schneider); Ugb. C-36 (Sailer, Huter);
        Ugb. C-38 (Steinmetzen); Ugb. C-43 (Gläser); Ugb. C-44 (Bäcker);
        Ugb. C-46 (Fischer); Ugb. C-50 (Leinweber); Ugb. C-52 (Bader); Ugb.
        C-53 (Gärtner); Ugb. C-54 (Buchbinder); Ugb. C-59 (Spengler, Weiss-
        bender); Ugb. D-2 (Steindecker); Ugb. D-3 (Weissgerber, Pergamen-
        ter); Ugb. D-9 (Schlosser); Ugb. D-11 (Wollenweber); Ugb. D-24 (Bier-
        brauer); Ugb. D-25 (Pastetchenbäcker); Ugb. D-26 (Barchantweber)
Freiburg in Breisgau, Stadtarchiv
    Eidbücher: Rep. B 3(0), no. 4, fols. 26–27, "Der hebammen Eyd mit der
        Ordnung"
Memmingen, Stadtarchiv
    Bürgerbücher: nos. 269, 270
    Criminalia
    Deutsche Schulwesen: no. 397
    Einnahmen und Ausgaben (1462–1488)
    Hebammen: 48, 102, 343, 406
    Ratsprotokollbücher (1510–1625)
    Spital: nos. 85, 87

Der stadt Denkbuch
Steuerbücher (1450)
Taglohner Taxe, Zucht- und Polizeiordnungen: no. 265
Zünfte: 311 (Zoller); 405 (Barbierer); 422 (Nadler, Kammacher, Gläser);
    430 (Merzler, Huckster); 441 (Strumpfstricker); 451 (Hutmacher,
    Hutschmucker); 453 (Metzger); 462 (Goldschmeid); 471 (Schneider);
    475 (Weber)
Munich, Stadtarchiv
    Gewerbeamt: nos. 1019, 1020, 1411, 1418, 1569, 2020, 2288, 2293, 2307,
        2730, 2794, 2866, 4535a, 5083, 5170, 5172, 5090a
    Heilig-Geist-Spital: nos. 9, 10, 249, 275, 310
    Kammereirechnungen (1380–1750)
    Ratsitzungsprotokolle (1459–1611)
    Ratsmandata: vols. 60A1, 60B1, 60B2, 60B3
    Stadtgericht: 87, 701, 713, 865 (Urgichten), 867 (Injurien und Ru-
        morsachen, Schuld- und Verbotssachen), 917, 919, 925 (Bussamts-
        protokolle)
    Steuerbücher (1410–1640)
    Zimilien: no. 29 (Eidbuch 1688); no. 41 (Eidbuch 1488)
Nuremberg, Germanisches Nationalmuseum
    "Schuld und Rechnungsbuch Dr. Christoph Scheurl"
Nuremberg, Staatsarchiv
    Aemterbüchlein: Rep. 62, nos. 1–139
    Amts- und Standbücher: Rep. 52b: nos. 100–106 (Eidbücher der Nürn-
        berg Aemter); nos. 189–193 (Halsgerichtsordnungen); nos. 221–227
        (Malefizbücher); nos. 232–233 (Wandelbuch Ordnung und Gesetze);
        no. 234 (Verschiedene Ordnungen); no. 250 (Kindtaufbüchlein);
        nos. 259–260 (Handwerkerordnungen); nos. 299–300, 305–306
        (Neubürgerlisten); nos. 307–309 (Meisterbücher); no. 324 (Ordnun-
        gen von vielen Handwerkssorten); no. 341 (Stiftungsbuch); no. 342
        (Frau Anna Erasmus Schurstab Stiftung)
    Jäger, Adolph, "Materialensammlung über Nürnberger Lehrfrauen"
    Nürnberger Testamenten: Rep. 78 (old. no. 92), no. 1253
    Nürnberger Totengeläutebücher und Ratstotenbücher: Rep. 65
    Ratsbücher: Rep. 60b (1441–1619)
    Ratschlagbücher: Rep. 51, nos. 10, 26, 29, 34, 61
    Ratsmandata: Rep. 63: vol. A, nos. 90, 114 (Ehen und Winckelehen be-
        treffend); vol. B, nos. 40, 144 (Bettelordnungen)
    Verlässe des Inneren Rats: Rep. 60a (1449–1619)
Nuremberg, Stadtarchiv
    Archiv der Nürnberger Handwerker und Innungen: Rep. E5/1
    Heilig-Geist-Spital Inventarbücher: Rep. D15/1, nos. 1138–1145,
        4021–6771
    Heiratsnotelbücher: no. 1 (1543–1596)
    Inventarbücher: nos. 1–4, 16–17
    Quellen zur Nürnbergische Geschichte: Rep. F5: nos. 68/I, 68/II, 68/III
        (Aller Handwerck Ordnung und Gesetze); no. 163 (Auszüge aus den

Nürnberger Ratsbücher 1, 1a, 1b, 1c, 2–7 [1440–1504] des Bayerische
Staatsarchiv Nürnberg über Nürnberger Handwerker geordnet nach
Berufen, prepared by Dr. Rudolph Wenisch); no. 168
Stadtgericht der Reichsstadt Nürnberg Grundverbriefungsbücher (Li-
bri Litterarum): Rep. B7/I, II, nos. 8–132
*Der Statt Nürmberg Verneuerte Reformation* (1564)
Nuremberg, Stadtbibliothek
    Norica Sammlung: P I, S II, *Eines Hoch-Edlen und Hochweisen Raths des*
    *heiligen Reichs Stadt Nürnberg verneuerte Hebammen-Ordnung*
Strasbourg, Archives Municipales
    Akten der XV (1571–1674)
    Akten der XXI (1601–1642)
    Der erneuerte grosse Rathsbuch der Statt Strassburg: vols. 1, 2
    Spitalordnungen: Serie VI, 302, no. 13
    Statuten: vols. 1–33
Stuttgart, Stadtarchiv
    Cannstadt Collection: nos. 439–440 (Spitalrechnungen); nos. 1093–
    1094 (Stadt- und Amtbuch); nos. 1098–1100 (Gerichtsprotokolle);
    nos. 1474–1475 (Steuerbücher); nos. 1477–1483 (Güterbücher)
    Stadt Stuttgart Historisches Archiv Findbuch
Stuttgart, Württembergisches Hauptstaatsarchiv
    Generalreskripta: A39
    Landwirtschaft, Gewerbe, Handel: A58
    Malefizakten: A43
    Oberrat Malefizakten: A209
    Polizeiakten: A38
    Strafakten Altwürttembergische Aemter: A309

## Printed Sources

Abel, W. *Agrarkrisen und Agrarkonjunktur.* Hamburg: Parey, 1966.
Abram, A. "Women Traders in Medieval London." *Economic Journal* 26 (June 1916): 276–285.
Alexander, Sally, Anna Davin, and Eve Hostettler. "Labouring Women: A Reply to Eric Hobsbawn." *History Workshop* 8 (Autumn 1979): 174–182.
Aveling, J. H. *English Midwives: Their History and Prospects.* 1872. Reprint. London: Hugh K. Elliott, 1967.

Baader, Joseph, ed. *Nürnberger Polizeiordnungen aus dem 13. bis 15. Jahrhundert.* Bibliothek des Litterarische Verein Stuttgart, vol. 63. Stuttgart: Litterarische Verein, 1861.
Bainton, Roland. *Women of the Reformation: In Germany and Italy.* Minneapolis: Augsburg, 1971.
Barrett, M. *Women's Oppression Today: Problems in Marxist and Feminist Analysis.* London: Verso, 1980.
Barth, Heinrich. "Systematische und kritische Darstellung der allgemeinen

Gütergemeinschaft des Nürnberg Stadtrechts auf der Grundlage der verneuerte Nürnberg Reformation vom Jahre 1564." Ph.D. diss., Erlangen University, 1903.

Baruch, Friedrich. "Das Hebammenwesen in Reichsstädtische Nürnberg." Ph.D. diss., Erlangen University, 1955.

Bastian, Fr. "Das Manuale des Regenburger Kaufhauses Runtinger und die mittelalterliche Frauenfrage." *Jahrbuch für Nationalökonomie und Statistik* 115 (1920): 417–426.

Bauer, Max. *Deutscher Frauenspiegel: Bilder aus dem Frauenleben in der deutschen Vergangenheit*. Munich: Georg Müller, 1917.

————. *Liebesleben in deutschen Vergangenheit*. Berlin: P. Langenscheidt, 1924.

Beck, Dieter. "Die privatrechtliche Stellung der minderjährige nach altem Nürnberger Stadtrecht unter besondere Berücksichtigung der Rechtserheblichen Altersstufe und des Mündelschützes." J.D. diss., Erlangen University, 1950.

Beech, Beatrice. "Yolande Bonhomme: A Printer of Religious Books." Unpublished paper.

Beer, Barrett. *Rebellion and Riot: Popular Disorder in England during the Reign of Edward VI*. Kent, Ohio: Kent State University Press, 1982.

Behagel, W. *Die gewerbliche Stellung der Frau im mittelalterlichen Köln*. Abhandlungen zur mittleren und neueren Geschichte, no. 23. Berlin and Leipzig: Walter Rothschild, 1910.

Bellamy, John. *Crime and Public Order in England in the Later Middle Ages*. London: Routledge and Kegan Paul, 1973.

Bender, Johann. *Handbuch des Frankfurter Privatrechts*. Frankfurt: Joseph Baer, 1848.

Beuys, Barbara. *Familienleben in Deutschland*. Reinbeck bei Hamburg: Rowohlt, 1980.

Bloch, Iwan. *Die Prostitution*. Berlin: Louis Marcus, 1912.

Bloch, Ruth H. "Untangling the Roots of Modern Sex Roles: A Survey of Four Centuries of Change." *Signs* 4, no. 2 (1978): 237–252.

Bock, Friedrich. *Der Nürnberger Hauptmarkt*. Nuremberg: Korn and Berg, 1924.

Boesch, Hans. *Kinderleben in der deutschen Vergangenheit*. Monographien zur deutschen Kulturgeschichte, no. 5. Leipzig: Eugen Diedrichs, 1900.

Bosl, Karl, ed. *Handbuch der historischen Stätten Deutschlands*. Vol. 7, *Bayern*. Stuttgart: Kröner, 1965.

Bosl, Karl, and Eberhard Weis. *Die Gesellschaft in Deutschland*. Munich: Lurz, 1976.

Bothe, Friedrich. *Beiträge zur Wirtschafts- und Sozialgeschichte der Reichsstadt Frankfurt*. Altenburg: Stephan Geibel, 1906.

————. *Die Entwicklung der direkten Besteuerung in der Reichsstadt Frankfurt*. Leipzig: Duncker und Humbolt, 1906.

————. "Das Testament des Frankfurter Grosskaufmanns Jakob Heller vom Jahre 1519." *Archiv für Frankfurter Geschichte und Kultur* 28 (1907): 356–380.

————. *Frankfurter Patriziervermögen im 16. Jahrhundert.* Berlin: Alexander Duncker, 1908.

————. *Frankfurts wirtschaftliche-soziale Entwicklung vor dem Dreissigjährigen Kriege und der Fettmilchaufstand (1612–1616).* Frankfurt: Joseph Baer, 1920.

————. *Geschichte der Stadt Frankfurt.* Frankfurt: Georg Schlosser, 1929.

Branca, Patricia. "A New Perspective on Women's Work: A Comparative Typology." *Journal of Social History* 9, no. 2 (1975): 129–153.

Braudel, Fernand. *Civilization and Capitalism in the Fifteenth–Eighteenth Centuries.* New York: Harper and Row, 1979.

Bridenthal, Renata, and Claudia Koonz, eds. *Becoming Visible: Women in European History.* Boston: Houghton Mifflin, 1977.

Brodmeier, Beata. *Die Frau im Handwerk.* Forschungsberichte aus dem Handwerk, vol. 9. Münster: Handwerkswissenschaftlichen Institut, 1963.

Brown, Judith. "A Woman's Place Was in the Home: Women's Work in Renaissance Tuscany." In *Rewriting the Renaissance: The Discourses of Sexual Difference in Early Modern Europe*, edited by Maureen Quilligan and Nancy Vickers. Chicago: University of Chicago Press, forthcoming.

Brown, Judith, and Jordan Goodman. "Women and Industry in Florence." *Journal of Economic History* 40 (1980): 73–80.

Brucker, J., ed. *Strassburger Zunft und Polizeiordnungen.* Strasbourg: Karl J. Trübner, 1889.

Bruford, W. H. *Germany in the Eighteenth Century: The Social Background of the Literary Revival.* Cambridge: Cambridge University Press, 1935.

Bücher, Karl. *Die Bevölkerung von Frankfurt am Main in 14. und 15. Jahrhundert.* Tübingen: H. Laupp, 1886.

————. *Die Frauenfrage im Mittelalter.* Tübingen: H. Laupp, 1910.

————. *Die Berufe der Stadt Frankfurt im Mittelalter.* Leipzig: Teubner, 1914.

Burke, Peter. *Popular Culture in Early Modern Europe.* New York: Harper and Row, 1978.

Busse, Ingrid. *Der Siechkobel St. Johannis vor Nürnberg (1234 bis 1807).* Schriftenreihe des Stadtarchivs Nürnberg, no. 12. Nuremberg: Stadtarchiv, 1974.

Chaytor, Miranda. "Household and Kinship: Ryton in the late 16th and early 17th Centuries." *History Workshop* 10 (Autumn 1980): 25–60.

Chrisman, Miriam U. *Strasbourg and the Reform: A Study in the Process of Change.* New Haven, Conn.: Yale University Press, 1967.

————. "Women of the Reformation in Strasbourg." *Archiv für Reformationsgeschichte* 63 (1972): 143–168.

————. *Lay Culture, Learned Culture: Books and Social Change in Strasbourg, 1480–1599.* New Haven, Conn.: Yale University Press, 1982.

*Die Chroniken der fränkischen Städte: Nürnberg.* Vols. 1–5. Leipzig: S. Hirzel, 1862–1874.

Clark, Alice. *Working Life of Women in the Seventeenth Century.* London: Routledge and Kegan Paul, 1919.

Clasen, Claus-Peter. *Anabaptism: A Social History, 1525–1618*. Ithaca, N.Y.: Cornell University Press, 1972.

———. *Die Augsburger Steuerbücher um 1600*. Augsburg: Mühlberger, 1976.

———. *Die Augsburger Weber: Leistungen und Krisen des Textilgewerbes um 1600*. Abhandlungen zur Geschichte der Stadt Augsburg, no. 27. Augsburg: Mühlberger, 1981.

Coulson, Margaret, Branka Magaš, and Hilary Wainwright. "The Housewife and Her Labour under Capitalism: A Critique." *New Left Review* 89 (1975): 59–71.

Crämer, Ulrich. *Die Verfassung und Verwaltung Strassburgs von der Reformationszeit bis zum Fall der Reichsstadt (1521–1681)*. Frankfurt: Elsass-Lothringen Instituts, 1931.

Cutter, Irvin S., and Henry R. Viets. *A Short History of Midwifery*. Philadelphia: Saunders, 1964.

Czok, Karl. "Die Bürgerkämpfe in Süd- und Westdeutschland im 14. Jahrhundert." *Esslinger Studien* 12/13 (1966/1967): 40–72.

Dale, Marian K. "The London Silkwomen of the Fifteenth Century." *Economic History Review* 4 (October 1933): 324–335.

Danckert, Werner. *Unehrliche Leute: Die verfemten Berufe*. Bern and Munich: Francke, 1963.

Davis, Natalie Zemon. *Society and Culture in Early Modern France*. Stanford, Calif.: Stanford University Press, 1965.

———. "Women in the Arts Mécaniques in Sixteenth-Century Lyon." In *Lyon et l'Europe: Hommes et sociétés. Mélanges d'histoire offerts à Richard Gascon*, 139–167. Lyon: Presses Universitaires de Lyon, 1980.

———. "God-Parentage: Conflict and Community in Sixteenth-Century Lyon." Unpublished paper.

Diepgen, Paul. *Frau und Frauenheilkunde in der Kultur des Mittelalters*. Stuttgart: Thieme, 1963.

Dieselhorst, Jurgen. "Die Bestrafung der Selbstmörder im Territorium des Reichsstadt Nürnberg." *Mitteilungen des Verein für Geschichte der Stadt Nürnberg* 44 (1953): 58–230.

Dietz, Alexander. *Frankfurter Handelsgeschichte*. 1921. Reprint. Frankfurt: Detlav Auvermann, 1970.

Dixon, E. "Craftswomen in the Livre des Métiers." *Economic Journal* 5 (June 1895): 209–228.

Douglass, Jane Dempsey. "Women and the Continental Reformation." In *Religion and Sexism*, edited by Rosemary Rudford Ruether, 292–318. New York: Simon and Schuster, 1974.

Dübeck, Inger. *Købekoner og Konkurrence*. Studier over Myndigheds Erhvervsrettens Udvikling med Stadigt Henblik pa Kvindens historiske Retsstillung. Copenhagen: Juristforbundets, 1978.

Ebel, Wilhelm. *Forschungen zur Geschichte des lübischen Rechts*. Veröffentlichungen zur Geschichte der Hansestadt Lübeck, no. 14. Lübeck: Max Schmidt, 1950.

Ebert, Marianne. "Geschichte des Nürnberger Lebkuchens vom Handwerk zur Industrie." *Mitteilungen des Verein für Geschichte der Stadt Nürnberg* 52 (1963/1964): 205–220.

Eccles, Audrey. *Obstetrics and Gynecology in Tudor and Stuart England*. Kent, Ohio: Kent State University Press, 1982.

Eckhert, Heinrich. *Krämer und Krämerzunft in süddeutschen Städten*. Berlin: Walter Rothschild, 1909.

————. *Die Krämer in süddeutschen Städten bis zum Ausgang des Mittelalters*. Abhandlungen zur mittleren und neueren Geschichte, no. 16. Berlin and Leipzig: Walter Rothschild, 1910.

Eisen, Ludwig. *Christliche Liebestätigkeit im alten Nürnberg*. Nuremberg: Buchhandlung des Vereins für Innere Mission, 1937.

Elliott, Vivien Brodsky. "Single Women in the London Marriage Market: Age, Status and Mobility, 1598–1619." In *Studies in the Social History of Marriage*, edited by R. B. Outhwaite, 81–100. New York: St. Martin's, 1981.

Endres, Rudolph. "Zur Einwohnerzahl und Bevölkerungsstruktur Nürnbergs im 15./16. Jahrhunderts." *Mitteilungen des Verein für Geschichte der Stadt Nürnberg* 57 (1970): 242–271.

Ennen, Edith. "Die Frau in der Mittelalterlichen Stadtgesellschaft Mitteleuropas." *Hänsische Geschichtsblätter* 98 (1980): 2–22.

————. "Die Frau im Mittelalter." *Kurtrierisches Jahrbuch* 21 (1981): 70–93.

Fleiss, Ulrich. "Das Hauswesen der Nürnberger Handwerker um 1500." Ph.D. diss., Göttingen University, 1957.

Forbes, Thomas. *The Midwife and the Witch*. New Haven, Conn.: Yale University Press, 1966.

Ford, Franklin L. *Strasbourg in Transition, 1648–1789*. Cambridge, Mass.: Harvard University Press, 1958.

*Frankfurt um 1600: Alltagsleben in der Stadt*. Kleine Schriften des Historischen Museums, no. 7. Frankfurt: Historische Museum, 1976.

Franz, Günther, ed. *Beamtentum und Pfarrerstand 1400–1800*. Vol. 5 of *Deutsche Führungsschichten in der Neuzeit*. Limburg and Lahn: C. A. Starke, 1972.

Freyberg, Maximilian Freiherr von, ed. *Sammlung historischen Schriften und Urkunden*. Stuttgart and Tübingen: J. G. Gotta, 1834.

Fromm, E. "Frankfurts Textilgewerbe im Mittelalter." *Archiv für Frankfurter Geschichte und Kultur*, ser. 3, 1899, no. 6:1–162.

Gardiner, Jean. "Women's Domestic Labour." *New Left Review* 89 (1975): 47–58.

Geiler, Johannes, von Kaisersberg. *Die aeltesten Schriften*. Freiburg in Breisgau: Herder'sche, 1877.

*Gesetze und Statutensammlung der freien Stadt Frankfurt*. Frankfurt: Weimer, 1817.

Gilligan, Carol. *In a Different Voice: Psychological Theory and Women's Development*. Cambridge, Mass.: Harvard University Press, 1982.

Glass, D. V., and Eversley, D. E. C. *Population in History: Essays in Historical Demography*. London: Edward Arnold, 1965.

Godelier, Maurice. "Work and Its Representations." *History Workshop* 10 (Autumn 1980): 164–174.

Goldman, Karlheinz. "Wie Nürnberger Handwerker Feste feierten." *Mitteilungen aus der Stadtbibliothek Nürnberg* 13, no. 1 (February 1964): 1–18.

Göttman, Frank. *Handwerk und Bundnispolitik: Die Handwerkerbände am Mittelrhein vom 14. bis zum 17. Jahrhundert*. Frankfurter Historische Abhandlungen, no. 15. Wiesbaden: Steiner, 1977.

Grönert, Walter. "Die Entwicklung des Gaststättenrechts in der freien Reichsstadt Nürnberg seit dem 14. Jahrhundert." Ph.D. diss., Erlangen University, 1967.

Grotefende, Hermann. "Hexen in Frankfurt." *Mitteilungen an die Mitglieder des Vereins für Geschichte und Altertumskunde in Frankfurt* 6 (1880/1881): 70–78.

Gutmann, Myron P. *War and Rural Life in the Early Modern Low Countries*. Princeton, N.J.: Princeton University Press, 1980.

Hacker, Barton C. "Women and Military Institutions in Early Modern Europe: A Reconnaissance." *Signs* 6, no. 4 (1981): 643–671.

Hampe, Theodor. *Fahrende Leute in der deutschen Vergangenheit*. Monographien zur deutschen Kulturgeschichte, no. 10. Leipzig: Eugen Diedrichs, 1902.

———. *Die Nürnberger Malefizbücher als Quellen der reichsstädtischen Sittengeschichte von 14. bis zum 18. Jahrhundert*. Neujahrsblätter der Gesellschaft für fränkische Geschichte, no. 18. Nuremberg: Gesellschaft für fränkische Geschichte, 1927.

Hanawalt, Barbara. "The Female Felon in 14th Century England." In *Women in Medieval Society*, edited by Susan Mosher Stuard, 125–140. Philadelphia: University of Pennsylvania Press, 1976.

Harksen, Sibylle. *Die Frau im Mittelalter*. Leipzig: Edition Leipzig, 1974.

Harris, Olivia. "Households as Natural Units." In *Of Marriage and the Market*, edited by R. Young and R. McCullagh, 136–155. London: C. S. E., 1981.

Hatt, Jacques. *Une ville du XVe siècle: Strasbourg*. Strasbourg: Collection historique de la vie en Alsace, 1929.

Heerwagen, Heinrich. "Aus einem Nürnberger Bürgerhaus zu Ausgang des 15. Jahrhunderts." *Mitteilungen aus dem Germanischen Nationalmuseum* 1902:31–36.

———. "Bilder aus der Kinderleben in den dreissiger Jahren des 16. Jahrhunderts." *Mitteilungen aus dem Germanischen Nationalmuseum* 1906:93–116.

———. "Beiträge zur Geschichte der Kunst und Kunsthandwerks in Nürnberg 1532–1542." *Mitteilungen aus dem Germanischen Nationalmuseum* 1908:106–126.

Henriques, Fernando. *Prostitution and Society*. Vol. 2, *Prostitution in Europe and the New World*. London: MacGibbon and Kee, 1963.

Herzog, Anton. *Die Lebensmittelpolitik der Stadt Strassburg im Mittelalter*. Abhandlungen zur mittleren und neueren Geschichte, no. 12. Berlin and Leipzig: Walter Rothschild, 1909.

Hess, Luise. *Die deutschen Frauenberufe des Mittelalters*. Beiträge zur Volkstumforschung, no. 6. Munich: Neuer Filser, 1940.

Hill, Christopher. "Puritans and the Poor." *Past and Present* 2 (November 1952): 32–50.

Hilton, Rodney. "Women Traders in Medieval England." *Women's Studies* 11 (1984): 139–155.

Hirschmann, G. "Frauen in Nürnbergs Geschichte." In *60. Jahre Deutsche Frauenkultur e.V. Nürnberg 1916–1976*, 18–26. Nuremberg: Krische, 1977.

*Eines Hochedlen und Hochweisen Raths des heiligen Reichs Stadt Nürnberg verneuerte Hebammen-Ordnung*. Nuremberg: Joseph Fleischmann, 1755.

Hollinsworth, T. H. *Historical Demography*. London: Sources of History, 1969.

Howell, Martha Congleton. "Women's Work in Urban Economies of Late Medieval Northwestern Europe: Female Labor Status in Male Economic Institutions." Ph.D. diss., Columbia University, 1979.

———. "Women, the Family Economy and the Structures of Market Production in Cities of Northern Europe during the Late Middle Ages." Unpublished paper.

Hufton, Olwen H. "Women and the Family Economy in Eighteenth-Century France." *French Historical Studies* 9 (1975): 1–23.

———. "Women, Work and Marriage in Eighteenth-Century France." In *Studies in the Social History of Marriage*, edited by R. B. Outhwaite, 186–203. New York: St. Martin's, 1981.

Illich, Ivan. *Gender*. New York: Pantheon, 1982.

Jacobsen, Grethe. "Women's Work and Women's Role: Ideology and Reality in Danish Urban Society, 1300–1550." *Scandinavian Economic History Review* 31, no. 1 (1983): 2–20.

———. "City Women in Danish Economy and Society 1400–1550: A New Look at the Late Middle Ages." Unpublished paper.

Jegel, August. "Heilkräutergebrauch im alten Nürnberg." *Suddeutsche Apotheker Zeitung* 21 (1933): 141–142.

———. "Nürnberger Gesundheitsfürsorge, vor allem während des 16. und 17. Jahrhunderts." Off-print from *Sudhoffs Archiv für Gechichte der Medizin* 26, no. 1 (1933): 25–48.

———. *Ernährungsfürsorge des Altnürnberger Rats*. Nuremberg: Sonderdruck des Nürnberger Stadtarchivs, 1937.

———. "Altnürnberger Hochzeitsbrauch und Eherecht." *Mitteilungen des Verein für Geschichte der Stadt Nürnberg* 44 (1953): 238–274.

———. *Bäder, Bader und Badesitten in alten Nürnberg*. Freie Schriftenfolge des Gesellschaft für Familienforschung in Franken, no. 6. Nuremberg: Gesellschaft für Familienforschung in Franken, 1954.

———. *Altnürnberger Handwerksrecht und seine Beziehung zu anderen*. Neustadt a.d. Aisch: C. W. Schmidt, 1965.

Kallmorgan, W. *Siebenhundert Jahre Heilkunde in Frankfurt a.M.* Frankfurt: Diesterweg, 1936.

Kampffmeyer, Paul. *Vom Zunftgesellen zum freien Arbeiter.* Berlin: Dietz, 1924.

Karant-Nunn, Susan. "Continuity and Change: Some Effects of the Reformation on the Women of Zwickau." *Sixteenth Century Journal* 13, no. 2 (1982): 17–42.

Kellenbenz, Hermann. *The Rise of the European Economy.* London: Weidenfeld and Nicolson, 1976.

Keller, Albrecht, ed. *Meister Franntz Schmidts Scharfrichters inn Nürnberg all sein Richten.* Leipzig: Wilhelm Helms, 1913.

Kelley, Donald. *The Beginning of Ideology.* Cambridge: Cambridge University Press, 1981.

Kelly, Joan [Joan Kelly Gadol]. "Did Women Have a Renaissance?" In *Becoming Visible: Women in European History,* edited by Renata Bridenthal and Claudia Koonz, 137–164. Boston: Houghton Mifflin, 1977.

———. "Early Feminist Theory and the Querelle des Femmes, 1400–1789." *Signs* 8, no. 1 (1982): 4–28.

Kennedy, Susan Estabrook, *If All We Did Was to Weep at Home: A History of White Working Class Women in America.* Bloomington: Indiana University Press, 1979.

Kessler-Harris, Alice. *Out to Work: A History of Wage-Earning Women in the United States.* New York: Oxford University Press, 1982.

Keyser, Erich. *Bevölkerungsgeschichte Deutschlands.* Leipzig: Hirzel, 1941.

———. *Württembergisches Städtebuch.* Deutsche Stadtbücher: Handbücher Städtischer Geschichte, no. 4. Stuttgart: Kohlhammer, 1962.

King, Margaret. "Thwarted Ambitions: Six Learned Women of the Italian Renaissance." *Soundings* 59, no. 3 (1976): 280–304.

———. "Book Lined Cells: Women and Humanism in the Early Italian Renaissance." In *Beyond Their Sex: Learned Women of the European Past,* edited by Patricia H. Labalme, 66–90. New York: New York University Press, 1980.

Kipfmüller, Bertha. "Die Frau im Recht der freien Reichsstadt Nürnberg: Eine rechtsgeschichtliche Darlegung auf grund der verneuerte Reformation des Jahre 1564." J.D. diss., Erlangen University, 1929.

Kiske, Bruno. "Die Frau im mittelalterlichen deutschen Wirtschaftsleben." *Zeitschrift für handelswissenschaftliche Forschung* 11, no. 3 (1959): 148–157.

Knapp, Hermann. *Das Lochgefängnis, Tortur, und Richtung im alten Nürnberg.* Nuremberg: Heerdegen-Barbeck, 1907.

Kober, Erich. *Die Anfänge des deutschen Wollgewerbes.* Abhandlungen zur mittleren und neueren Geschichte, no. 8. Berlin and Leipzig: Walter Rothschild, 1905.

Köhler, Ingeborg. "Bestimmungen des Rates der Reichsstadt Nürnberg über die Kleidung seiner Bürgerinnen." Munich, 1953.

Kopitzsch, Franklin. *Aufklärung, Absolutismus und Bürgertum in Deutschland.* Munich: Nymphenburger, 1976.

Kowaleski, Maryanne. "Women's Paid Work in a Market Town: Exeter in the Late Fourteenth Century." In *Women and Work in Pre-Industrial Europe*, edited by B. Hanawalt. Bloomington: Indiana University Press, forthcoming.

————. "Women and Work in Medieval English Seaports." Unpublished paper.

Krause, J. "The Medieval Household: Large or Small?" *Economic History Review*, 2d ser., 9, no. 3 (1957): 420–432.

Krebs, Peter-Per. "Die Stellung der Handwerkswitwe in den Zünfte von Spätmittelalter bis zum 18. Jahrhundert." J.D. diss., Regensburg University, 1974.

Kreutzer, B. "Beiträge zur Geschichte des Wollengewerbes in Bayern." *Archiv für vaterländische Geschichte* 20 (1897): 427–450.

Kriedte, Peter. *Peasants, Landlords and Merchant Capitalists: Europe and the World Economy, 1500–1800*. Cambridge: Cambridge University Press, 1983.

Kriegk, Georg. *Aerzte, Heilanstalten und Geisteskranke im mittelalterlichen Frankfurt a.M.* Frankfurt: August Österrieth, 1863.

————. *Deutsches Bürgerthum im Mittelalter.* 2 vols. Frankfurt: Rutten und Loning, 1871.

Kroemer, Barbara. "Die Einführung der Reformation in Memmingen." *Memmingen Geschichtsblätter*, 1980: 11–23.

Kuhn, Annette, and Ann Marie Wolpe, eds. *Feminism and Materialism: Women and Modes of Production.* London: Routledge and Kegan Paul, 1978.

Kunstmann, Hartmut. *Zauberwahn und Hexenprozess in der Reichsstadt Nürnberg.* Schriftenreihe des Stadtarchivs Nürnberg, no. 1. Nuremberg: Stadtarchiv, 1970.

Kussmaul, Ann. *Servants in Husbandry in Early Modern England.* Cambridge: Cambridge University Press, 1981.

Kuster, Fritz. "Nürnberg in der Geschichte der Arbeitverwaltung." *Arbeit und Beruf* 9 (1977): 258–260.

Leffte, Jean-Pierre. "Aperçu historique sur l'obstétrique de Strasbourg avant la grande révolution." M.D. diss., Strasbourg University, 1952.

Leipner, Kurt, ed. *Altwürttembergische Lagerbücher aus der österreichischen Zeit, 1520–1534.* Veröffentlichungen der Kommission für Geschichte der Land Baden-Württemberg, ser. A, vol. 8. Stuttgart: Kohlhammer, 1972.

Lenhardt, Heinz. "Feste und Feiern des Frankfurter Handwerks." *Archiv für Frankfurter Geschichte und Kultur*, ser. 5, 1910, nos. 1–2: 1–120.

Lenk, Leonard. *Augsburger Bürgertum im Späthumanismus und Frühbarock, 1580–1700.* Augsburg: Mühlberger, 1968.

Lerner, Gerda. *The Majority Finds Its Past.* New York: Oxford University Press, 1979.

Lewenhak, Sheila. *Women and Work.* New York: St. Martin's, 1980.

Lindemann, Mary. "Love for Hire: The Regulation of the Wet-Nursing Business in 18th-Century Hamburg." *Journal of Family History* (Winter 1981): 379–392.

Lochner, G. W. K. *Die Einwohnerzahl der ehemaligen Reichsstadt Nürnberg.* Nuremberg: F. V. Campe, 1857.

Lorenzen-Schmidt, Klaus-Joachim. "Zur Stellung der Frauen in der frühneuzeitlichen Städtegesellschaft Schleswigs und Holsteins." *Archiv für Kulturgeschichte* 61 (1979): 317–339.
Lotter, J. M. *Sagen, Legenden und Geschichten der Stadt Nürnberg*. Nuremberg: Raw, 1899.

MacLean, Ian. *The Renaissance Notion of Woman*. Cambridge: Cambridge University Press, 1980.
Malos, E., ed. *The Politics of Housework*. London: Allison and Busby, 1980.
Martin, Alfred. *Deutsches Badewesen in vergangenen Tagen*. Jena: Eugen Diedrichs, 1906.
Maschke, Erich. *Die Familie in der deutschen Stadt des späten Mittelalters*. Heidelberg: Winter, 1980.
———. *Gesellschaftliche Unterschichten in den südwestdeutschen Städten*. Protokolle über die V. Arbeitstagung des Arbeitskreis für südwestdeutsche Stadtgeschichtsforchung. Stuttgart: Kohlhammer, 1967.
———. "Verfassung und soziale Kräfte in der deutschen Stadt des späten Mittelalters." *Vierteljahrsschrift für Sozial- und Wirtschaftsgeschichte* 46 (1959): 289–469.
Maschke, Erich, and Jürgen Sydow, eds. *Städtische Mittelschichten*. Protokoll der 8. Arbeitstagung des Arbeitskreis für südwestdeutsche Stadtgeschichtsforschung. Stuttgart: Kohlhammer, 1972.
Mauersberg, Hans. *Wirtschafts- und Sozialgeschichte zentraleuropäischer Städte in neuerer Zeit*. Göttingen: Vandenhoeck und Ruprecht, 1960.
Mayr, L. "Memminger Bader and Bäder." *Memmingen Geschichtsblätter* 5, no. 6 (1920).
McBride, Theresa. "The Modernization of 'Women's Work.'" *Journal of Modern History* 49 (June 1977): 231–245.
McClelland, Charles. *State, Society, and University in Germany, 1700–1914*. Cambridge: Cambridge University Press, 1983.
Medick, Hans. "The Proto-Industrial Family Economy: The Structural Function of Household and Family during the Transition from Peasant Society to Industrial Capitalism." *Social History* 1 (1976): 291–315.
Middleton, C. "Sexual Division of Labour in Feudal England." *New Left Review* 113–114 (1979): 147–168.
Midelfort, H. C. Eric. *Witchhunting in Southwestern Germany, 1562–1684*. Stanford, Calif.: Stanford University Press, 1972.
Miller, Max, ed. *Handbuch der historischen Stätten Deutschlands*. Vol. 6, *Baden Württemburg*. Stuttgart: Kröner, 1965.
Mistele, Karl-Heinz. *Die Bevölkerung der Reichsstadt Heilbronn im Spätmittelalter*. Heilbronn: Veröffentlichungen des Archivs der Stadt Heilbronn, 1962.
Mitterauer, Michael. "Geschlechtsspezifische Arbeitsteilung in vorindustrieller Zeit." *Beiträge zur historische Sozialkunde* 11, no. 3 (1981): 77–87.
Mone, F. G. "Die Weberei und ihre Beigewerbe von 14–16. Jhd." *Zeitschrift für Geschichte des Oberrheins* 9 (1858): 129–189.
Monter, E. William. "Women in Calvinist Geneva." *Signs* 6, no. 2 (1980): 189–209.

Müller, Johan. "Aus dem deutschen Familienleben des 16. Jahrhunderts: Von alter Kochweise." *Westermanns Jahrbuch des Illustrierte Deutsche Monatshefte* 5 (1859): 16–23.

Müllerheim, Robert. *Die Wochenstube in der Kunst: Einen Kulturhistoriche Studie.* Stuttgart: Ferdinand Emke, 1904.

Mummenhoff, Ernst. "Geschichtliches zur Heilkunde in Nürnberg." In *Nürnberg: Festschrift der Gesellschaft Deutscher Naturfolger und Aerzte*, 84–86. Nuremberg: J. H. Schrag, 1892.

———. *Die öffentliche Gesundheits- und Krankenpflege im alten Nürnberg: Festschrift zur Eröffnung des neuen Krankenhauses der Stadt Nürnberg.* Nuremberg: Korn, 1898.

———. "Das Findel und Waisenhaus zu Nürnberg." *Mitteilungen des Verein für Geschichte der Stadt Nürnberg* 21 (1915): 57–335.

———. "Frauenarbeit und Arbeitsvermittlung: Eine Episode aus der Handwerksgeschichte des 16. Jahrhunderts." *Vierteljahrsschrift für Sozial und Wirtschaftsgeschichte* 199 (1926): 157–165.

Nübling, Eugene. *Ulms Baumwollweberei im Mittelalter.* Staats- und sozialwissenschaftliche Forschung, vol. 9, no. 5. Leipzig: Duncker und Humblot, 1890.

Oellrich, Ludwig. "Der Strafprozess in Nürnberg während der letzten drei Jahrhunderte der selbstständigkeit der freien Reichsstadt." J.D. diss., Erlangen University, 1948.

O'Faolain, Julia, and Lauro Martines, eds. *Not in God's Image: Women in History from the Greeks to the Victorians.* New York: Harper and Row, 1973.

Ott, Caspar. *Bevölkerungsstatistik in der Stadt und Landschaft Nürnberg in der ersten Hälfte des 15. Jahrhundert.* Berlin: R. Trenckel, 1907.

Ozment, Steven. *When Fathers Ruled: Family Life in Reformation Europe.* Cambridge, Mass.: Harvard University Press, 1983.

Petrelli, Richard L. "The Regulation of French Midwifery during the Ancien Regime." *Journal of the History of Medicine* (July 1971): 276–292.

Pfaff, Karl. *Geschichte der Stadt Stuttgart.* Stuttgart: Sonnewald, 1845.

Pfeiffer, Franz. "Alte deutsche Kochbücher." *Serapeum* 9 (1948): 273–285.

Pfeiffer, Gerhard, ed. *Nürnberg: Geschichte einer europäischen Stadt.* Munich: C. H. Beck, 1971.

Pinchbeck, Ivy. *Women Workers and the Industrial Revolution.* 1930. Reprint. London: Virago, 1981.

Pisan, Christine de. *The Book of the City of Ladies.* Translated by Earl Jeffrey Richards. New York: Persea, 1982.

Pitz, Ernst. *Wirtschafts- und Sozialgeschichte Deutschlands im Mittelalter.* Wiesbaden: Steiner, 1979.

Planitz, H. *Die deutsche Stadt im Mittelalter.* Graz and Cologne: Böhlau, 1954.

Pollock, Linda. *Forgotten Children: Parent–Child Relations from 1500 to 1900.* Cambridge: Cambridge University Press, 1984.

Power, Eileen. *Medieval Women*. Edited by M. M. Postan. Cambridge: Cambridge University Press, 1965.

Püchner, Otto. "Das Register des Gemeinen Pfennigs (1497) der Reichsstadt Nürnberg als bevölkerungsgeschichtliche Quelle." *Jahrbuch für fränkische Landesforschung* 34–35 (1974/1975): 909–948.

Purucker, Albrecht. "Das Testamentrecht der Nürnberger Reformation." J.D. diss., Erlangen University, 1948.

Rathgeber, Julius. *Strassburg im 16. Jahrhundert*. Stuttgart: Steinkopf, 1871.

"Das Rechnungsbuch der Nürnberger Grosskaufmanns Hans Praun von 1471 bis 1478." *Mitteilungen des Verein für Geschichte der Stadt Nürnberg* 55 (1968): 90–105.

Reicke, Emil. "Ein Blick in das Alltagsleben der Pirckheimerzeit." *Fränkische Heimat* 19 (1940): 84–87, 20 (1941): 10–12.

Reininghaus, Wilfried. "Zur Entstehung der Gesellengilden im Spätmittelalter." Ph.D. diss., Münster University, 1980.

Reiser, Otto. "Beweis und Beweisverfahren im Zivilprozess der freien Reichsstadt Nürnberg." J.D. diss., Erlangen University, 1955.

Renard, Georges. *Guilds in the Middle Ages*. New York: Kelley, 1968.

Reynolds, Robert. *Europe Emerges: Transition toward an Industrial World 600–1750*. Madison: University of Wisconsin Press, 1961.

Richards, E. "Women in the British Economy since about 1700: An Interpretation." *History* 59 (1974): 337–357.

Roberts, Michael. "Sickles and Scythes: Women's Work and Men's Work at Harvest Time." *History Workshop* 7 (Spring 1979): 3–29.

Roetzer, Karl. "Die Delikte des Abtreibung, Kindstötung sowie Kindsaussetzungen in der Reichsstadt Nürnberg." J.D. diss., Erlangen University, 1957.

Roper, Lyndal. "Urban Women and the Household Workshop Form of Production: Augsburg, 1500–1550." Unpublished paper.

Rösslin, Eucharius. *Die swangere Frawen und hebammen Roszgarten*. Hagenau, 1513. Facsimile reprint in the series Alte Meister der Medizin und Naturkunde, no. 2. Munich, 1910. With notes by Gustav Klein.

Roth, Johann F. *Fragmente zur Geschichte der Bader, Barbierer, Hebammen, Ehrbare Frauen und Geschworene Weiber in Nürnberg*. Nuremberg: Six, 1792.

———. *Lebensbeschreibungen und Nachrichten von merkwürdigen Nürnbergern und Nürnbergerinnen*. Nuremberg: Six, 1796.

———. *Geschichte des nürnbergischen Handels*. Vol. 4. Leipzig: Herzil, 1803.

Ruether, Rosemary Radford. *Sexism and God-Talk*. Boston: Beacon, 1983.

Rüger, Willi. *Die Almosenordnungen der Reichsstadt Nürnberg*. Nürnberger Beiträge zu den Wirtschafts- und Sozialwissenschaften, no. 31. Nuremberg: Krische, 1932.

Russell, Josiah Cox. *British Medieval Population*. Albuquerque: University of New Mexico Press, 1948.

Sachs, Carl L. "Nürnbergs Reichsstädtische Arbeiterschaft während der Amtszeit des Baumeisters Michel Behaim (1503–1511)." *Mitteilungen aus dem Germanischen Nationalmuseum* 1914/1915: 141–209.

Safley, Thomas Max. *Let No Man Put Asunder: The Control of Marriage in the German Southwest, 1550–1600*. Kirksville, Mo.: Sixteenth Century Journal, 1984.

Sankovitch, Tilde. "Inventing Authority of Origin: The Difficult Enterprise." In *Women in the Middle Ages and the Renaissance: Literary and Historical Perspectives*. Edited by Mary Beth Rose, pp. 227–243. Syracuse: Syracuse University Press, 1985.

Schallhammer, Herbert. "Das Schulwesen der Reichsstadt Memmingen von den Anfängen bis 1806." *Memmingen Geschichtsblätter*, 1962:15–26.

Schanz, Georg von. *Zur Geschichte der deutschen Gesellenverbände*. Leipzig: Duncker und Humblot, 1877.

Scherr, J. *Geschichte der deutschen Frauenwelt*. Leipzig: Otto Wiegand, 1865.

Schichthörle, Anton. *Die Gewerbsbefügnisse in der Königliche Haupt- und Residenzstadt München*. Erlangen: J. J. Palm, 1844.

Schmelzeisen, G. K. *Die Rechtstellung der Frau in der deutschen Stadtwirtschaft*. Arbeiten zur deutschen Rechts- und Verfassungsgeschichte, no. 10. Stuttgart: Kohlhammer, 1935.

Schmid, Reinhold, ed. *Kaiser Karl des fünften peinliche Gerichtsordnung (Carolina Constitutio Criminalis)*. Jena: A. Schmid, 1835.

Schmidt, Benno, and Karl Bücher. *Frankfurter Amts- und Zunfturkunden bis zum Jahre 1612*. Veröffentlichungen der historische Kommission der Stadt Frankfurt a.M., vol. 6. Frankfurt: Joseph Baer, 1914.

Schmidt, Gertrud. "Die berufstätige Frau in der Reichsstadt Nürnberg bis zum Ende des 16. Jahrhunderts." Ph.D. diss., Erlangen University, 1950.

Schmoller, Gustav. *Die Strassburger Tucher und Weberzünft: Urkunden und Darstellung*, 2 vols. Strasbourg: Karl J. Trübner, 1879.

Schochet, Gordon. *Patriarchalism in Political Thought: The Authoritarian Family and Political Speculations and Attitudes Especially in Seventeenth-Century England*. Oxford: Blackwell Scientific, 1975.

Schoen, Erhard. *Der Handwerker in der deutschen Vergangenheit*. Monographien zur deutschen Kulturgeschichte, no. 5. Leipzig: Eugen Diedrichs, 1900.

Schönfeld, Walter. *Frauen in der abendländische Heilkunde*. Stuttgart: Ferdinand Enke, 1947.

Schöppler, Hermann. "Die erste gedruckte Hebammenordnung der freien Reichsstadt Nürnberg." *Mitteilungen des Verein für Geschichte der Stadt Nürnberg* 18 (1908): 258–265.

Schornbaum, Karl. "Ein altes Haushaltsbüchlein (1545–1549)." *Mitteilungen des Verein für Geschichte der Stadt Nürnberg* 43 (1952): 491–498.

Schulte, Aloys. *Geschichte des mittelalterlichen Handels und Verkehrs zwischen Westdeutschland und Italien*. Vol. 1. Leipzig: Duncker und Humblot, 1900.

Schulz, Alwin. *Deutsches Leben im XIV. und XV. Jahrhundert*. Vienna: F. Tempsky, 1892.

Schuster, Dora. *Die Stellung der Frau in der Zunftverfassung*. Quellenhefte zum Frauenleben in der Geschichte, no. 7. Berlin: Herbig, 1927.

Secombe, Wally. "The Housewife and Her Labour under Capitalism." *New Left Review* 83 (1974): 3–24.

———. "Domestic Labour: Reply to Critics." *New Left Review* 94 (1975): 85–96.

Seebass, Gottfried. "Das Problem der Konditionaltaufe in der Reformation." *Zeitschrift für bayerische Kirchengechichte* 35 (1966): 138–168.

———. "Die Vorgeschichte von Luthers Verwerfung der Konditionaltaufe nach einem bisher unbekannten Schreiben Andreas Osianders an Georg Spalatin von 26. Juni 1531." *Archiv für Reformationsgeschichte* 62 (1971): 193–206.

Shammas, Carole. "Food Expenditures and Economic Well-Being in Early Modern England." *Journal of Economic History* 43, no. 1 (March 1983): 89–100.

Shorter, Edward. "Women's Work: What Difference Did Capitalism Make?" *Theory and Society* 3, no. 4 (Winter 1976): 513–527.

Siebenkees, Johann C., ed. *Materialen zur nürnbergische Geschichte.* 4 vols. Nuremberg: Schneider, 1792.

———. *Nachrichten von Armenstiftungen in Nürnberg.* Nuremberg: Schneider, 1792.

———. *Nachrichten von den Nürnbergische Armenschulen und Schulstiftungen.* Nuremberg: Schneider, 1793.

Snell, Keith D. M. "Agricultural Seasonal Unemployment, the Standard of Living and Women's Work in the South and East: 1690–1860." *Economic History Review*, 2d ser., 34, no. 3 (1981): 407–437.

———. "The Apprenticeship of Women." Unpublished paper.

Soliday, Gerald Lyman. *A Community in Conflict: Frankfurt Society in the Seventeenth and Early Eighteenth Centuries.* Hanover, N.H.: University Press of New England, Brandeis University Press, 1974.

Solleder, Fridolin. *Zur wissenschaftliche Auswertung der ältesten Nürnberger Ehebücher.* Freie Schriftenfolge der Gesellschaft für Familienforschung in Franken, no. 2. Nuremberg: Gesellschaft für Familienforschung in Franken, 1951.

———. *München im Mittelalter.* 1938. Reprint. Aalen: Scientia, 1962.

Springer, Jacob, and Institorius, Heinrich. *Malleus Maleficarum.* Translated by Montague Summers. London: Pushkin, 1951.

Stahlschmidt, Rainer. *Die Geschichte des eisenverarbeitende Gewerbes in Nürnberg von der ersten Nachrichten im 12.–13. Jahrhundert bis 1630.* Schriftenreihe des Stadtarchivs Nürnberg, no. 4. Nuremberg: Stadtarchiv, 1971.

*Der Statt Franckfurt erneuerte Reformation.* Frankfurt: Johann Bringen, 1578.

Steinhausen, Georg. *Der Kaufmann in der Vergangenheit.* Monographien zur deutschen Kulturgeschichte, no. 2. Leipzig: Eugen Diedrichs, 1899.

———. *Deutsche Privatbriefe des Mittelalters.* 2 vols. Denkmäler der deutschen Kulturgeschichte. Berlin: Weidmann, 1907.

Stone, Lawrence. *The Family, Sex, and Marriage in England 1500–1800.* New York: Harper and Row, 1979.

Strauss, Gerald. *Nuremberg in the Sixteenth Century: City Politics and Life between Middle Ages and Modern Times.* Bloomington: Indiana University Press, 1976.

Stricker, Wilhelm. *Geschichte des Heilkunde und der verwandeten Wissenschaften in der Stadt Frankfurt a.M.* Frankfurt: Johann Kessler, 1847.

Strobel, Margaret. "Current Research in African Women's History." Unpublished paper.

Sudhoff, Karl. *Die ersten Massnahmen der Stadt Nürnberg gegen die Syphilis in den Jahren 1496 und 1497*. Leipzig: J. A. Barth, 1912.

Tawney, R. H. *Religion and the Rise of Capitalism*. New York: Harcourt, Brace, 1926.

Theime, Hans. "Die Rechtstellung der Frau in Deutschland." *Recueils Société Jean Bodin* 12 (1973): 351–376.

Thirsk, Joan. "The Fantastical Folly of Fashion: The English Stocking-Knitting Industry 1500–1700." In *Textile History and Economic History*, edited by N. B. Harte and K. G. Ponting, 50–73. Manchester: Manchester University Press, 1973.

———. *Economic Policy and Projects: The Development of a Consumer Society in Early Modern England*. Oxford: Clarendon, 1978.

Till, Rudolph. "Die berufstätige Frau in mittelalterlichen Wien." *Wiener Geschichtsblätter* 25 (1970): 115–119.

Tilly, Louise, and Joan Scott. *Women, Work and the Family*. Chicago: University of Chicago Press, 1978.

Tucher, Anton. *Haushaltbuch (1507 bis 1517)*. Edited by Wilhelm Loose. Bibliothek des Litterarische Verein Stuttgart, vol. 134. Stuttgart: Litterarische Verein, 1877.

Uitz, Erika. "Zur gesellschaftlichen Stellung der Frau in der mittelalterlichen Stadt." *Magdeburger Beiträge zur Stadtgeschichte* 1 (1977): 20–34.

Unwin, George. *Industrial Organization in the Sixteenth and Seventeenth Centuries*. New York: Kelley, 1963.

Vann, Richard T. "Toward a New Lifestyle: Women in Pre-Industrial Capitalism." In *Becoming Visible: Women in European History*, edited by Renate Bridenthal and Claudia Koonz, 192–216. Boston: Houghton Mifflin, 1977.

Wachendorf, Helmut. *Die wirtschaftliche Stellung der Frau in den deutschen Städten des späteren Mittelalters*. Quackenbrück: C. Trute, 1934.

Weinhold, Karl. *Die deutschen Frauen in dem Mittelalter*. 2 vols. Vienna: Gerold, 1851.

Weisser, Michael. *Crime and Punishment in Early Modern Europe*. Brighton, Sussex: Harvester, 1979.

Weith-Knudsen, K. A. *Kulturgeschichte der europäischen Frauenwelt*. Stuttgart: Franckh'sche Verlagshandlung, 1927.

Wensky, Margaret. *Die Stellung der Frau in der stadtkölnische Wirtschaft im Spätmittelalter*. Quellen und Darstellungen zur hänsische Geschichte. Cologne: Böhlau, 1981.

Werner, Hermann, and Neuhauser, Erika. *Die Schwäbin*. Stuttgart: Franckh'sche Verlangshandlung, 1947.

Wertheimer, Barbara Mayer. *We Were There: The Story of Working Women in America*. New York: Pantheon, 1977.

Westermann, Oscar. "Die Bevölkerungsverhältnisse Memmingens in ausgehende Mittelalter." *Memmingen Geschichtsblätter* 2 (1913).

Wiesner, Merry E. "Early Modern Midwifery: A Case Study." *International Journal of Women's Studies* 6, no. 1 (January–February 1983): 26–43.

Wilda, Wilhelm. *Das Gildenwesen im Mittelalter.* Aalen: Scientia, 1964.

Willen, Diane. "Guildeswomen in the City of York, 1560–1700." *Historian* 46, no. 2 (February 1984): 204–218.

———. "Women and Poor Relief in Pre-Industrial Norwich and York." Unpublished paper.

Winckelmann, Otto. "Die Almosenordnungen von Nürnberg (1522), Kitzingen (1523), Regensburg (1533) und Ypres (1525)." *Archiv für Reformationsgeschichte* 10 (1912/1913): 242–279.

———. *Das Fürsorgewesen der Stadt Strassburg.* Quellen und Forschungen zur Reformationsgeschichte, no. 5. Leipzig: Heinsius, 1922.

Winter, Annette. "Studien zur sozialen Situation der Frauen in der Stadt Trier nach der Steuerliste von 1364." *Kurtrierisches Jahrbuch* 15 (1975): 20–45.

Wissell, Rudolph. *Das alten Handwerks Recht und Gewohnheit.* 2 vols. Berlin: Colloquium, 1971, 1974.

Wolf, Armin, ed. *Die Gesetze der Stadt Frankfurt am Main im Mittelalter.* Frankfurt: Kramer Verlagsbuchhandlung, 1969.

Wood, Merry Wiesner. "Paltry Peddlers or Essential Merchants: Women in the Distributive Trades in Early Modern Nuremberg." *Sixteenth Century Journal* 21, no. 2 (1981): 3–13.

Woodward, Donald. "Wage Rates and Living Standards in Pre-Industrial England." *Past and Present* 91 (May 1981): 28–46.

Wunder, Gerd. *Die Bürgerschaft der Reichsstadt Hall von 1395–1600.* Württemburgische Geschichtsquellen, no. 25. Stuttgart: Kohlhammer, 1956.

———. "Die Bewohner der Reichsstadt Hall im Jahre 1545." *Württemburgische Franken* 49 (1965): 34–50.

———. *Die Stuttgarter Steuerliste von 1545.* Veröffentlichungen des Archivs der Stadt Stuttgart, vol. 26. Stuttgart: Klett, 1974.

Wunder, Heide. "Zur Stellung der Frau im Arbeitsleben und in der Gesellschaft des 15.–18. Jahrhunderts: Eine Skizze." *Geschichtsdidaktik* 3 (1981): 239–251.

———. "L'espace privé and the Domestication of Women in the Sixteenth and Seventeenth Centuries." Unpublished paper.

Yost, John. "The Value of Married Life for the Social Order in the Early English Renaissance." *Societas* 6 (Winter, 1976): 25–39.

———. "Changing Attitudes toward Married Life in Civic and Christian Humanism." *Occasional Papers of the American Society for Reformation Research* 1 (1977): 151–166.

Zagorin, Perez. *Rebels and Rulers 1500–1660.* Cambridge: Cambridge University Press, 1982.

Zaretsky, Eli. *Capitalism, the Family and Personal Life.* New York: Harper and Row, 1976.

Zatschek, Heinz. "Aus der Geschichte des Wiener Handwerks während des 30 Jährigen Krieges: Eine soziologische Studie." *Jahrbuch des Verein für Geschichte der Stadt Wien* 9 (1951): 30–40.

Zoepf, Friedrich. *Deutsche Kulturgeschichte.* Vol. 1. Freiburg in Breisgau: Herder, 1928.

# Index